THE ORGANIZATION OF WAR
UNDER EDWARD III, 1338–62

The
Organization of War
under Edward III

1338–62

by

H. J. HEWITT
M.A., Ph.D.

MANCHESTER UNIVERSITY PRESS
BARNES & NOBLE, INC., NEW YORK

Printed in Great Britain by Butler & Tanner Ltd, Frome and London

Contents

Illustrations

Author and publishers are indebted to the Trustees of the British Museum for permission to reproduce the four Plates, and to Editions E. de Boccard, Paris, for Map 4, which is taken from *Mélanges d'archéologie et d'histoire* (Ecole française de Rome), tome LXII.

PLATES

MAPS

Preface

WAR, it has been said, is much too serious a thing to be left to military men. It might equally be said that the history of war is much too serious a thing to be left to military historians. It is true that they 'tell a good tale', and that during the drama of war, a nation's attention is concentrated on the soldier, for he is the hero. Such indeed is his role and so gripping is the struggle, that in accounts of many wars—especially those of distant centuries—the very existence of those who stay at home is overlooked. Yet the non-combatants of the warring nations are never mere spectators. They too are participants: their efforts to clothe, feed, arm and transport the soldiers, their hopes, fears, sufferings are inseparable from the drama: their fate is at stake. They witness the destruction, endure the heartbreak and bear much of the cost. What they see, do, experience, think, belongs to the conflict; and the conflict is not fully understood unless their experiences form part of the study. Unfortunately, however, the non-combatants have not interested the military historian: they do not fit into the Art of War.

This gap in the study of war has not escaped the notice of other historians. From time to time, hints of the need to widen existing military studies have appeared both in England and in France. To quote the most recent and the most emphatic, Professor Piero Pieri, writing in *Annales* (juillet-août, 1963), states 'War cannot be studied as a closed reality. . . . It must be linked with all man's activities. . . . Military history must overflow into other fields of study.'

I think the new and wider conception of the field of study will no longer be the army-at-war, but the people-at-war. It may therefore cover the work of all who directly or indirectly further or hinder the nation's effort, and the experience of all whose lives are affected by the war.

With these principles in mind, I have tried to throw a little light on some obvious and rather down-to-earth, yet fundamental questions concerning the 'Home Front' (on both sides) in the war between England and France during the years 1338–1362. I have not treated every non-combatant aspect, nor do I claim to have said the last word on any aspect: I have merely put forward a few supplementary studies for a broader view of the war. In some places, however, I have sought to explore topics to which little, if any, attention has so far been given. The *garde de la mer*, for example, has not, so far as I know, formed the subject of research. Nor am I aware of any study of the collection of victuals either by men in England or by the army in France. And no English writer appears to have given an account of the transfer of territory after the treaty of Bretigny. On these topics—especially the first—my conclusions are set out tentatively.

Some features may need explanation. Concerning the limits of time and space, the period between the beginning of the war and the execution of the treaties of peace forms an obvious and convenient 'unit'. The amount of attention which should be given to the Anglo-Scottish aspects of the struggle will remain a matter of individual judgement. (The Scots are not over-looked but the French absorbed far more of England's resources.) If I follow the armed men *after* their array and even describe their chief activities during the campaigns, it is always as part of the experience of the populace among whom they moved.

In order to differentiate my work from military history as commonly understood, I had thought of calling it 'The Civilian in the Hundred Years War, 1338–62', for it deals almost wholly with the work and experiences of men and women who took no part in the actual fighting. The distinction between soldier and civilian, however, had not yet been made. I hope that the title ultimately adopted will not lead any reader to look for aspects of the Art of War but rather for the wide, detailed and co-ordinated preparations for the landing of an army in France or Flanders, the effects of victualling, looting and destruction in the invaded areas and the steps taken to influence opinion in England.

I am indebted to Professor J. le Patourel for helpful suggestions about sources, to Professor E. Perroy for drawing my attention to 'La mission charitable de Bertrand Carit', to Professor G. E. Trease for help in connection with medical supplies, to Dr K. A. Fowler for permission to print the list of ships in Appendix II from his thesis on Henry of Lancaster, and Mrs J. Nicolls for help with the maps and the proof-reading.

H. J. HEWITT

Saltash, 1965

Abbreviations

Baker	*Chronicon Galfridi le Baker de Swynebroke*, ed. Thompson, E. M.
Bardonnet	*Procès Verbal de délivrance des places françaises*
B.P.R.	*The Black Prince's Register*
C. Close R.	*Calendar of Close Rolls*
C. Inqn. Misc.	*Calendar of Inquisitions Miscellaneous*
C. Pat. R.	*Calendar of Patent Rolls*
Froissart	Froissart, J., *Oeuvres*, ed. de Lettenhove, K.
Froissart (Macaulay)	*The Chronicles of Froissart*, ed. Macaulay, G. C.
Hewitt, *B.P.E.*	Hewitt, H. J., *The Black Prince's Expedition of 1355–57*
Moisant	Moisant, J., *Le Prince Noir en Aquitaine*
Registres	*La Guerre de Cent Ans vue à travers les Registres du Parlement, 1337–69*, ed. Timbal
R.P.	*Rolls of Parliament*
Rymer	*Foedera*, ed. Rymer
Trans. R.H.S.	*Transactions of the Royal Historical Society*

ix

CHAPTER I

Defence

THE war that was to last so long began quite gradually. In view of the circumstances in Gascony on the one hand and in Flanders on the other, in view of the unceasing Anglo-French rivalry (formerly feudal and political, now becoming commercial), in view also of king Edward's descent from the Capetian line, both Philip VI of France and Edward III of England probably regarded war as inevitable. Both made preparations for many months; both involved themselves in the complicated affairs of Flanders. Brutal clashes at sea between French and English sailors intensified hostile feelings on both sides of the Channel. In November 1337, Sir Walter Manny made a successful raid on Cadsand which was occupied by a Flemish garrison. The French retorted by a series of raids on English ports. The long conflict had begun.

The first incidents of war experienced by people in England occurred in June 1338 when French privateers burned Portsmouth. In October of that year they made a very serious attack on the unwalled (or only partly walled) town of Southampton; and there were raids on the Isle of Wight, on Swanage and elsewhere in England, and on the Channel Islands, Guernsey and the smaller islands being taken and occupied by the French till 1340.

Boldly moving here and there in the Channel—often in galleys[1]—the French continued their attacks. Harwich was burned in March 1339. From June onward there were demonstrations and some degree of damage from the Thames estuary to Cornwall, particularly at Sandwich, Dover, Folkestone, Rye, Hastings, Portsmouth and Plymouth. In the summer of 1340, notwithstanding the English victory at Sluys, French ships appeared—this time with Spanish allies[2]—off the Isle of Wight.

---

[1] The galleys were usually Spanish. Russell, P. E., *English Intervention in Spain and Portugal*, 229–33, gives a good description of these vessels.

[2] In *Les Journaux du Trésor* (ed. Viard, J.), no. 1981, there are notes of payment to the king of Castile for 200 ships of Spain. There were serious

They burned Teignmouth and would have made a second attack on Plymouth had it not been defended.

French attacks on England's southern ports had occurred at earlier dates. A great part of Dover, for example, had been burned in 1295, but the repeated appearances of French fleets along the Channel coast in 1338–40 and the damage they inflicted were not maritime counterparts of locally organized border raids, nor the enterprises of spirited pirates. They were an expression of French policy.

It is not our purpose to examine that policy at length. It may have been aimed at the destruction of English shipping or—as the chevauchées usually appeared to have been aimed—at the infliction of material and psychological damage. It may indeed have had both these aims and been part of the preparation for an invasion of England, plans for which were drawn up in March 1339.[1] It may have been intended to compel Edward (who could enter France without having first to capture a French port) to keep forces in England for the defence of his own land.

Whatever the purpose, we are concerned mainly with the results: serious damage was done and alarm was widespread. In his biased account, Baker belittles the effects. At Harwich, he says, a breeze limited the spread of the fire; though the French made their threats to the Isle of Wight, they did not land there but went to worse defended places and committed many evils; they appeared many times off Dover and Folkestone and burned fishing vessels, as they did off the coasts of Devon and Cornwall; at Plymouth they did some damage both to ships and the town.[2]

But Southampton had been sacked. Baker admits it. Froissart adds that the spoils were carried off to Normandy.[3] And official records reveal something of the extent of the damage: the destruction of the houses, the flight of the inhabitants, their reluctance—even under great pressure—to return, the loss of quantities of wool and wine and even of the seals and weighing beam used for the customs, the order to remove the king's horses

Franco-Spanish attacks on the towns of the south coast again in 1377. Russell, op. cit., 239–40.

[1] *Rolls of Parliament*, II, 158–9; *Black Book of the Admiralty*, vol. I, 420, 426–7; Avesbury, 205; Coville, A., *Les Etats de Normandie*, 48.

[2] Baker, 62, 64.

[3] Froissart (Macaulay), 48.

to a safer place, and the looting, as the raiders withdrew, of goods belonging to some foreign merchants.[1]

The likelihood of an attempt by the French to invade England had been foreseen for several months as hostile galleys and ships of war assembled in the Channel. (The government may have been aware also of the French invasion scheme already mentioned.) From April 1338 onward, there were predictions of French intentions, and instructions for counter measures (or notes that such measures were being taken) in Holderness, in Norfolk, Suffolk, Essex, Kent, Sussex and Devon, and general directions for guarding all the ports.[2] Steps were even taken towards detaching some of the Genoese armed galleys, hired by the French, in order that they might be used *against* the French.[3] Yet in spite of all these precautions, Southampton had been sacked and utterly destroyed. There were reports of 'disgraceful neglect of duty on the part of those who should have defended the town'. An enquiry into their conduct was ordered.[4]

The lesson was learned. One year later in the Thierache,[5] Edward spread devastation on a vastly greater scale than the town of Southampton or all the English towns attacked had suffered and, at intervals during the following twenty years, the dreadful havoc was repeated in many parts of France. Nevertheless, it was evident that more resources must be devoted to defence even at a time when the king was bent on leading expeditions to Flanders.

The steps taken were for the most part traditional, but their operation had to be more widespread and more thorough than previous generations had known. The enemy could land—as he had done at Swanage and Teignmouth—without the need for port facilities: no part of the south coast could be regarded as immune from attack. He could do great damage by burning ships in harbour without landing at all. It was necessary therefore to be prepared to counter a hostile landing almost anywhere, necessary to ensure that men were aware of the enemy's presence if he came ashore, necessary—whenever possible—to warn men of impending invasion.

[1] There is no adequate history of medieval Southampton, but references in the records are numerous, e.g. *C. Close R.*, 1339–41, 375 (seal and beam), 143 (wine), 40 (burning), 40 (wool), 236 (horses).
[2] *C. Close R.*, 1337–9, 370.   [3] *C. Pat. R.*, 1338–40, 190.
[4] Ibid., 180.   [5] Vide infra, pp. 124–6.

We consider first the warnings. These—as is shown more fully in a later chapter[1]—were of three kinds: the plain statement that the French (or the Scots) are preparing to invade England, the more precise declaration that the enemy is expected to land in this or that county, and the prediction that an attempt at invasion is not only imminent but will be accompanied, if the enemy lands, by terrible evils.

The source of the warnings was twofold: in Baker's words 'manifest signs and reliable reports'.[2] The signs commonly quoted were the massing of French galleys and ships; the reliable information came from 'intelligence received', for both Philip and Edward employed, or received news from, agents who should no doubt be regarded as spies. Froissart, like Baker, was aware of their work and frequently mentions the result. 'Of all these (preparations)', he says in 1337, 'king Philip was well informed', and 'they made current war whereof the English lords . . . were well informed'.[3] The signs and the agents' reports convinced the English government of French intentions.

Again and again predictions of the enemy's intention to invade England were sent to sheriffs for proclamation throughout their bailiwicks and to the officers responsible for the defence of the coast.[4] And such phrases as 'the custody of the maritime lands . . . against the incursion of hostile aliens' or 'to set out against the king's enemies if they presume to invade the realm', occurring frequently in correspondence, kept vividly in men's minds the danger in which England stood.[5]

The fact that no invasion occurred, and that coastal attacks lessened and were not renewed on a serious scale till 1360, does not prove that the statements of French plans broadcast to the English people were groundless. (Predictions in 1588 and 1805 were based on 'manifest signs and reliable reports'.) The French had indeed several plans but usually lacked the necessary means, namely mastery of the seas and sufficient shipping to transport a large army.

By long tradition, news of a hostile landing in England was to be spread over a wide area by means of a system of beacons on well known lofty sites. The control of these warning signals

---

[1] Vide infra, chapter VII.   [2] Baker, 61.

[3] Froissart (Macaulay), 42; and cf. 'The French king wrought as much as he could to the contrary for he knew much of their intents', ibid., 46.

[4] Vide infra, chapter VII.   [5] C. Close R., 1339–41, 233, 266.

in the coastal areas lay with the keepers of the maritime lands. In September 1337, the keepers in Somerset, Dorset and Devon were directed to have the beacons in their coastal areas prepared without delay and guarded by four, five or six attendants.[1] In the following August, the sheriffs throughout England were ordered to have beacons made ready on hilltops far from the sea as well as on the coasts because massed French galleys sailing in the Channel portended an invasion.[2]

The 'four, five or six' men attending the beacon were no doubt the 'watch' described by Froissart: 'empty wine tuns filled with sand were set one on another and on the top a man would sit keeping watch, looking across the sea'.[3] As for the material to be burnt to produce the light, in Kent in 1337 it was to be pitch. It 'showed better' and lasted longer than twigs.[4]

An additional means of spreading news appeared in November 1338 when sheriffs of south coast (and some other maritime) counties were instructed to arrange that at churches ordinarily only one bell should be rung. The ringing of all the bells was to signify a French attack.[5]

We turn to measures for the defence of the realm and more particularly of those parts which were most exposed to attacks from the French. First came the restoration of shattered towns. With great promptitude Southampton was walled, garrisoned, supplied with arms and with engines of war.[6] A succession of

---

[1] *C. Close R.*, 1337–9, 179. [2] Rymer, II, ii, 1055.

[3] Rickert, E., *Chaucer's World*, 302 (quoting Froissart). Empty tuns filled with stones were used for a wall near Guines. Baker, 92. Empty and well cleaned, they were used for water, flour, arms. Vide infra, Appendix I, B.

[4] From Philipot, T., *Villare Cantianum*, 6.

[5] Rymer, II, ii, 1066. Bells were used to sound the alarm in Valenciennes and in Brittany, Froissart (Macaulay), 57, 75, and in Paris in 1358 and in the Ile de France, *Jean de Venette*, ed. Newhall, R. A., 85, 94.

[6] Rymer, II, ii, 1077; *C. Close R.*, 1339–41, 55, 57, 101, 215 (walls); ibid., 64, 82, 83, 135, 185, 215 (arms); ibid., 297 (poverty and withdrawals). An indenture between the Black Prince and the earl of Warwick (1339) sets out the arrangements for the custody of the town, the garrison, the wages and the arms. It refers also to the measures to get people to return and live there. *The Sign Manuals and Letters Patent of Southampton to 1402*, vol. I, 46–7. There are indications that the 'wall of stone and lime' was not completed or not satisfactory in 1355. The burgesses were granted murage for ten years by letters patent of 28 June 1355. *The Oak Book of Southampton*, II, 118–21.

competent officers were put in charge of its defence and periodically it was surveyed as a fortress. The former inhabitants were
urged to return and live in the town—or lose their lands and
houses.[1]

Next, energy was concentrated on the strengthening of fortifications. Defensive works, arms, victuals and garrisons were
surveyed or increased at Dover, Hastings, Porchester, Portsmouth, Winchester, Carisbrooke, Corfe, Exeter, Old Sarum,
Gloucester, Bishop's Lynn, the castles of North Wales and even
those of Ireland.[2] The men of Southwark were ordered to be
ready to guard their town and the men of London to defend
the river front and to cause piles to be fixed in the Thames.[3]
To the Channel Islands (important because of their nearness to
the French coast and their position on the medieval sea route
to Gascony), supplies of food were sent and the garrison of
Jersey was reinforced.[4]

But the most important measures taken were those for general
defence. In order to ward off the threatened invasions, the men
of the coastal counties, and especially those bordering the
English Channel, were called on to fulfil their military obligation to defend their localities.[5] The militia thus mobilized (or
rendered very quickly available) operated in a coastal strip
called 'the maritime lands', a region deemed to extend inland
from the shore for six leagues. (The area thus enclosed must
have had a boundary conventionally and traditionally under-

[1] *R.P.*, II, 108.
[2] Dover: *C. Close R.*, 1337-9, 568; ibid., 1339-41, 11, 69, 150, 174, 208;
ibid., 1341-3, 342.
 Hastings: *C. Close R.*, 1339-41, 113, 215.
 Porchester: *C. Close R.*, 1337-9, 564; ibid., 1339-41, 113, 345, 446.
 Portsmouth: ibid., 218.
 Winchester: *C. Close R.*, 1339-41, 346; *C. Pat R.*, 1338-40, 180.
 Carisbrooke: *C. Close R.*, 1339-41, 368; *C. Pat R.*, 1338-40, 212.
 Corfe: *C. Pat R.*, 1338-40, 556.
 Old Sarum: *C. Close R.*, 1339-41, 35.
 Gloucester: *C. Close R.*, 1337-9, 571.
 Bishop's Lynn: *C. Close R.*, 1339-41, 102.
 Wales: *C. Close R.*, 1337-9, 543, 577.
 Ireland: ibid., 244; Rymer, II, ii, 1087-8.
 And see *V.C.H. Sussex*, I, 506, 509.
[3] *C. Close R.*, 1337-9, 537, 612.
[4] Ibid., 544, 547, 606; ibid., 1339-41, 32, 358.
[5] '. . . all men should be compelled to repel enemies if they invade the
realm'. *C. Close R.*, 1337-9, 172.

stood rather than mathematically defined.) During the period we are considering, men living in this strip were not only exempt from service in overseas expeditions, they were directed to stay in their shires for the defence of the realm.[1] Men living elsewhere in the coastal counties were liable for service in the maritime lands. Thus was constituted the defence force whose function was known as *Garde de la Mer*.

In each county there were officers—often two or three local magnates—called 'keepers of the maritime lands' to whom were entrusted extensive powers for the defence of their own county. In 1340, a typical statement[2] of their duties runs:

A, B and C are appointed

— to guard the coast of (Kent) and the whole of the maritime land of that county (coast being defined as 'all places where ships can put in' and thus including creeks and estuaries);
— to resist invaders whether they come by sea or by land;
— to take all steps necessary for the safety of the realm;
— to make suitable appointments;
— to require that, after due warning, the sheriff shall parade the posse before them.

Arrayers are appointed to array fencible men according to their condition and to lead them as the keepers direct.

By 1346, the arraying is included in the statement of the keepers' duties;[3] the men are to be furnished with arms and grouped in constabularies, centaines and vintaines; beacons are to be made ready on the hills and elsewhere; keepers can distrain on defaulters or arrest those who resist. By 1356, the only significant addition[4] is that to the sheriff's obligation to assemble

---

[1] I am not sure that these principles were operative in 1338–40, but they were made very clear in 1346. Rymer, III, i, 81, and in 1353, *C. Close R.*, 1349–54, 545.

[2] Gascon Roll, C 61/50, m. 8.

[3] Treaty Roll, C 76/23, m. 20.

[4] Treaty Roll, C 76/24. In 1295, the *terrae maritimae* were called *partes maritimae* and the keepers' powers were defined: *ita quod idem Adam vos omnes et singulos ad custodiam et defensionem parcium illaram compellere possit quociens necesse fuerit et prout securitati parcium illarum melius viderit expediri. Parliamentary Writs*, I, 270. Details of the arrangements (in 1295) for Essex, Sussex, Norfolk and Suffolk are set out in ibid., 272.

In 1336, the duties of the keepers in North Wales and South Wales include the arrest, if necessary, of ships and their fitting out with *duplex eskippamentum*. And the keeper in South Wales has *providere navige pour le sauve*

the posse at such places and times as the keepers (or one of them) shall direct, are added the words 'as often as danger threatens'. In all instances, the public in general and the sheriffs in particular are notified of the keepers' appointment and powers, and directed to give their assistance.

This then is the core of the organization for the defence of the realm. The keepers are responsible to the Council or the king; they can enforce the obligation to serve and have all other powers necessary for the performance of their duties. But the powers and duties are restricted to their own counties.

Two questions arise: first, are there any arrangements for the co-ordination of defence in adjoining coastal counties? The terms of appointment make no reference to co-ordination but, both before and during the period of this study, there are instances of joint custody of maritime lands in neighbouring coastal counties. In 1324, for example, the following counties are linked: Norfolk and Suffolk, Kent and Sussex (and Surrey), Devon and Cornwall; and in 1336, South Wales is treated as one unit and North Wales as another.[1]

Secondly, in the event of an emergency, does the whole burden of defence fall on the coastal county or counties the enemy chooses to attack? Here the answer—in theory at any rate—is quite clear. Since the obligation to render military service for home defence rests on all men between sixteen and sixty years of age, men resident in counties remote from the sea may be sent to serve in the maritime lands. A scheme, dated March 1346, directs the arrayers that the men of Rutland and Leicestershire will go to the maritime land in county Lincoln, the men of Middlesex and Hertford to Essex, the men of counties Worcester and Hereford to Gloucester, those of Wiltshire, Oxford and Berkshire to Hampshire, and so on. In this scheme, the arrayers of the inland counties have to obey the requests of the keepers of the maritime lands of the counties with which they are linked, and the sheriffs of the coastal counties are associated with the keepers of those counties.[2]

Commissioners were appointed in the summer of 1338 to

---

garde des portz et coustiers de la meer celes parties. Exchequer Various Accounts E 101/612/34, E 101/19/13.

[1] *Parliamentary Writs*, II, ii, 660, no. 3; Exchequer Various Accounts E 101/612/34, E 101/19/13.

[2] Treaty Roll, C 76/22, mm. 25, 27.

array the men of each county (even those of Cumberland and Northumberland)[1] 'to be ready to repel invasions of the French at the request or summons of the keepers of the coast';[2] and the formula is seen in operation in such words as 'send men chosen and arrayed in the county of Oxford as often as hostile attacks are expected in the county of Hampshire and as the arrayers are forewarned by the said keepers'.[3]

These then are the means by which a force was to be raised to counter invasion. Neither the obligation to serve, nor the *Garde de la Mer*, nor the maritime lands were devised to meet the policy of Philip VI. Still less were they due to the blow inflicted by the French at Southampton. They were parts of a defence system which—together with the 'watches' and the beacons—may be traced back in essence to pre-Norman times.[4] But the circumstances of 1338–40 threw into prominence principles which had not been put into operation on so large a scale by any earlier generation.

The operation of the defence system was at all times less simple than the principle, for it had to be applied in a particular historical context. In 1338–40, so far as the evidence is available, the arraying took place normally and there was some resort to the power to call in men from non-coastal counties (from Wiltshire to Hampshire, for example),[5] but three aspects gave rise to difficulties.

The first was the problem of ensuring that the maritime lands were not evacuated. Fear, prudence or the desire to evade the financial or military burdens of defence tended to cause an exodus not only from the Isle of Wight and the neighbourhood of Portsmouth and Southampton, but from other regions where

[1] For clearness and convenience, this study deals only with counties bordering the Channel.

[2] *C. Pat. R.*, 1338–40, 134.

[3] *C. Close R.*, 1339–41, 19.

[4] Not uncommonly the instructions (of this period) imply the continuance of long established practice: commissioners are appointed in July 1338 to array men 'pursuant to the statutes of Winchester and Northampton', *C. Pat. R.*, 1338–40, 13; beacons are prepared 'as was wont to be done' or 'as is customary', *C. Close R.*, 1354–60, 215; measures are taken for the defence of the Isle of Wight 'as was wont to be done in the time of our forefathers during the disturbances of war', Gascon Roll, C 61/50. The obligation to serve is treated at length in Powicke, *Military Obligation in Medieval England*.

[5] *C. Close R.*, 1339/41, 226.

French attacks had occurred, or were threatened, or even officially predicted. Evacuation would facilitate the enemy's task. There are therefore repeated orders to all who live in the coastal strip to remain there. To those normally resident some distance inland but possessed of estates on or near the coast, there are directions to go and live in the maritime lands. And for those who have moved away for safety, there are peremptory instructions to go back to their homes on the coast.[1] It is on holding the population where it should be that the defence of the realm—and incidentally the use and cultivation of fertile tracts of land—depends.

A second feature arises directly from the first. Since the size of the resident population was to be maintained (and even increased by enlarging garrisons and bringing men, if necessary, from inland counties to the coast), it was necessary to prevent the carrying off of victuals by purveyors or traders.[2]

Thirdly, there was administrative confusion—which may have been inevitable—over the place at which or the manner in which obligatory service should be, or was being, rendered. The keepers not only reported to the Council the absence from the maritime lands of those who by virtue of their estates owed service; they promptly applied pressure by distraint or other means on the absentees. Such distraint was intelligible to the culpable, but there were two classes of men for whom it was unjust: those who were about to embark with the king's armies or already serving overseas,[3] and those who were performing

---

[1] E.g. John de Mowbray was ordered to go to Sussex and stay there 'while danger is imminent', *C. Close R.*, 1337–9, 540; Bartholomew de l'Isle (who had withdrawn from the Isle of Wight) received the rebuke '. . . it is not becoming for belted knights to eloign themselves from places where deeds of war may take place but rather to go to those places and stay there . . .' ibid., 1339–41, 444. The mayor and bailiffs of Sandwich are directed to proclaim that the men who have left their town must return and bear their share of the expense or lose their lands and goods, ibid., 237; the sheriff of Hampshire is instructed that men are to build houses (in Southampton) 'and dwell therein for the safe-keeping of the town', ibid., 101, and vide infra, 13–14.
The tendency to move away from dangerous areas may be seen again in instructions of January 1347 that people having lands in the Isle of Wight must be compelled to stay there to render the services they are wont to render in time of war. Rymer, III, i, 104.

[2] *C. Close R.*, 1339–41, 352.

[3] Ibid., 1337–9, 124, 516; ibid, 1339–41, 121, 223, 224.

their duties in the maritime lands of other counties. In the latter class were those whose estates were widely scattered. The abbot of Hyde, for example, had lands in Sussex, Surrey, Dorset and Wiltshire, and was helping in the defence of the maritime lands of Hampshire.[1] Bartholomew de Lisle was in charge of the maritime lands in the Isle of Wight but held estates in Dorset, Somerset and Northampton as well as in the Isle of Wight.[2] The bishop of Exeter was actively arraying in Devon and finding men at his own cost for the defence of the maritime lands of Devon but, owing to the location of his estates, he was under pressure to find men in Sussex also.[3] The prior of the hospital of St John of Jerusalem was finding men for the defence of Southampton, but was pressed also to find men in Dorset. Roger de Chaundos, serving in Dorset[4] with men-at-arms representing his full quota for all his lands in England, was being pressed to provide men also in Kent.[5]

Such men protested that they were already discharging their duties as fully as they were able. With the Council lay the task of investigating their complaints. In many instances, keepers were ordered to withdraw the distraint (or other pressure) they were applying.[6]

There were, of course, attempts to escape the burdens of the period: men claiming to be members of the retinue of the bishop of Salisbury argued that they were exempt from duty in the maritime lands;[7] men in Wiltshire failed to send the wages of Wiltshire men serving in the garrison of Porchester castle;[8] in Kent, some men tried to avoid serving in Sheppey, others tried to avoid contributing to the cost of defence,[9] and there was a dispute over the manning of ships at Sandwich.[10] Such attempted evasion would however be common in any period and of little consequence.

[1] Ibid., 1337–9, 109. [2] Ibid., 117.

[3] Ibid., 1339–41, 123. John de Grandison, the very active bishop of Exeter 1327–69, described elsewhere as 'chief arrayer of men in county Devon and keeper of the maritime lands there', ibid., 226.

[4] Ibid., 1337–9, 124–5. [5] Ibid., 1339–41, 337.

[6] There are many orders to 'supersede the distraint' or 'supersede the exaction' or 'desist from the distraint', and orders 'not to compel' X or Y to find men in ibid., 1339–41, 109, 123–4, 215–24; ibid., 1337–9, 580–1.

[7] Ibid., 1339–41, 122. [8] Ibid., 123.

[9] Ibid., 123. C. Pat. R., 1338–40, 359–60.

[10] C. Close R., 1339–41, 238.

To the general measures for defence may be added the removal of French monks from the priories of Lewes and of St Michael's Mount.[1]

While, therefore, the king was concentrating his efforts on drawing military resources to the ports of Orwell and Great Yarmouth and leading his forces in Flanders, the counties between Cornwall and Kent suffered attacks on their ports and witnessed the flight of people from the coastal regions and the Isle of Wight. They saw also the strengthening of the castles, the combination of the fleet of the Cinque Ports with the fleet of the Admiral towards the West,[2] the reluctant return of men to the maritime lands, the movement to those areas of others who normally lived further inland, and the mobilization of the local militia.

We add a few details for the several counties between the spring of 1338 and the autumn of 1340 (the truce of Esplechin). The numbers of men to be arrayed[3] as laid down in February 1339, were:

	Men-at-arms	Armed men	Archers
Cornwall	25	100	100
Devon	35	140	140
Dorset	25	100	100
Hampshire	30	120	120
Sussex	50	20	200
Kent	35	140	140

In Cornwall, Philip de Columbariis was keeper of the maritime lands. Men between Saltash and Fowey were to be arrayed.[4]

In Devon, Hugh Courtenay, earl of Devon was keeper and his son deputy keeper.[5] The bishop of Exeter, John de Stoford and William de Braybrook were also keepers and engaged in arraying.[6] The sheriff was co-operating in defence work.[7] In February 1340, an invasion of the county was predicted.[8]

In Dorset, the earl of Devon and Philip de Columbariis were keepers.[9] Elizabeth de Burgh was finding men for the Portland

---

[1] Rymer, II, ii, 1061.

[2] Ibid., 1133.   [3] Ibid., 1071-2.

[4] C. Close R., 1339-41, 255, 449; C. Pat. R., 1338-40, 279.

[5] C. Close R., 1339-41, 86, 449.   [6] Ibid., 449, 226.

[7] Ibid., 534.   [8] Ibid., 449.

[9] C. Pat. R., 1338-40, 134. John de Bello Camp had been the keeper in 1337; ibid., 1337-9, 179.

area.[1] The bishop of Bath and Wells was arraying.[2] The abbots and priors of ten religious houses and a large group of laymen were ordered to move to manors near the sea for the defence of the realm.[3] Corfe Castle was to be surveyed with a view to making repairs.[4]

In Hampshire, Richard earl of Arundel was keeper and Bartholomew de Lisle had held that post.[5] They called in the aid of men from Oxfordshire.[6] People were being sent to the coastal area.[7] The men of Winchester were fortifying their city and levying money to defray the expenses.[8] The abbots of Hyde and of Reading each provided six men for defence.[9] At one time the keeper regarded Portsmouth as being in greater danger than Southampton.[10]

At Southampton, the inhabitants had been compelled to return but many were impoverished and homeless. The building of town walls and of houses was proceeding. Quantities of arms and of engines of war were brought in. The abbots of Beaulieu and the abbess of Romsey each provided two men, and the prior of the Hospital of St John in England provided thirty men, for defence.[11]

The labour and expense of defending the Isle of Wight were recognized and some payments were respited.[12] Stocks of food were taken to Carisbrooke castle and orders given that no corn should be taken from the island.[13] Bartholomew de Lisle was ordered to stay on the island, and Henry Trenchard and the

[1] Ibid., 1339–41, 12. The very extensive lands of Elizabeth de Burgh are treated in Holmes, G. A., *The Estates of the Higher Nobility in Fourteenth-Century England*, 35–8 et passim.

[2] *C. Close R.*, 1339–41, 216.

[3] Rymer, II, ii, 1062. They were the abbots of Sherborne, Cerne, Bindon, Abbotsbury and Milton, the priors of Wareham, Cranborne, Frompton, Lodres and Horton and thirty other persons.

[4] *C. Pat. R.*, 1338–40, 556.

[5] And Arundel had power to call for troops from Oxfordshire. *C. Close R.*, 1339–41, 19, 254, 444.

[6] See note above, and ibid., 233.

[7] *C. Pat. R.*, 1338–40, 149–50.

[8] Ibid., 180; *C. Close R.*, 1339–41, 131.

[9] Ibid., 218; ibid., 1337–9, 571.

[10] Ibid., 1339–41, 218.   [11] Ibid., 67, 123, 215, 297.

[12] Ibid., 506, 540. The men of the island later protested that they were 'supporting great labour and heavy expense in the defence', ibid., 1339–41, 285. Further respite was granted in February 1340. *C. Pat. R.*, 1338–40, 423.

[13] Ibid., 212, 423, 425; *C. Close R.*, 1339–41, 352.

lord of Glamorgan to return there.[1] The abbot of Quarr was
providing ten men-at-arms and some archers for the defence of
the island.[2]

In Sussex, the earls of Surrey and of Huntingdon were
keepers of the maritime lands.[3] Fortifications were increased at
Chichester.[4] Building and repairs were proceeding at Porchester
castle; food was being stocked there and a garrison of fifty men
maintained.[5] The garrison at Hastings castle was to be prepared
against an invasion predicted in June 1339.[6] The hundred
archers arrayed in the county for service overseas with the king,
were kept in Sussex for local defence.[7] The abbot of Battle and
his men were staying on the coast near Winchelsea for the
defence of those parts.[8] Churchmen as well as laymen from the
highest downwards were ordered to live with their servants and
retinues on their manors near the sea and to stay there for the
defence of the realm.[9]

The earls of Surrey and of Huntingdon were keepers of the
maritime lands of Kent. The earl of Huntingdon was also constable of Dover castle, which he was charged to victual speedily
and guard securely. For the latter purpose he had a garrison of
100 men (20 men-at-arms, 40 armed men, 40 archers).[10] The
prior of St Martin's, Dover, made engines of war, armour and
walls for the defence of the town.[11] As in Sussex, churchmen and
laymen were to live on their manors near the sea.[12] Archers were
not to be taken from the maritime lands.[13] No victuals except
wine were to be purveyed anywhere within twelve leagues of the
sea, because it was considered that the existing provisions would
hardly suffice for the maintenance of the defence forces.[14]

A few details of the arrangements made for those forces are
available; the hundreds were assessed for men-at-arms and
hobilers, and assembly points were laid down. Night watches

---

[1] *C. Pat. R.*, 1338–40, 444, 455.   [2] Ibid., 6 and see ibid., 26.
[3] Ibid., 215.   [4] Rymer, II, ii, 1078.
[5] *C. Close R.*, 1337–9, 564; ibid., 1339–41, 113, 345.
[6] Ibid., 215.   [7] Ibid., 1341–3, 66.
[8] Ibid., 1337–9, 547, 587. He appears to have served also in the maritime
land of Kent, ibid., 1339–41.
[9] Ibid., 1337–9, 413–14.
[10] Ibid., 568; ibid., 1339–41, 11, 22, 69, 150, 174.
[11] Ibid., 1341–3, 342.
[12] Ibid., 1337–9, 413–14.
[13] Ibid., 402.   [14] Ibid., 402.

were appointed all along the water front and the coast from Dartford, Gravesend, and Faversham in the north, round to Dungeness in the south.[1] The steward of the archbishop of Canterbury was helping in the defence of the maritime land.[2] The bishop of Rochester, the prior of Rochester and the abbot of Boxley were required to send men to defend the Isle of Sheppey which was said to be threatened in October 1338 with invasion.[3] Once in that island, the defenders had to stay there or be punished.[4] The men of Thanet were ordered to stay in Thanet for its defence though the men of Sandwich contended that they should man ships.[5]

Dover, Winchelsea and Rye suffered in their trade because of the war, and Rye had been burned by the French.[6] Sandwich had the life of a busy port providing ships for the king's service, and through the port a large quantity of hurdles and gangways made in Kent for horse boats, were forwarded to Orwell.[7] Some of the inhabitants were leaving in order to avoid the charges for the defence of the town 'against hostile invasion'. They were ordered to return and bear their share of the expense or lose their lands and goods.[8]

In the Channel Islands, the warden, Thomas Ferrers, was ordered to arm the levies and be prepared for French attacks. The attacks came and only Jersey remained in English hands till the French were driven from the other islands in 1340.[9]

When, in September–October 1340, the armed conflict was suspended, England had not been invaded nor, in spite of the French plan of March 1339, had any invasion been attempted. To infer that French intentions had been thwarted by England's preparedness would be to enter a military sphere with which this study is not concerned. (King Edward had indeed felt able to go overseas and take a considerable body of troops with him.) Yet the mobility of naval power had enabled France to threaten a long coast line, to choose successfully where she would inflict damage, to keep thousands of people in a state of anxiety and,

[1] Philipot, T., *Villare Cantianum*, 4–5.
[2] *C. Close R.*, 1337–9, 614; ibid., 1339–41, 266.
[3] Ibid., 1337–9, 609.   [4] Ibid., 1339–41, 123.
[5] Ibid., 238.   [6] Ibid., 1341–3, 8, 342.
[7] Ibid., 1339–41, 505.   [8] Ibid., 237.
[9] Le Patourel, J., *The Medieval Administration of the Channel Islands*, 62. References to the garrison and to the dispatch of victuals are fairly numerous, e.g. *C. Close R.*, 1337–9, 544, 547, 560, 606; ibid., 1339–41, 32.

in brief, to cause social and economic dislocation out of proportion to the effort she had expended. That—for our purpose—is the significant aspect of the events of 1338–40 along the south coast of England.

For nearly two decades few English ports suffered serious damage at the hands of the enemy but the possibility, and at times the likelihood, of French attacks were kept constantly in mind. During the negotiations for an extension of the truce in 1341, sheriffs of the south coast (and those of some east coast) counties were warned that king Philip had assembled a big fleet of armed galleys to destroy English shipping. English fleets would be assembled and all men must be ready to repel attack.[1] In the following year, in the light of an expected attack on the Isle of Wight, defence measures were ordered and all who had moved inland for safety were required to return and live in the maritime region or lose their lands.[2]

There were predictions of invasion and strict orders against evacuation in 1345 (Thanet),[3] early 1346 (Southampton and Essex),[4] again in July 1346[5] and early in 1347.[6] A meeting between the Council on the one side and men thoroughly acquainted with the problems of guarding the maritime lands on the other, was ordered for March 1347.[7] The ostensible grounds for summoning Parliament in 1348 were French preparations for an attack on the realm and the need to thwart them.[8] In 1351 the clergy were informed of French intentions, and keepers were newly appointed for the maritime lands from Cornwall to Lincoln.[9] Invasion, especially of the Isle of Wight, was again predicted in 1352: no victuals were to be taken out, men were to be arrayed and beacons made ready in the island.[10]

And in 1355 and 1356—years in which the English intended to invade France—extensive measures were taken for defence.

[1] Rymer, II, ii, 1165–6. The earl of Huntingdon was now captain and admiral of the 'fleet towards the west'.

[2] Ibid., 1194.   [3] Ibid., III, i, 53.
[4] Ibid., 77–8.   [5] Ibid., 87.
[6] Ibid., 105, 106. A French invasion of England was under consideration in 1347. Coville, *Les Etats de Normandie*, 60.
[7] Rymer, III, i, 106.
[8] *R.P.*, II, 200.
[9] *C. Close R.*, 1349–54, 356; Rymer, III, i, 217.
[10] Ibid, 239, 245. In this instance instructions cover the maritime lands round the whole coast except in Wales, Cheshire and Lancashire.

In July 1355, port authorities from Dover to Fowey and sheriffs of the counties from Kent to Cornwall, were directed to safeguard their shipping, prepare their town for defence and take the usual measures with their beacons.[1] In August, the keepers from Dorset to Norfolk received the usual warning about French ships and prospective invasions together with clear instructions to prepare the beacons and to take steps for the defence of their counties. In Dorset, men were to be armed according to their estate and in the remaining six counties, the mounted men were to be grouped in constabularies, the foot in centaines and vintaines, and the sheriffs and all other officers were to comply with the keepers' plans.[2]

In January 1356, the king wrote from Newcastle that if the French knew that southern England lacked defence forces, they would invade it. He ordered, therefore, a strengthening of London, Southampton and Kent.[3] In August all fencible men in the coastal counties between Norfolk and Hampshire were to be arrayed and furnished with arms and horses to resist invasion, beacons were to be made ready and in Sussex and Kent, once more the order was given that arrayed men must be kept near the coast.[4]

During these years instructions for the safety of shipping became more explicit: ships were not to leave harbour unless they were well armed; ships in harbour were to be kept as near land as possible; finally ships were to be drawn up on the shore.[5]

It is not practicable to follow in detail the effect of such orders on the keepers of the maritime lands and the men under their command. How often they were assembled, for what periods they served, what kinds of activity filled the hours of service, what degree of economic loss arose from their removal from their homes to the coast—on all such questions the evidence is insufficient for judgement.

Inevitably there were complaints. One of them is interesting for the light it throws on the service itself. The keepers, it was said (1337), were too punctilious in maintaining men continuously on the coast. This drew from the king the reply that if the

[1] C. Close R., 1354–60, 214, 215.
[2] C 76/34, m. 9.   [3] Rymer, III, i, 315–17.
[4] Ibid., 337–9. C 76/34, m. 9.
[5] Rymer, III, i, 471; C. Close R., 1354–60, 214–15; C. Inqn. Misc., III, 150.

beacons were properly manned by four, five or six men and lit when danger threatened, that would suffice.[1] The other complaints relate to the cost of the defence system. The prior of Canterbury declared that his convent was not used to be called on to contribute to the *Garde de la Mer*;[2] the men of Kent and the men of Budleigh complained of the burden of the cost;[3] the men of Surrey and of Sussex sought to evade that burden;[4] in Parliament the Commons petitioned that the *Garde* should be maintained at the king's costs;[5] the bishop of Exeter instanced the cost of the *Garde* in an effort to excuse the men of Devon for their reluctance to comply with royal requests for supplies. The county, he said, was unfertile; money was scarce but, above all, there was the *Garde de la Mer*: the county had so many open ports; (French) galleys had sailed round Devon and Cornwall, surveying these ports and, should they presume to invade the realm, landing would be easy.[6]

From Hampshire and Dorset there is an interesting side-light: representations had been made by the keepers to the Council about the continuous watch ordered by the Council in the maritime lands. After investigation, the Council decided that in view of the men's health and of the insufficiency of the goods and chattels needed, 'during the prevailing wintry weather'— it was 3 December 1346—the men might be allowed to go to their homes 'without loss or aspersion on their character', provided that they should be immediately available in case of danger. 'During the present wintry weather', the keepers were not to hold men to continuous duty.[7]

The period saw the growth of complaints in the nation as a whole concerning burdens resulting from the war. Such injustices as the 'prise' of victuals without payment for the king's service, were not confined to the counties bordering the Channel, but some of the southern ports were enduring economic and social distress. The people of Dunwich, for example, complained that in addition to the pestilence and the loss of trade, they had

[1] Rymer, II, ii, 996.
[2] *Literae Cantuarienses*, ed. Sheppard, J. B., II, 206–7.
[3] *R.P.*, II, 194, 213.
[4] Rymer, II, ii, 1025.
[5] *R.P.*, II, 161.
[6] *Register of John de Grandison*, ed. Hingeston-Randolph, F. C., I, 300.
[7] C 76/23, m. 8 dors.

suffered losses of their ships.[1] The men of Budleigh showed that French attacks had caused heavy destruction of their ships.[2] Men resident in the maritime lands and doing their full service in the *Garde* were nevertheless oppressed by sheriffs who fined them for failure to provide men-at-arms and archers or expected them to serve elsewhere.[3]

But the circumstances in the coastal counties were not wholly depressing. During the truces there had been opportunities for resuming trade with France and her allies. When the nations were at war, there was a big demand for shipping. Portsmouth, Southampton, Plymouth had been ports of embarkation for the armies proceeding to Normandy, Brittany and Gascony. Dover had enjoyed much business in supplying Calais with men, munitions and food. From Sandwich the armies had crossed to Calais in 1359. Losses of shipping had occurred but there had been no invasion, not even a serious attack on any part of the coast.

Suddenly, in mid-Lent 1360, a blow fell. King Edward and most of his eminent, military leaders were out of the kingdom. (They were moving northwards between Guillon and Paris.) Early in March messages had been sent out widely to inform the people of England—as so often before—that a French fleet was about to attempt an invasion. Southampton, Portsmouth, Sandwich 'or elsewhere' were mentioned as places likely to be used for a landing; killing, spoiling, burning and other evils would follow—if they landed; the rescue of king John was among their aims.[4]

On Sunday, 15 March, the French 'landed at Winchelsea in a great host of armed men with their horses, took the town, barbarously slew the men therein found, and' an official message continued, 'are riding over the country slaying, burning, destroying and doing other mischief; and greater damage will shortly be done unless they be speedily and manfully opposed'.[5] Actually, the invaders stayed in England only one night.

[1] *C. Close R.*, 1349–54, 620; *R.P.*, II, 210.
[2] Ibid., II, 213.
[3] *R.P.*, II, 53, 160.
[4] Rymer, III, i, 471–2, 475; *C. Pat. R.*, 1358–61, 404–5. Concerning the custody of king John and other French prisoners, see Rymer, III, i, 470, 472, 475.
[5] *C. Close R.*, 1360–64, 101.

As Denifle observes, 'If the French seized the opportunity to do evil and practise crimes, it is nothing compared with the evils the English had wrought in France for twenty three years.'[1] M. Perroy comments that the French attack struck in English hearts 'the panic of a landing which since 1340, they had thought impossible'.[2] In view of all the evidence we have quoted, we cannot hold that English people regarded a landing as 'impossible'.

But the official response to the blow does indicate panic. Immediately messages were sent to the arrayers in a score of counties to raise men; to the ports for the assembly of fleets; to commissioners to arrest ships fit for war, man them and victual them for one month; to residents in the coastal areas to guard the ports; to Flanders for the withdrawal of English ships. Large numbers of the arrayed men were to proceed to London for its defence and London was to provide mariners for the fleets.[3]

In short the administrative effect was out of all proportion to the military cause. By a brief and relatively inexpensive attack on a single port—and that of second-rate importance—the French had caused a very serious dislocation of 'civil' life over a great part of England. The dislocation had at least four aspects. First, there was the sudden withdrawal of men from their necessary work (which included preparation for the year's crops). Next, was the speedy diversion of shipping from the trade of the ports. Thirdly—as the government foresaw—there had to be comprehensive arrangements for the transfer of victuals from inland counties to the coast line where men would assemble for the defence of the realm, to the ports where men would meet for embarkation, and to the ships which were to be stocked for a month.[4] In particular, along the roads of Kent, the public authorities were everywhere directed to ensure that bakers, brewers and victuallers had food and drink available for the troops converging on Sandwich; and supplies of corn and malt were demanded from many counties for transfer to Sand-

[1] *La Desolation des Eglises*, II, 350n.2.
[2] *La Guerre de Cent Ans*, 113. Delachenal wrote that the undertaking was 'mal conçue, mal preparée et médiocrement dirigée', *Histoire de Charles V*, II, 182.
[3] Rymer, III, i, 476–8; C. Close R., 1360–64, 15–20; C. Pat. R., 1358–61, 349–50, 411, 413; Rymer, App. E, 51.
[4] C. Pat. R., 1358–61, 349–51.

wich itself.[1] Finally, very many men did not reach the appointed rendezvous or port by the day stated in the time-table. Other men therefore were enrolled to make up the numbers—and paid wages.[2]

Viewed in the perspective of the war, the two brief episodes on the south coast—separated by more than twenty years—were of trifling importance. 'He never voided his realm but that he left ever enough at home to keep and defend the realm, if need were', wrote Froissart.[3] The men left at home to guard the coasts had been organized and kept in readiness to repel invasion. They gained no ransoms, no spoils, no fame. The chroniclers do not even mention them, nor do the military historians. Yet their presence and the function they performed were factors in the war.

*   *   *   *

The Channel and the North Sea were not only the scenes of occasional, menacing displays of French naval power. They were also the theatres of much violent activity that was independent of formal, international relations but became merged in the war. As this activity concerned the ports from which the English expeditionary forces sailed, the vessels in which they were transported and the crews who manned those vessels, it is convenient to treat it very briefly here.

[1] Ibid., 350–1, 411, 413.

[2] Rymer, III, i, 503; C. Close R., 1360–4, 22–4, 34–5. The collectors of the tenth and fifteenth granted for the expenses of these troops who did not reach the rendezvous by the appointed time, were ordered to pay over to the treasurer specified sums in respect of the moneys collected in their counties, but exceptions were made for the city of Winchester and the towns of Portsmouth and Southampton 'because of divers expenses and charges borne by them for the defence of the realm . . . and for the poverty which they are undergoing in these days . . .', ibid., 90. Soon after peace was declared, some of the moneys hastily collected in every county were repaid, ibid., 50–7.

[3] Froissart (Macaulay), 93.

In his *Military Obligation in Medieval England*, Professor Michael Powicke has many references to 'coast defence'. Twice he mentions the use of men from inland counties for service on the coast (pp. 93 and 203). Only once does he refer to the maritime lands and the keepers ('custodes in maritime or marcher districts', p. 121). He never uses the term *garde de la mer*. The aim of his volume is of course quite different from that of this chapter.

In the middle of the fourteenth century, seafarers in the English Channel and the North Sea had to face four hazards:

1. The natural dangers arising from storms while with imperfect instruments and imperfect steering gear, they navigated uncharted seas.[1]
2. War.
3. Violations of the truces.
4. Piracy.

If we set aside the naval encounters of Sluys and Les Espagnols sur Mer and the organized attacks on the southern ports, then acts of war and acts (by either side) in violation of the truces are scarcely distinguishable from piracy. Indeed at sea, war and truces were but brief episodes in the enduring drama of piracy, for the sea was No-Man's-Land and, though piracy was an obstacle to commerce, the international cooperation necessary for its suppression was not yet forthcoming. No doubt some men sought to gain a livelihood wholly or mainly by robbery at sea, but there was a widespread tendency among seafaring people to take advantage of opportunities for enrichment at the expense of a national enemy, of a neutral, or even of their own countrymen without regard to the circumstances of war or peace.

Chaucer's well-known line about his Shipman—'of nice conscience took he no keep'—indicates an absence of squeamishness concerning victims, and a contemporary guide for confessors says that sailors not only kill men on land, but at sea they practise piracy, seizing the goods of merchants and cruelly killing them.[2]

The exact effect of the war on this kind of enterprise cannot be determined. It may have sharpened the desire to attack while diminishing the opportunities, since vessels used for piracy were as liable as other vessels to be arrested for national needs. Correspondingly the truces and the peace liberated shipping for commerce and for piracy.

Official English concern may be seen in the condemnation of

[1] Lights were maintained at the entrances to the harbours of Yarmouth, Dover, Calais, on St Catherine's Point in the Isle of Wight (and there was a lighthouse on a rock in the sea at the mouth of the Gironde). Concerning ships sailing in convoy, see *Black Book of the Admiralty*, I, 13–19.

[2] Pantin, W. A., *The English Church in the Fourteenth Century*, 273.

an attack by English sailors on the ships of a friendly alien as 'in contempt of the king and to the shame and scandal of the whole realm and the delay of business'.[1] It is seen also in the acknowledgement by the government that English sailors had plundered ships of Portugal (1343), of Gueldres (1340 and 1345), of Spain (1345 and 1346), of Pisa (1352) and of Genoa (1354). It is demonstrated in the orders for restoration or compensation for the losses suffered by the merchants or masters in these incidents.[2]

But it is shown at its fullest in a series of measures aimed at the suppression of piracy or at least the safe-guarding of English interests. At the beginning of our period the fleet is equipped for war 'to repel and destroy the galleys and ships of war gathered at sea for the king's annoyance'.[3] Then a fleet is raised to scour the seas in order to suppress pirates.[4] Later the government develops the convoy system: the wine ships sailing to Bordeaux in the 'reck' season are to assemble off the Isle of Wight or off Plymouth and proceed together for safety. At another time, it arranges to police the mouth of the Thames for the protection of shipping.[5] In 1359, it forms a fleet of ships of war, one of the purposes being to 'conduct and defend ships crossing to and from England with goods and merchandise;[6] and in the same year when the seneschal of Gascony sails with new ships to Bordeaux, he is granted 'duplex eskippamentum' because of pirates and other enemies of the king who stay at sea spying for the said ships'.[7]

Contemporary French records are not readily accessible but it is probable that French shipping interests needed similar protection.

Even in their own harbours, safety for ships was not assured. The French attacks on the south coast of England in 1338–40 and 1360 included the destruction of shipping and ultimately led to the precaution of drawing ships on shore. The English on their part burnt a large number of ships at Boulogne in 1340[8]

[1] C. Pat. R., 1340–3, 593.
[2] Portugal, Gueldres and Spain, C. Fine R., 1337–9, 162, 406, 448. Spain, C. Pat. R., 1340–43, 306, ibid., 1345–8, 38. Pisa, Rymer, III, i, 248. Genoa, C. Close R., 1349–54, 548–9; C. Pat. R., 1354–8, 92.
[3] C. Close R., 1337–9, 526.
[4] Rymer, App. E, 46–7, 51.
[5] C. Close R., 1341–3, 474.   [6] Ibid., 1354–60, 600.
[7] E 372/207 m.   [8] Baker, 67.
c

and, in revenge for the damage done at Winchelsea in 1360, made descents on the French coast and landed at the mouth of the Seine.[1]

Note must also be taken of the uncertain fate of ships of any nation when, seeking refuge from storm, they put into a foreign port. We cite some examples illustrative of the hazards of merchant vessels during this period: ships of Hartlepool trading with Hanse ports are 'taken by evildoers';[2] a ship of Santander is robbed in the port of Dartmouth;[3] the merchants of Sandwich can get no satisfaction for goods taken from their ships by men of Santander;[4] the master and crew of the *Katerine* of Yarmouth are killed in the port of Zwyn, the ship and goods being taken;[5] the *Julyane* of Wight laden with Cornish tin is taken at sea and the crew killed;[6] the *Elayne* of Heachem, fishing off the coast of Norfolk, is taken by men of Estland and sunk, the master and crew being killed;[7] two ships carrying wine and iron for Norman merchants are attacked in the Channel and brought into Dartmouth where the cargo is shared out.[8] A ship carrying wheat from London to Flanders is attacked by sailors from Calais who take the ship and its cargo.[9]

Examples of the work of English sailors during the single year, 1354, include the plundering of the ships of Genoa already mentioned, attacks on a ship sailing to Ireland near the Scillies,[10] on a Lübeck ship near Berwick-on-Tweed,[11] on a Norman ship from which the goods were landed in the Isle of Wight,[12] on another Norman ship from which the cargo was unloaded at Shoreham[13] and on a ship sailing from Flanders whose crew they murdered.[14] Other ports at which pirates put ashore the goods they had obtained at this period include Fowey, Looe, Plymouth and Chichester.[15]

In this general climate of lawlessness, a few episodes not necessarily officially directed, may be regarded as acts of war.

---

[1] Delachenal, op. cit., II, 183–4.
[2] *C. Inq. Misc.*, II, 1660, 1731. See also *C. Pat. R.*, 1358–61, 427.
[3] *C. Inq. Misc.*, II, 1679.
[4] Ibid., 1722.   [5] Ibid., 1865.   [6] Ibid., 1867.
[7] Ibid., 1916.   [8] Ibid., 1814.   [9] Ibid., 1909.
[10] *C. Pat. R.*, 1354–8, 56.
[11] Ibid., 120.
[12] Ibid., 66.   [13] Ibid., 68.   [14] Ibid., 118.
[15] Ibid., 1340–3, 306; ibid., 1358–61, 585.

The *Elyne* of Lynn for example took a cargo of wheat for Stirling Castle and, in returning, was captured and burnt by Scots near Airth in the Firth of Forth.[1] The crew were released on payment of a heavy ransom. The *Maudelayne* of Sluys was taken by the French and used by them to convey victuals and letters to Scotland. It was captured by men of Berwick-on-Tweed.[2] Such episodes may, however, equally be regarded as ordinary practices. The French attitude may be seen in an Ordinance of December 1355 aimed at the encouragement of attacks which, while enriching the attacker, would trouble the enemy and weaken his military effort. In the *guerre de course*, the French had many opportunities for attacks on ships conveying victuals for English armies serving in the various theatres of war.[3]

Temporary cessations of war did not diminish the practice of piracy. They may even have increased the opportunities, for not only was shipping set free for commerce, but also the truces laid down that merchants of France and her allies and those of England and her allies were free to trade at their will in the lands of their opponents. The terms also included the appointment of officers for the investigation of alleged violations of the truce.[4] Except, therefore, those instances in which French or English sailors plundered the ships of their own countrymen, any attack on a ship at sea might be deemed not only piracy (which, though deplorable, had to be endured), but also a violation of the truce which should be formally reported to, and investigated by, the home government and then passed forward to the other government for action and compensation or restitution.

It was to the advantage of the governments and the merchants of all the countries concerned that the terms of the truces should be strictly observed,[5] but the inevitable slowness of the procedure of investigation and reporting from one side to the other,[6] made it ineffective. Merchants and king sought speedier remedies and resorted to retaliation for losses sustained at sea.

---

[1] *C. Inqn. Misc.*, II, 1908.

[2] *C. Close R.*, 1339–41, 560–1.

[3] *Registres*, 260. [4] Baker, 94–5.

[5] And there are instances of the desire to observe the terms on the English side. Cf. (after an episode off the coast of Brittany) 'the king does not wish that trespass to go unpunished because it was committed during the truce', *C. Close R.*, 1341–3, 356.

[6] Cf. ibid., 1354–60, 32–3, 277, 366.

At the highest level, the English king on hearing that one of his subjects had been robbed at sea by a French master and crew of goods valued at a certain sum, directed English port authorities to seize goods of the same (total) value from any French ships which were in, or came into, their harbours.[1] At a lower level, aggrieved masters or merchants or their fellows seized opportunities as they occurred of paying off old scores. (Several south coast towns, as already mentioned, had been burned by the French.) Both forms of reprisal led to counter-reprisal and the process was capable of indefinite extension—and confusion.

Under the circumstances, no balance sheet of gains and losses can be drawn up. Some of the instances of English piracy we have quoted occurred during the truces. There were others in 1340 shortly after the truce of Esplechin, and in 1341 in the western part of the Channel,[2] while pirates based on Winchelsea not only attacked aliens but hindered the assembly of the king's fleet at Sandwich in 1345.[3] On the other hand, there are instances of French attacks on a Fowey ship[4] in 1344, on a ship sailing from Sluys[5] in 1346, on a Boston ship[6] sailing from Bruges in 1348, and on a ship bringing tin to London[7] in 1354. But there must have been many attacks (made by the men of both sides) news of which did not reach the English government.

Though reprisals at one level or another appeared to be the only effective course open to the king or the aggrieved trader or ship's master, they were unsatisfactory as tactics, wounding and exasperating guiltless merchants and sailors without furthering the aims of the war or of the truce. In 1355, when peace negotations were in progress, instructions were sent to the Captain of Calais that while reprisals should neither be made nor tolerated during the truce, certain reprisals instituted at the

---

[1] C. Close R., 1354–60, 32–3, 277, 366; ibid., 1341–3, 435, 447. But there was a proposal on the part of marshal D'Audrehem early in 1355 'to do justice to all merchants and others of England for all damage inflicted upon them by the French, provided the king will do the like on his part'. The captain of Calais was ordered to release the ships and goods of French merchants which he held and to confer with the marshal on this basis. Ibid., 1354–60, 44.

[2] C. Pat. R., 1340–3, 185, 448, 540, 557.

[3] C. Close R., 1343–6, 581.

[4] Ibid., 334.   [5] Ibid., 1346–9, 3.

[6] C. Inqn. Misc., II, 2079.

[7] C. Close R., 1354–60, 87.

king's direction should be ended.[1] In 1357, the issue appeared
to have been settled by an agreement of reciprocal compensation for damage sustained since the preceding truce by subjects
of the English and French kings. This agreement was to be
embodied in a peace treaty.[2] The expected treaty was, however,
rejected by the French and war was resumed in 1359.

Peace came in 1360, but piracy was rife throughout the
century.

[1] Rymer, III, i, 293.
[2] C. *Close R.*, 1354–60, 366.

CHAPTER II

Men going to the War

THE size, composition, recruitment and pay of English armies in the fourteenth century have received much attention during the last thirty or forty years, and more recently the history of military obligation has been the subject of detailed study.[1] The surveys thus produced have been made from heights which enabled scholars to view their subjects over a century or more of development and to offer judgements on questions of national importance in the fields of military and constitutional history. Our task is lowlier, simpler, briefer. It is—to continue the figure —no more than a survey on the ground, not for the purpose of studying a specific topic, but with the aim of seeing events as contemporaries saw them during our quite limited period. We are concerned with the individual rather than the nation, with the locality more than the country. It is unnecessary to repeat what has been competently stated about soldiers' pay and military obligation. We attempt to answer the question, 'why and how did men go to the war at this time?' The motives are well known, but a statement is essential for our picture. The general process by which a 'civilian' became a soldier and reached, say, Sandwich or Plymouth, is also understood, but we shall offer illustrations from many counties.

That there was some degree of national consciousness need not be doubted though it is very difficult to analyse; that there was anti-French feeling is certain, for attacks on south-coast towns had been serious and, as we shall show in a later chapter, steps were repeatedly taken to inform opinion about the great likelihood, indeed the imminent danger, of French invasion and the dire consequence that would follow.[2] Steps were taken also to explain to the people in general the causes of the war, to gain the church's aid in requests for God's blessing on English campaigns, and to spread news of the victories of English arms.[3]

[1] See the Bibliography under Lewis, N. B., Prince, A. E., Powicke, Michael.

[2] Chapter VII. [3] Ibid.

But participation sprang from personal rather than general reasons, and there were reasons enough to attract men of widely different status and circumstance to take up arms. We glance therefore at the conditions out of which voluntary participation arose.

In a period in which crimes of violence were very numerous and murderers were declared (after due procedure) to be outlaws, it was held that murder (and other crimes leading to outlawry) could be expiated by notable service. Only the king, however, could grant charters of pardon.[1] During years of peace, therefore, there were many scores—at times several hundreds —of men suffering the gravest penalty short of death and longing for a means of regaining the status of free citizens.

The outbreak of war enabled the king to take advantage of this situation by offering to grant such men pardons in return for military service or the manning of his ships.[2] Though a few pardons were granted in advance, for the great majority of men indicted of murder or other serious felonies, charters of pardon were withheld till the services had been performed and attested by the leaders in whose companies the men had served. Even then the pardons were frequently subject to further conditions.

A straightforward instance is seen in an offer made in 1342 to a group of sailors whose piracy had involved the king in the payment of heavy compensation. If they would go to the port of Orwell and do two months service at sea, then on receipt of a satisfactory report on their bearing, they would receive charters of pardon.[3]

Very often three conditions were imposed; that the man pardoned stand his trial if anyone proceed against him for the

[1] See Hunnisett, R. F., *The Medieval Coroner*, especially p. 77.

[2] Ibid., especially p. 68. Recent studies of outlaws include Keen, M., *The Outlaws of Medieval Legend*; Aston, T. H., 'Outlaws of Medieval Legend' and articles or notes on Robin Hood by Hilton, R. H., Holt, J. C., and Keen, M., in *Past and Present*, nos. 20, 14 and 19; Stones, E. L. G., 'The Folvilles of Ashby-Folville in Leicestershire', *Trans. R.H.S.*, 5th series, vol. 7, 1957. Only the last of these studies has any direct relation to the subject of this chapter. It deals with six brothers—all criminals—four of whom gained pardons in 1327 for service against the rebellion of the earl of Lancaster, and a fifth received pardon in return for service against the Scots.

[3] *C. Pat. R.*, 1340-43, 538. The certificates in Ancient Correspondence XL, numbers 10 to 20 appear to refer to these men.

trespasses of which he is indicted; that he find sufficient security to be henceforth of good behaviour; that he come to the king wherever he may be, when called upon, to stay for one year at the king's wages (or sometimes at his own charges). And, when pardons were granted during the course of a campaign, the following condition was often inserted: that he do not withdraw from the king's service so long as he shall stay on this side the seas, without his special licence.

There were also general pardons in which no conditions were inserted.

Many of the charters of pardon are dated in the months following the return of companies to England; some follow several years later. Normally the recipient is discharged of all felonies committed before a certain date (e.g. a battle) and of any consequent outlawries.

It is not, of course, possible to know what proportion of outlaws offered themselves for military service, nor of those who offered what proportion was accepted, nor of those accepted what proportion qualified for pardon or survived to beg for charters. Some idea of the relation of pardons to military service may, however, be gained from the following figures: in 1339–40, at least 850 charters of pardon were granted to men who had served in the wars; in 1346–7 several hundred for service in Scotland, or with the king in northern France, or with Henry of Derby in Gascony; after the Poitiers campaign, about 140; in the autumn of 1360 and the year 1361, over 260; and many more at other dates. (The proportion of murderers in these numbers is considerably above three-quarters.) It seems probable that from two to twelve per cent of most of the armies of the period consisted of outlaws.[1]

In a very broad generalization, it may be said that men of the northern counties received pardons for service in Scotland.[2] No doubt because of the practice of holding men living near the Channel for the defence of England, relatively few pardons appear to have been received by men of the south coast counties. But there are many exceptions: deeds leading to outlawry occurred in every county and men as eminent as Sir Robert Knolles and Sir Hugh Calveley received pardons for the felonies they had

[1] The figures are drawn from the Calendars of *Patent Rolls*, e.g. 1338–40, 217–36 and ibid., 1358–61, 375–402.
[2] E.g. *C. Pat. R.*, 1354–8, 354, 369.

committed, though such born leaders needed no incentive to take up arms.

Incentives, however, both worthy and less worthy, were not lacking. It is true that the campaigns of the period were not comfortable jaunts, that Derby's men had to withstand a siege at Aiguillon (1346), the king's troops to endure the winter cold at Calais (1346–7), the prince's men to ford or swim the swollen rivers of Languedoc in November 1355, the king's soldiers to face winter in the lowlands of Scotland in 1356, and his large army to march in appalling weather to Rheims in 1359 and wait in the snow outside that city. It is true that at times in all campaigns, food was short for man and horse. But such rigours were not unusual in the fourteenth century.

It is true also that the early campaigns in Flanders are now described as 'disappointing', 'fruitless' and merely ending in a truce (at Esplechin), that the early campaign in Brittany ended in a truce (at Malestroit) which was followed by negotiations and a further truce. But these summary judgements are made in references to the aims and achievements of the enterprises.[1] They do not reflect the views of individual knights, men-at-arms and archers who had seen foreign lands, experienced the companionship of arms, felt the excitement of witnessing burning towns, shared the loot—and, in some instances, earned pardons too.

But from 1346, almost all aspects of the war appeared to be favourable to recruitment. English power and skill were displayed in the devastating march through Normandy, the approach to Paris, the victory of Crécy, the capture of Calais, the successes of Henry of Derby in Gascony and the triumph over the Scots at Neville's Cross. Victory was in the air, confidence in the hearts of men.[2] A desire to participate in the great undertaking was natural.

Fame soon surrounded some of the leaders. It was good to serve under Henry of Derby (Lancaster) for, when a town was sacked, he took little or nothing for himself.[3] Audley was a most valiant knight: the prince himself recognized his worth. Chandos 'a simple knight with very meagre fief holdings, could muster in 1359 a contingent which surpassed in size and quality that of most of the baronage, and even of one or two earls'.[4]

---

[1] McKisack, 130, 131, 165. [2] Walsingham, 292.
[3] Ibid., 284. [4] Prince, *Indenture System*, 283.

The circumstances of the war were evolving men for whom the profession of arms provided an honourable and even remunerative career. That nobles such as the earls of Lancaster, Northampton, Warwick, Oxford, Suffolk, Salisbury played conspicuous parts in several of the campaigns was not surprising. Equally important was the eminence achieved by non-nobles some of whom had inherited little wealth but gained distinction by their valour or skill. Prominent among them were John Chandos, Hugh Calveley and Robert Knolles (while Bertrand du Guesclin affords a French parallel). We are very far from *la carrière ouverte aux talents*, but a few talented men did contrive to carve distinguished careers in arms. For such men—and for less distinguished men also—there were material rewards. John Copeland was handsomely paid for capturing the Scots' king and Robert Bertram received 100*l* from the king for a Scottish prisoner of war.[1] John Chandos received a large estate in Lincolnshire and, later, lands in the Cotentin.[2] A score or two of the prince's personal followers were given lands or other sources of income for their services in Gascony. The capture of a French noble might lead to a fortune; the arrest of an enemy ship to riches; the bringing of first news of a victory to a very substantial gift.[3]

And there was plunder to be had in France. Furs and finery brought back to England revealed the excellence of French goods while instances of gold and silver articles and beautiful leatherwork could be quoted. Wine was so abundant that looters smashed the vats and let the precious liquid drain away.[4] Even on the battlefield of Poitiers, Cheshire archers picked up a silver ship (probably a large salt cellar) belonging to the French king, and the prince of Wales bought it from them.[5]

Behind it all in the landed class lay a strain of chivalry and of the romance of war, lingering from the ideals of earlier cen-

[1] *C. Pat. R.*, 1338–40, 177.

[2] Hewitt, *B.P.E.*, 160–1; *C. Pat. R.*, 1358–61, 255, 329.

[3] Hewitt, *B.P.E.*, chapter VII, and 138 (news of Poitiers); *C. Pat. R.*, 1345–8, 198 (news of Neville's Cross); *C. Fine R.*, 1347–56, 437 (arrest of ship with valuable cargo).

[4] Froissart (Lettenhove), V, 379, 385 ('ils . . . effondraient les tonnials plains de vins'). In B.M. Royal, 20 C VII, fol. 41v (illustrating the looting of a house) soldiers are depicted smashing one vat and drinking from another.

[5] *B.P.R.*, III, 254.

turies, warmed by stories of Alexander and of Arthur and the
Round Table, fostered by the Order of the Garter and exempli-
fied by the king who loved war, especially war with the trap-
pings of chivalry.[1] At its best, it is honourable even when artifi-
cial and utterly remote from the realities of war. At its second
best, it signifies intense loyalty to a leader and a desire for personal distinction. At its worst, it is a veneer covering an exciting
materialism. Our very 'parfit gentil knyght' after years of travel
and experience of war, is unassuming in manner and still loves
chivalry and the great social virtues. Our 'young squyer' though
only twenty years of age, has already seen military service in
Flanders, Artois and Picardy and 'born him wel', his motive
being 'hope to standen in his ladies grace'. He is (in modern
terms) a well-bred young fellow; but we feel that he has less hold
on fundamentals than his father. It will be sufficient for him if he
stands well in his lady's grace or that of his followers. He will
of course go overseas in the next campaign and prove a quite
satisfactory soldier. With him will be many who know how 'to
sitte on hors and fairē ryde', who delight in 'hors and harness
noyse and clateryng', who love chivalry 'and wolde seek to have
a noble name', young men desiring 'honourable and noble adven-
tures of feats of arms'. Their ideals are not high but they are not
mercenary.

Finally, the years of this study fall in the period in which paid
service was being added to, or substituted for, obligatory service
—not as a single stroke of policy, but gradually as circumstances
revealed the necessity for the change. The feudal army had
proved unsuitable for war; the machinery by which it was assembled was cumbrous, the period of obligatory service insufficient for operations even in Scotland or Wales, the discipline
unsatisfactory. In the early years of his reign, king Edward had
relied on obligatory service to provide the nucleus of his
mounted troops and used the incentive of pay to augment it with
volunteers. By 1337, 'the process of reducing the compulsive and
increasing the voluntary element was carried still further'.[2] In

---

[1] See, e.g., *Sir Gawain and the Green Knight* (Penguin Classics, 1959) or
'Sir Gawayne and the Grene Knight' in *The Age of Chaucer* (Pelican, 1954),
351 to 430.
[2] Lewis, N. B., 'The recruitment and organization of a contract army,
May to November, 1338', *Bulletin of the Institute of Historical Research*,
XXXVII, No. 95 (May 1964), 5.

the 1340's recruitment by contract was widely used and a scale of wages was evolved that was applicable not only to the archer but also to the earl.[1] Moreover, for the mounted archer at any rate, the wages were good. They were 6d. a day—the wages of a skilled, even of a master craftsman. There was also an additional payment or war bonus called a 'regard' which was paid over to the leader of a group once a quarter.[2]

The results of the change were important. The nobility still served as cavalry but they now became recruiting agents, contracting to supply given numbers of men to be paid at the standard rates, the men themselves having undertaken to serve for specified periods.

For the adventurous, the ambitious, the romantically-minded, for men conscious of gifts of leadership, for the gentry, for nobles carrying forward a family tradition, for the mercenary-minded, for the discontented, the ne'er-do-well, the outlaw—provided they were fit in body and of suitable age—some aspect or aspects of war in the mid-fourteenth century had sufficient appeal to make service acceptable, even attractive.

Such men joined the companies which leaders undertook to raise for the king's service. Among the numerous contractors were the six nobles already mentioned and, for the expedition of 1359, they were joined by the king's sons, Edward, prince of Wales, John, earl of Richmond, Lionel, earl of Ulster, Edmond of Langley, with the earls of March and of Stafford, and very many others of whom the following may be a representative dozen: Guy de Brian, Bartholomew de Burghersh, Roger de Clifford, Reginald de Cobham, William Farlee, Ralph Ferrers, Roger de Hampton, Thomas Moigne, Richard de Pembrigge, Henry de Percy, Thomas de Roos, Thomas Ugthred.[3]

As already stated the contracts made between a captain and the king or other leader specified the number of men of different ranks to be raised, with their rates of pay and the period of service undertaken. At first this was only 40 days, but allowance was commonly made for an extension at the given rates of pay, and later contracts were made to run for nine weeks, a quarter of a year, a half year, a year or 'as long as the king desires'.

As examples of the groups to which a man might attach him-

[1] Prince, *Indenture System*, 287, 291.
[2] Ibid., 293.
[3] *C. Pat. R.*, 1358–61, 375–402.

self, we cite undertakings made in 1341 (for 40 days) by the following leaders:[1]

	Bannerets	Knights	Men-at-arms	Armed men	Archers
Earl of Warwick	3	26	71	40	100
		100			
Earl of Northampton	7	74	199	200	250
		280			
Earl of Gloucester	1	30	69	—	—
		100			
John de Beaumont	1	24	36	40	40
		61			
Robert de Ferrers	1	10	40	30	100
		51			

And in 1342:[2]

	Bannerets	Knights	Esquires	Mounted archers
Earl of Derby	earl & 5	50	144	200
		200		
Earl of Devon	2	12	36	60
		50		
Earl of Stafford	3	16	31	50
		50		

In 1345, Henry of Derby undertook to lead 250 men-at-arms and 250 mounted archers for his campaign in Gascony.[3] No written indentures for the Crécy campaign appear to have survived.[4] In 1355, the prince of Wales had a retinue of 433 men-at-arms, 400 mounted archers and 300 foot archers[5] and Sir John de Lisle (who accompanied him) had a total of 100 men, namely himself, 20 knights, 39 esquires, 40 mounted archers.[6]

Equally a man might seek service in the march of Scotland where in 1342 Thomas Lucy undertook to stay with 5 knights, 20 men-at-arms and 30 archers. In 1355, the same Thomas

[1] C. Pat. R., 1340–43, 264–7.
[2] C. Close R., 1341–3, 565, 569, 571–2.
[3] Prince, Indenture System, 289n.6.   [4] Ibid., 287–8.
[5] B.P.R., IV, 143–5.   [6] E 372/200, m. 7.

agreed to be responsible for the garrison, castle and town of Carlisle. In addition to himself (a banneret), there were to be 5 knights, 55 esquires, 60 mounted archers and 20 foot archers.[1] Under the same indenture system, men were raised for the defence of the Isle of Wight.[2]

The 'accustomed wages of war' specified in the agreements between a leader and the king were: for an earl 6s. 8d. a day, a banneret 4s., a knight 2s., a man-at-arms 1s., a mounted archer 6d., a foot archer 3d. Welsh lancemen drew 2d. a day.

In many instances, leaders produced the exact number of men they had undertaken to raise.[3]

To the large numbers thus raised by contract, the king sought to add still more by extending the ancient duty of military service. It was necessary, therefore, to resort to the *posse comitatus* and to the use of commissions of array in order to select the men most suitable for service in the expeditionary forces. The practice gave rise to controversies over the legality of demanding service outside the counties in which the chosen men lived, over the expenses of equipping such men, and over the date or point from which the 'conscripted' men should be paid. With the legal and constitutional issues we are not here directly concerned. Our aim is to follow the process by which a man became a soldier and went to the war.

Arrayers operated within single counties[4] and, although they were at times subject to supervision,[5] it would be an error to infer that the procedures adopted and the standards of fitness and skill looked for were uniform. Nor, though the number of men demanded from the counties varied broadly with their size, can it be assumed that the proportion of men to be raised was the same in different counties.[6]

[1] Indentures of War, E/Box 68, file 3, numbers 51 and 44.

[2] Ibid., file 4, number 74.

[3] Prince, *Indenture System*, 289, 289 n.6.

[4] Neighbouring counties forming the bailiwick of one sheriff were of course combined, but the argument is unaffected.

[5] C 76/22, m. 21, contains a long statement (20 Edward III) with names of counties.

[6] In 1341, arrayers appointed to raise 160 archers from the counties of Northampton and Rutland jointly, charged Rutland with 40. The men of Rutland protested that the county of Northampton 'contains twenty six hundreds whereof the smallest is larger than the whole of Rutland', *C. Close R.*, 1341–3, 190. Another aspect of proportional recruitment is seen in

PLATE I. Archery practice (from the Luttrell Psalter)

Arrayers were instructed to carry out the following tasks:

1. to choose, test and array a certain number of men.
2. to clothe them.
3. to equip them.
4. (in some instances) to mount them.
5. to pay them.
6. (*a*) to send them, under a leader, to a given place.

or

(*b*) to hold them in readiness for departure till further instructions were received.

Though a few arrayers were held to have been incompetent or dishonest,[1] it is likely that the majority discharged their duties competently, visiting each hundred, township and liberty, and selecting (in accordance with their instructions) the *meliores, fortiores, validiores, potentiores* or *aptiores, les meillors et plus suffisantz, les plus forcibles et plus vigerous, les plus suffisantz et plus vaillanz*, of the archers.

Good health and good archery were not always combined. There was a complaint in 1341 that some archers were 'feeble'.[2] Henry of Lancaster was directed in 1346 to pick out the 'ailing and weakly' from some Welsh troops before they embarked.[3] And in 1355, just before he sailed from Plymouth, the prince of Wales sent home some men from Flint and North Wales because they were ill.[4]

From 1343 onward, men who were opposed to inclusion in the selected body might gain exemption by a money composition.[5] The sums accepted (described as 'reasonable fines') varied widely according to men's means, and the practice of thus avoiding service does not seem to have been widespread.[6] The

---

instructions to arrayers in Lincolnshire in 1359: they are 'to enquire as to the customary proportion of men to be levied from different parts of the county', *C. Inqn. Misc.*, III, No. 369.

[1] *R.P.*, II, 149.   [2] *C. Close R.*, 1341–3, 369.
[3] C 76/22, m. 22.   [4] *B.P.R.*, III, 216.
[5] Baker, 76; see Powicke, 197–8.

[6] The subject has not been fully investigated. The Black Prince instructed the Justice of Chester in 1346 to raise men 'without sparing anyone for gift or favour', *B.P.R.*, I, 14 and ibid, III, 449. But he ordered the release of seven Welshmen in 1347 who had been imprisoned for failure to go to the war 'as they have made fines with the prince for this trespass and have paid

city of London, having voluntarily raised 40 armed men and 60 archers in 1338, secured acknowledgement that its action should not prejudice its liberty as a precedent, and in 1359 the citizens paid 500*l* in lieu of the service of 150 mounted archers.[1]

(Occasionally also a pseudo-exemption or a protection against the arrayers had to be conceded to seaports, the men of which were rendering equivalent naval service, as at Great Yarmouth in 1338, at Kingston-upon-Hull in 1355, and at Great Yarmouth and King's Lynn in 1359.)[2]

These conditional exemptions, however, did not really lessen the total number of men raised, for the sums received in lieu of service could, of course, be used for the wages of other troops; and manning the ships was indispensable for expeditionary forces. There were times when archers were raised explicitly for service against pirates.[3]

In addition to the archers, the levies contained footmen from North Wales[4] equipped with 'lances and other suitable arms'; and a few men who were needed for their civilian skills such as smiths, miners, pavilioners, carpenters, mortarers, ditchers, but these craftsmen were found by other means.[5] The miners— usually from the Forest of Dean—needed transport for their tools.[6]

Beside the fighting men and craftsmen already mentioned, the king and the prince took with them groups of personal attendants and a few administrative officers. In 1355, for example, the prince had (among others) his chamberlain, tailor,

---

the fines'. *B.P.R.*, I, 62. C 76/22, m. 21, contains instructions to treat with those men in counties Worcester, Hereford, Oxford and Berkshire who wish to make fines in lieu of service (1346). Sums ranging from one mark to ten marks are stated to have been paid as fines for release from military service in 1346, *C. Pat. R.*, 1345–8, 122. And see *C. Fine R.*, 1337–47, 498–500.

[1] *C. Pat. R.*, 1338–40, 108; ibid., 1358–61, 256.

[2] *C. Close R.*, 1337–9, 323; ibid., 1354–60, 142, 555.

[3] Rymer, Appendix E., 47, 'impressment of archers to be employed in scouring the sea during the absence of the king' (1359).

[4] *B.P.R.*, I, 49, 52. Welsh lancemen provided with swords and lances, were sent also to Scotland, ibid., III, 494.

[5] Rymer, III, i, 417 (1359); C 76/22, m. 20 (1346). In the forts round Calais there were also springalders, carters, victuallers, boatmen. E 101/27/8.

[6] E 372/191, m. 9 dors. A body of miners from the Forest of Dean with six master miners set off in October 1346 with six horses to carry their 'instrumenta'.

baker, butler, pavilioner, two friars preachers, three clerks, some minstrels, two farriers, his physician (William Blakwater) and John Wengfeld, soon to be known as the Governor of the prince's business.[1] With the king in France in 1344 was a military band consisting of five trumpeters, five pipers, three waits, two clarioners, 1 taborer, 1 nakerer, 1 fiddler. They ranked among the archers of the royal household.[2] A large staff, which included Master Jordan of Canterbury, the king's physician, accompanied the king in 1346, and he is said to have taken mounted falconers in 1359.

Other non-fighting (or not primarily fighting) men are also to be found such as the chaplains, interpreters and occasionally physicians who accompanied Welsh contingents, the 'guide to Gascony' who served the prince in the autumn of 1355[3] and miscellaneous men whose chief work was with the baggage-train or in the kitchen.

We turn to the soldiers' clothing. Writs of the period commonly state that the troops raised in a given county are to be supplied with a suit or 'clothed in one suit' (at the county's expense) and the records of London (1334) reveal purchases of cloth for 'gowns' and 'hoods' for some mounted troops and a sum paid for making the 'gowns'.[4] The writs state no reason for adopting uniform and, except in one limited region, they do not mention the colour or size or form of the suit. Probably experience had shown that the soldier should be not only adequately armed but also adequately clothed.

Only in the records of Cheshire and Flint are there details of the clothing of the archers and of the Welsh lancers. In these two counties, the material used was woollen, the articles supplied were short coats and hats, the colours were green and white (green on the right side of both articles, white on the left), and these colours were ordered for every group of men raised in our period. It was the duty of the chamberlain of Chester to buy the cloth and deliver a suit and a hat to each arrayed man, but how and by whom they were made is not clear. At times, when men of Flint were arrayed at short notice, they received their uniforms in London.[5]

[1] Hewitt, *B.P.E.*, 22–3; *B.P.R.*, IV, 208.
[2] Rickert, E., *Chaucer's World*, 287.   [3] Hewitt, *B.P.E.*, 65.
[4] Sharpe, R., *London and the Kingdom*, 189–90.
[5] *B.P.R.*, I, 13, 14, 49; ibid., III, 29, 30, 32, 249, 449.

The equipment provided (at the county's expense) for the archers consisted of bows, arrows and 'competent arms', the last terms being undefined but (on the evidence of the sheriffs' rolls and the Black Prince's Register) tending to mean swords and knives. The arrows here delivered were no more than an initial supply—one sheaf per man—and as further supplies would have to be drawn from national stores for which the sheriffs made large purchases, national and local supplies are treated together in a later chapter.[1]

Though it was evident that arrayed men had to have wages, the point at which paid service should begin needed definition. Within their own counties, unpaid service could be demanded, and it was arguable that active service did not begin until the men had embarked or at least reached the port from which they would sail. Alongside these partly legal aspects stood three practical considerations, namely the mens' unwillingness to start on a long journey without money, their probable conduct on the way if they had to march penniless to the port and, of course, the source from which the moneys required for wages should be drawn.

The Cheshire men were in the clearest position, for their service in the Welsh wars had led to a definition of their obligations in a charter of 1216, and further evidence lay in an Inquest of Service of 1288. Barons in the palatine county owed the earl (in our period, the Black Prince) no service 'beyond the Lyme except of their own good will' and at his expense; serjeants of the peace 'as soon as they shall cross the Dee or go elsewhere out of Cheshire, it shall be at the king's charges'.[2] During the years of this study, payment for out-of-county marches of the Cheshire archers was never in dispute. In 1346 it was for the period 'till their arrival at Sandwich'; in 1347, they were given sixteen days' wages for the journey to Calais; in 1355, twenty-one days' wages for the march to Plymouth and in 1359, seven days' wages for the journey to Northbourne. These periods were laid down by the prince's council and the wages were paid in advance by the chamberlain of Chester.[3]

The men of North Wales usually received similar treatment

[1] Chapter III.

[2] *Cheshire County Court Rolls*, Chetham Society, 1925, xliii–liv, 115.

[3] *B.P.R.*, I, 13; ibid., III, 204, 350, 357. See also ibid., I, 49–52, 63, 68, 80 and Powicke, 205n.3.

respecting the number of days' pay, but their rates of pay were lower. In 1336 the issue had arisen over the manning of ships in the ports of North Wales to resist a possible Franco-Scottish invasion. The Welsh had demanded that they be paid in advance and the king, though maintaining that 'all are compelled as a duty to defend the realm against invasion', had been obliged to concede their demand. Henceforward the principle of pre-payment was accepted—at first grudgingly: 'not wishing to delay the start of the seven hundred men thus chosen', runs a dispatch to the chamberlain of North Wales in 1338, 'we order you to pay them, their leader or leaders their daily wages from the date they leave their own parts till they reach Norwich'.[1]

In other parts of the realm no such clear principle was operative. Moreover, a principle was needed for men proceeding to war in Scotland. In 1339 the Commons agreed that the men arrayed in the counties of Derby, Nottingham and York were to go as far as Newcastle-on-Tyne at the cost of their counties, and the men of Lancashire, Westmorland and Cumberland as far as Carlisle at their county's expense. From these two assembly points, they would proceed at the king's wages.[2]

The circumstances of the period were posing new problems or old problems on a new scale. The king, the barons, the Commons had conflicting interests and, for some years, a lasting principle could not be reached. An ordinance of 1344 laid down that men chosen to go on the king's service out of England should be at the king's wages from the day they left the counties in which they were chosen, till they returned.[3] The ultimate outcome was that arrayed men marched without pay to their county boundary, then at the county's expense to the sea. Thereafter they were at the king's wages—even when there was a delay before embarkation.[4] (Contracting barons and other

---

[1] Evans, D. L., *Wales under the Black Prince*, 52; Rymer, II, ii, 1018.

[2] *R.P.*, II, 110, 119.

[3] *The Statutes at Large*, II, 13. Sometimes arrangements were made to pay men at certain points on their march to the ports, e.g. in 1325 footmen from North Wales were to receive wages at Shrewsbury and Hereford. *Parliamentary Writs*, II, ii, 708.

[4] The subject may be pursued at length in Powicke, especially 197, 201–9.

leaders also counted their service from the day they arrived with their men at the sea.)[1]

It was impracticable to direct each individual sheriff to pay men for a given number of days' travelling time: they were told to pay 'reasonable wages'—and had to pay them in advance. Fairly often they stated the distance in justification of the sums they disbursed, and about twenty miles a day appears to have been regarded as a distance which men might achieve and auditors approve. (This is more than a contemporary army on

TABLE I

Some movements of archers in 1345*

County	Archers	Place of Assembly	Start	Days' Pay	Port
Stafford	125	Lichfield	25 May	6	Southampton
Wiltshire	40	Marlborough	1 June	—	Sandwich
Cambridge	50	—	10 ,,	5	,,
Huntingdon	20	Fenstanton	12 ,,	5	,,
Gloucester	50	Lechlade	16 ,,	6	,,
Warwick	40	Dunchurch	14 ,,	6	,,
Leicester	20	Bosworth	9 ,,	6	,,
Lincoln	50	Stamford	2 ,,	6	,,
Salop	100	Bridgnorth	12 ,,	7	,,
Somerset	40	Bruton	4 ,,	9	,,
Dorset	40	Blandford	6 ,,	8	,,
Buckingham	22	Aylesbury	10 ,,	2	,,
Worcester	20	Campden	4 July	5	,,

* Pipe Roll, 19 Edward III, E 372/190 (chiefly m 6).

the march could maintain, but the archers had little impedimenta and seldom needed more than seven or eight days for their journey.)[2]

At some point, steps were taken to safeguard the interests of the men during their absence from England: attorneys were appointed by those who had considerable possessions; letters of

[1] The date from which payment shall start is laid down in the indenture, and confirmation for knights who die during a campaign may appear in an inquisition. Sir John de Lisle, for example, accompanied the prince to Gascony in 1355 and was fatally wounded on 13 October of that year. That he and his men reached Plymouth on 9 July (from which date payment was due) is revealed in Pipe Roll, Edward III, m. 7.

[2] See Tables I and II.

protection were issued and, in various places where legal action was pending against an archer or a leader, orders were given for the operation of the law to be suspended till his return.[1]

The last step was the dispatch of the selected men to the port or other rendezvous. A place of assembly was appointed and some kind of review held to ensure that the required number of men were sent and that each one was properly equipped. The place chosen for the assembly was not necessarily central. It is from such towns as Lechlade, Bruton, Shaftesbury, Alton, Lichfield, Bridgnorth, Stamford that the men set out. On the first day's—in some instances, in the first hour's—march they would cross the county boundary.

If the number of men was large, they were organized in hundreds and in scores (vintaines). A leader—generally mounted and, for all large parties, appointed by the king—took charge, usually carried the wages[2] and a nominal roll, and had the duty of 'delivering' the men to an official appointed to receive them.

Several of the major expeditions appear to have been intended to depart after the hay harvest. At that part of the year, hours of daylight and warmth of atmosphere may have rendered the march tolerable, even easy. With twenty-one days' wages available, the Cheshire archers enrolled for service in Gascony in 1355 needed to cover no more than an average of thirteen miles a day to reach Plymouth. On the other hand, inevitable delays in assembling shipping, emergencies and occasional lack of forethought might necessitate a start in any month. In 1346, some small groups set out in December, and a few began their march in January, 1347.

Equipped with arms and wearing their uniforms, the archers set out for the port of embarkation or the rendezvous. The weather, the speed of movement necessary, the nature of the lands through which they passed no doubt influenced the mood of the marchers. How they ate and where they slept cannot be traced. Unaccustomed to discipline, as they advanced further

---

[1] Where men were about to set out in the king's service or were already serving overseas, sheriffs or justices or other officers received instructions under various formulae: 'X should have respite till . . .', 'things are to stay in the same state as they now are', 'the execution of the commission to enquire . . . should be superseded', 'Y's homage is deferred'. In the courts, the formula may run 'the case is postponed indefinitely . . . as Z is serving . . .'.

[2] *C. Close R.*, 1333–7, 26–7. 'Order to pay the leaders of the men elected . . . wages for themselves and the said men.'

TABLE II

Some movements of archers in 1346*

County	Archers	Place of Assembly	Start	Days' Pay	Port
Wilts	50	Salisbury	17 Aug.	12	Winchelsea
,,	30	,,	14 Oct.	6	Sandwich 130 miles
,,	30	,,	2 Jan.†	6	,,
Surrey & Sussex	30	?	9 Oct.	—	,,
Cambs & Hunts	20	Cambridge?	3 Jan.†	6	,, 118 miles
Worcs	12	Worcester?	14 Oct.	4	(Lambeth)
,,	12	Worcester?	18 Dec.	4	Sandwich
Warwick	20	Coventry	—	7	,,
Kent	20	Canterbury	—	2	,,
,,	20	,,	—	7	(The king)
Staffs	20	Stafford	14 Dec.	7	Sandwich 140 miles
Hants	12	Alton	10 Oct.	5	,,
,,	12	Winchester	16 Dec.	6	,,
,,	50	,,	18 Aug.	12	(The king)
Essex	20	Chelmsford	3 Jan.†	5	Sandwich
Herts	20	Cheshunt	3 Jan.†	6	,,
Somerset	80	Somerton	24 Aug.	12⎫	Southampton, then
Dorset	60	Shaftesbury	25 ,,	12⎭	Winchelsea
Somerset	30	Somerton	22 Dec.	12	Sandwich 182 miles
Dorset	30	Shaftesbury	8 ,,	12	,, 166 miles
Salop	20	Shrewsbury	8 Oct.	7	,, 160 miles
,,	20	,,	11 Nov.	7	,, 160 miles

* Pipe Roll, 20 Edward III, E 372/191.   † 1347.

and further from their villages, they were liable to experience
two temptations: first, to commit acts of lawlessness ('felonies,
trespasses and oppressions commited by men coming to Portsmouth to go on the king's service beyond the seas'),[1] and second
—on the journey or after reaching the port—to desert. In 1338,
some archers from the county of Cambridge, equipped, clothed
and mounted, reached Newcastle-on-Tyne on their way to
Scotland, were paid, and then disappeared.[2] Before leaving
Plymouth in 1355, the prince's officers listed twenty-one men of

[1] *C. Pat. R.*, 1345–8, 113. Giles de Beauchamp and Aleyn de Cherlton,
appointed to lead some Welsh troops to Portsmouth in 1325, were instructed
to ensure that the men did no harm (*mal ne damage*) during their march.
Parliamentary Writs, II, ii, 708, No. 248.

[2] *C. Pat. R.*, 1339–41, 72.

Flint, fourteen men of North Wales and four Cheshire men who had 'withdrawn themselves . . . whither the prince knows not' (and one of the Cheshire deserters took more than 6*l* with him!).[1] But references to such lawlessness and desertion are not numerous.

On the other hand, victuallers were tempted to take advantage of the large numbers of men marching towards the ports of embarkation. Though the price of wine was regulated by ordinance, wholesale dealers contrived by secret sales to evade the regulation even in peace time. News of war quickly sent up the price. In June 1355, the mayor and sheriffs of London and the king's butler were ordered to search all wine cellars and storeplaces for wine, to list the quantities found and to enable the army leaders to buy wine at the ordained prices.[2] In 1359 it was believed that large quantities of bad wine had been obtained for sale at Rochester to troops marching towards Sandwich. The castellan was ordered to investigate the matter and in the event of the wine's being as bad as it was reported to be, to have it taken out of the taverns and poured away.[3] In the same year, in order to deal with the problem of feeding troops as they marched towards Sandwich and waited there before embarkation, two steps were taken: first, the hosts of all inns on the direct highway from London to Sandwich were to be encouraged to sell victuals 'at a reasonable price' to the men as they passed; secondly, all markets in Kent and all fairs for the sale of victuals were closed except those at Canterbury, Dover and Sandwich.[4]

Contingents from different counties did not, and were not expected to, arrive all on the same day. (Instructions usually mentioned a final, not an arrival date: 'by three weeks from Midsummer', 'without fail by Palm Sunday', but it was to their financial advantage to avoid delay.) Concerning meals and sleeping places for the hundreds of men who crowded into the ports, very little evidence appears to have survived. At Portsmouth in 1346, Robert Houel, acting in the place of the marshal of England, had the task of lodging 'outside the verge of the [king's] household' all men arriving for service overseas;[5] and

---

[1] *B.P.R.*, III, 214–15.
[2] *C. Close R.*, 1354–60, 134.
[3] Ibid., 590.   [4] Ibid., 647.
[5] *C. Pat. R.*, 1345–8, 79.

in preparation for the prince's arrival in Plymouth in 1355, the sheriff of Cornwall was directed to have wine, oats, wheat and brushwood conveyed to that port. Sir Bartholomew de Burghersh appears to have been sent down to make further arrangements.[1]

Drawn from widely different regions with differences of accent and even of vocabulary, the men must have experienced some difficulties in communication during the early days of their acquaintance. Moreover, the presence of the local men of the port, of groups of mariners from distant ports and of archers from remote shires, produced the conditions under which quarrels become likely. In one such contention at Portsmouth in 1346, between 'mariners and others', the ears of a Londoner and of a Devonian were 'maliciously cut off' by mariners.[2] The inevitable delays at the ports might also affect morale adversely.

At some point or points during the time spent in the port, the men received wages. They were of course paid at the standard rates of the period, but the records of payment often throw light on the date at which this or that group reached the coast, or the composition of an expeditionary force, or some other item which has not survived elsewhere. Arrival dates and up to four weeks' delay, for example, are illustrated in the payments at Ipswich and Yarmouth on 22 February 1339 to the following groups awaiting their passage to Sluys:[3]

60 archers from the county of Oxford						waiting since 25 January
60	,,	,,	,,	,,	,, Huntingdon	,, ,, 26 ,,
30	,,	,,	,,	,,	,, Hereford	,, ,, 29 ,,

And it is from accounts of wages paid at Plymouth in 1342 to men proceeding to Brittany that we know the size and composition of the following contingents:[4]

Kenwrick Dein, leader of the Welsh men from England, a chaplain, an interpreter, a standard-bearer, a crier, a physician, four vinters and one hundred archers;
Griffith ap Yerward, leader of the Welsh men from Merioneth with a standard-bearer, a physician, four vinters and eighty archers;

[1] *B.P.R.*, II, 77–8.
[2] *C. Pat. R.*, 1345–8, 146, 154.
[3] E 372/184, m. 7 (Pipe Roll, 13 Edward III).
[4] E 101/23/22, m. 5.

William Breton, leader of archers from various parts of England whose group of four vinters and ninety archers included twenty from the county of Gloucester and twenty nine from the county of Worcester.

The first contingent (Kenwrick Dein's) received twenty-one days' pay for service while waiting between 5 and 25 November.

The tedium of waiting for the arrival of ships, for their adaptation and loading, and for a favourable wind, was usually shared by the leader of the expedition. In 1346, for example, the king was lodged at Porchester castle while waiting for the completion of his plans; in 1355, the prince stayed at Plympton priory for several weeks, and in 1359 both prince and king were near Sandwich during the autumn, the prince staying some of the time at Northbourne manor.

* * * *

In view of the widespread support of the war and the variety of incentives for direct participation, the departure of knights and archers from so many counties—mainly south of the Mersey and the Trent—can have caused little surprise, though in the family, the village, the town, there may have been regret.

Absences might last for periods of from one to two years but a high proportion of the men returned. A few were seriously injured in limb or eye, but many were apparently in satisfactory health and some joined later expeditions.

Since we cannot discover the exact geographical distribution of the homes of the recruits, the local, economic effects cannot be considered, but the aggregate effect of the withdrawal of fifty or even a hundred men from an average-sized county for a year would not dislocate the economy excessively. Though the demands made on the counties were understood to be roughly proportionate to their populations, it is likely that Cheshire—relatively unpopulous and directly under the Black Prince's rule—bore the greatest weight.

The homes of those who joined the contracting nobles and other leaders are even more difficult to trace. Many knights are known to have had lands in this or that county, and very many of the charters of pardon state the counties in which the murders had been committed—not necessarily those in which the murderers had lived—but it is quite impracticable to state the geographical origin of the great majority of the indentured troops. Still less therefore can we estimate the economic effect of their recruitment on localities.

An attempt to visualize the many movements of troops and their impact on the public mind must take into account such journeys as those of the men of North Wales who marched to Ipswich, to Sandwich, to Portsmouth, to Southampton, to Plymouth.

TABLE III

*Some movements of armed men**

The mayor and sheriffs of London, the mayor and bailiffs of other towns were ordered to provide and send the following:

	1346 To Portsmouth	1350 To Sandwich
Abingdon	10	6
Barnstaple	10	3
Bath	6	3
Bodmin	20	8
Boston	10	4
Bridgnorth	6	4
Bristol	40	20
Cambridge	20	6
Chelmsford	4	3
Chichester	20	—
Coventry	40	10
Ely	15	3
Exeter	30	10
Gloucester	20	10
Helston	5	—
Hereford	30	10
Launceston	15	5
Lewes	4	3
London	—	100
Lostwithiel	6	3
Lynn	—	20
Northampton	35	8
Shrewsbury	30	10
Stafford	8	3
Taunton	6 .	4
Truro	5	—
Winchester	30	10
Worcester	20	8

* Rymer, III, i, 71, 193–4.

TABLE IV

Some movements of archers, 1338*
(directions for)

From	To	
	Norwich	*Portsmouth*
Bedford	45	10
Berkshire	30	10
Buckingham	40	20
Dorset	50	20
Essex	80	80
Gloucester	100	20
Hampshire	60	20
Kent	70	40
Middlesex	20	20
Oxford	40	40
Somerset	80	20
Surrey	80	20
Warwick	60	20
Wiltshire	70	20
Worcester	60	20

* Rymer, II, ii, 1018.

We leave the troops at the port and turn to supplies of food, arms and other goods necessary for their journey or for the campaign they were about to undertake.

CHAPTER III

Supplies

VICTUALS

IN the chronicles of the period, the impracticability of having a great baggage-train and hence the need to 'live on the land', are assumed. Glimpses of the importance of food emerge here and there in the narratives: a storm dispersed the ships bringing victuals; the king devastated a region that the enemy might not profit therefrom; victuals were plentiful here and scarce there; for 'lack of victuals' the king was obliged to take this or that course.

But the chroniclers make no reference to the initial supplies needed by an army as it landed on foreign soil, awaited the unshipping of horses, arms and armour and then proceeded—sometimes after many miles marching through friendly territory—into enemy lands where such food as remained, could be seized. Nor do they mention the fact that bodies of men far outnumbering the whole population of a port commonly had to wait in that port for several weeks before embarking. Finally, the needs of the many hundreds of men who manned the transports (and themselves often waited for weeks in harbour) are unmentioned. The organization of supplies was not a topic for the chroniclers.

Yet organization on a large scale was, of course, indispensable. It was understood that all the king's castles were kept provisioned, that periodically the stores were changed, and that at times of emergency they were increased. The garrisons at Carlisle and Berwick needed assured supplies, and there were outlying dependencies—the Channel Islands, the castles at Perth, Stirling and Edinburgh, the fortresses of Tonnay and Taillebourg—to which victuals had to be sent, while the deficiencies of corn in the great wine-producing region of Gascony had to be made good by shiploads of grain from England. For the movements of the king's household large quantities of food and provender were prepared. For the household of the prince of Wales at Kennington great herds of cattle were driven from Cheshire and North Wales and even at times from Cornwall.[1] To these standing requirements were added, during periods of war, the large quantities of victuals required for the expeditionary forces, for their reinforcements, and for the mariners conducting the armies overseas, or suppressing pirates, or defending England's coast and shipping against French attacks, or idly waiting in harbour. For the troops during the prolonged siege of Calais and subsequently for the maintenance of English power in that town, very large supplies were needed also.

Broadly, the task was to ensure the collection of various foodstuffs for man and horse in many counties, and their carriage to a port from which they could be sent to Scotland, to Flanders, to France or to Gascony. The task had to be accomplished promptly and without the aid of forecasts of regional surpluses. Lack of ships or lack of wind might delay the departure of expeditionary forces. It is not known that any were delayed for lack of victuals. The manner in which supplies were taken inevitably led at times to serious criticism, and payments in this field (as in others) were often unpunctual but, when allowance is made for the slowness of communications and for the impossibility of accurate forecasts of needs, the organization may be regarded as remarkably efficient.

The victuals obtained in England were:

Meat: beef, mutton, pork—mainly salted—all reckoned in carcases, though beef was sometimes counted in sides. It is seldom clear whether salted pork (*bacones*) means flitches of bacon or sides of pork or whole carcases (but there are 'half *bacones*').

Oats, peas and beans: bought in quarters, peas and beans usually being grouped together.

Wheat: bought in quarters but ground into flour before being shipped.

Cheese: bought in 'weys' or in stones.(A wey = 26 stones in southeast England.)

Fish: commonly stockfish or herrings or 'dried fish', bought in hundreds or thousands, and chiefly for Gascony.

In view of the differences in the quantities of goods needed at different times, in the units of measurement and in the availability of water transport, uniform procedure would not be expected. Wherever there are navigable rivers, river boats

[1] *B.P.R.*, III, 76, 279, 307, 349, 393, 419, 423; ibid., II, 69.

(*navicula*) are used. Often, corn is bought 'with advantage' (21 quarters for the price of 20) and the bushel measure is 'rased' (the grain in the full measure being level, not 'heaped'). Prices, even within a single county, are by no means uniform. Where private carts have to be used to convey goods to ports or river-ports, the haulage distance is usually quoted; where no distance is stated, there is commonly an agreement to carry corn at so much a quarter.

For the victualling of a fleet, the admiral may be empowered to purchase and collect cattle and commodities. In 1336, Geoffrey de Say had three mounted men buying on his behalf, in Hampshire, Sussex and Kent, nine men driving the cattle thus bought to the ports, and a man at each of his depots at Sandwich and Winchelsea, receiving goods and cattle, and distributing supplies to masters of the ships.[1]

Or a great seaport, called on to provide transport for military purposes, may victual its own ships. In 1340, when Yarmouth supplies 30 ships for 40 days' service between England and Flanders, the town authorities obtain stocks for all their ships. Their bailiffs' account contains details of the amounts of each commodity delivered to each ship calculated on the basis of the number of mariners serving on board. The rations include wheat flour, ale, beef, salt, salted pork, salt fish, butter, cheese, peas for pottage, oat flour. The number of vendors is small: two men supply 377 quarters of wheat flour; three persons provide the ale thus:

Johanna Hikkeson	400 gallon at 1*d.*		1. 13. 4*d.*
Peter Grymbolp	30,000	,, ,,	125. 0. 0*d.*
John Gayter	30,000	,, ,,	125. 0. 0*d.*

This amounts to 60,400 gallons and allows (as explicitly stated) for each of the 1,510 men in the ships one gallon a day. (The supplies include, of course, fuel.)[2]

We turn to army supplies. In an operation carried out in 1340 in the basin of the Trent, wheat and barley are collected at Nottingham, Newark, Torksey, Gainsborough and Retford, carried in river-boats to Hull, stored in granaries and then

[1] Pipe Roll, 13 Edward III, E 372/184, m. 3 dors; *C. Close R.*, 1337-9, 508.

[2] E 101/22/25. In the same year, Lynn gave the sailors additional pay in place of victuals 'because of the dearness of victuals in those parts'. E 372/185, vii dors (Pipe Roll, 14 Edward III).

(with purchases made in Beverley and Hedon in Holderness) transported in six ships to Flanders and delivered to the king's receiver of victuals.[1] In the same year, stores are gathered from south Essex and north Kent—from Brentwood, Ashbridge, Stonefleet, Southfleet, Northfleet, Faversham—into a granary at Billingsgate, London, and taken thence by sea to Sandwich.[2]

Often, the sheriffs and their staffs are made responsible for the work. In 1338-9, the sheriff of Hampshire sends supplies to the Channel Islands; and, for the fleet, he purveys 108 quarters 2 bushels of corn (making 'with advantage' by 'rased measure' 114 quarters), 41 carcases of beef, 16 tuns of cider, all of which he puts on board the ships at Hamel on Sea.[3] In the same year, the sheriff of York provides victuals for the stores of the king's castles in Scotland and also for the king's expedition. The quantities bought from individuals are mostly quite small[4] as are those taken in the county of Bedford in 1346.[5] Even smaller quantities are taken in Kesteven in 1345.[6]

But the most illuminating examples of the sheriffs' work emerge when a large expedition is being prepared. Some rough estimate of total needs is made and county contributions to achieve this aggregate are worked out. Sheriffs in certain counties are then directed to obtain their allotted quotas and deliver them to the 'receiver of victuals'.

Three things are evident to each sheriff: large containers will be needed. Empty tuns, therefore, are bought, conveyed to suitable places, cleaned, dried and carted—they are bulky—to the corn mills. Secondly, depots must be arranged at several points for storing the various commodities. Since goods will have to be moved over considerable distances, it will be advantageous if the depots stand on the banks of navigable rivers and the goods are brought down by water to quite large warehouses at a seaport. Thirdly, river-boats must be provided by the sheriff, and the admiral will be expected to provide sea-going vessels to convey the accumulated stores to their destination. It follows that in loading and unloading, some of the goods will be

[1] E 101/22/27 (account of William de la Pole).
[2] E 101/22/28 (account of John de Pulteney).
[3] E 372/184, m. 7.
[4] E 101/21/5 (victuals provided in Yorkshire).
[5] E 101/25/14 (persons from whom corn was taken).
[6] E 101/531/24 (roll of John de Malteby).

handled many times especially if the sea-going vessel is not in port as the river-boats arrive there.

If the county is large, it is divided into regions; depots are established in each region and men are appointed to ride about searching for stores and cattle. By negotiation, by threat, or by force, stores and cattle are bought; values are calculated; tallies are handed over. Orders are given for the slaughter and dressing of the cattle. Carts and wagons are taken. The goods and carcases are loaded into them and conveyed to a depot where they are unloaded or, if a river-boat is available, put straight into the boat. A man is appointed to receive and guard the accumulated goods.

The river-boat is brought downstream to a port. If the appointed sea-going vessel is already lying in the port, the goods (except the wheat) are transferred by windlass to the ship. Commonly, however, they have to be placed in the central warehouse for a period. The wheat is unloaded from the boat into carts and taken to the mills where it is unloaded, ground, sifted, packed into the empty tuns which are now bound and fastened up. They have to be carted to the central warehouse or, if the ship is available, hoisted on board. A man is employed at the port warehouse to receive and guard the stores.

When the supplies have been received from the various depots and put on board, the sheriff and the receiver of victuals (or his deputy) add up the several quantities to be handed over and agree the figures. Indentures are written and sealed. Each party retains a memorandum stating in detail the costs of all the goods transferred (including the number and price of the tuns), the expenses of carriage, the wages of the men employed on the work, even payments for windage. For the sheriff, the indenture is a receipt. For the modern student, it is a valuable source for that branch of the history of war which goes far beyond 'military' history.

We illustrate the above generalized sketch by using the indenture-receipts of several sheriffs for goods purveyed in a large victualling operation for the king's expedition of 1346.[1] The port of embarkation was Portsmouth; the receiver of victuals[2] was William de Kelleseye. The scale of the operation may be seen in Table V.

[1] E 101/25/16 (receipts by William de Kelleseye).
[2] The receiver of victuals is never a passive recipient. He is actively

TABLE V

Victuals supplied to William de Kelleseye,
receiver of the king's victuals, 1346*

COUNTY	FLOUR										PORT
	Corn bought	*Flour produced*	*Packed in*	*Oats*	*Salt Pork*	*Carcases of mutton*	*Sides of beef*	*Weys of cheese*	*Peas and beans*		
	qrs.	qrs.	tuns	qrs.						qrs.	
Cambridge and Huntingdon	450	392	60	243	100	38	26	2	63		Lynn
Essex and Hertford	412½	340	55	—	160	—	42	13	—		Maldon and London
Lincoln	652½	552½	87	300	135	213	32	12	100		Boston and Hull
Northampton	240	208	32	112	180	140	14	—	—		Lynn
Notts and Derby	375	310¼	50	134	100	—	20	—	77		Hull
Rutland	153	131¼	20	100	60	8	—	—	—		Lynn
Yorkshire	620	580	80	170	15	—	—	—	91¼		Hull

* Exchequer Various Accounts E 101/25/16.

In Yorkshire, ten mounted men (four in the East Riding, three in the North, and three in the West Riding) were employed for fifteen days purveying, buying and taking the goods. Seven depots were established for their collection (at Wansford, Beverley, Doncaster, Selby, Tadcaster, Boroughbridge and York) and premises in the port of Kingston-upon-Hull were rented for twelve weeks as storehouses. Corn, unloaded at Hull, was ground at Wawne Mills (4 miles away) and Skiter Mills (7 miles away), packed into eighty tuns (with a little salt at the top to keep it sweet) and then taken back to the port and loaded into ships. Seven men were employed for eight days dealing with transport, loading and unloading. The purchase price of wheat ranged between three and four shillings a quarter, and the 'market measure' (21 for 20) had been used.

Similar details are available for nine other counties. The sheriff of Lincoln bought his empty tuns in Lincoln, Spalding and Grimsby. He provided an analysis of the figures quoted for

concerned with the completion of an operation by a given date and therefore with transport in the provision of which the sheriff's co-operation is indispensable. See, for example, *C. Pat. R.*, 1340–43, 252, 272; *C. Close R.*, 1341–3, 303.

E

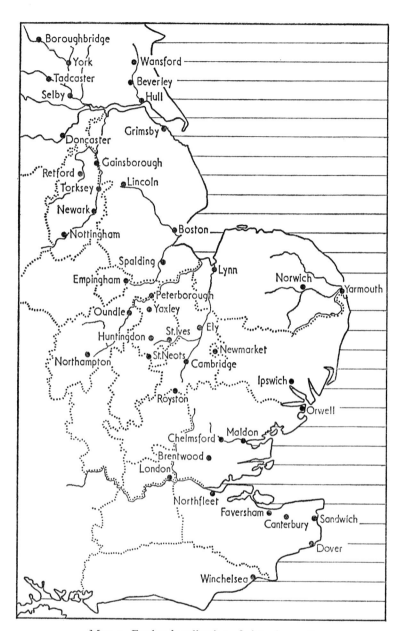

MAP 1. England: collection of victuals, 1346

each main item and showed in detail the prices paid for carcases of different values and corn of different qualities. Part of his stores he sent to Hull and the remainder to Boston from where it was carried in the ship *Margaret* to Portsmouth.

In the county of Northampton, victuals were gathered at Oundle and Northampton, carried by road to Yaxley,[1] unloaded into boats in the river Nene and conveyed to Lynn for transport to Portsmouth.

Rutland's quota, gathered together at Empingham, was also sent (34 miles in 20 carts) via Yaxley to Lynn. The empty tuns had been bought at Peterborough.

In Huntingdon, the tuns had been fetched from Ely and St Neots to St Ives. In Cambridge they were brought from Ely, Newmarket and Royston to Cambridge. From both centres they were sent by water to Lynn.

The goods from the counties of Nottingham and Derby were sent to Hull (except ten of the *bacones* which were sold). Those of Essex were assembled at the port of Maldon for shipping to London, the corn having been ground at Chelmsford.

For other counties, no such detailed statements of the purveyances of 1346 remain, but the direction of the traffic may be inferred from instruction to the sheriffs: victuals from Hereford are to be sent through the port of Bristol, those of Kent through Sandwich, those of Oxford and Berkshire through London.[2] So far as is known, all such shipments were made to Portsmouth or direct to the coast of Normandy.

When Edward reached Calais (on 4 September), his supplies were very limited and a prolonged siege of the town appeared probable. Order after order, therefore, was sent to sheriffs in England for still further quantities of victuals to be forwarded —this time, to Sandwich or direct to Calais.

As already stated, no accurate forecast of the demands that would have to be satisfied could be given. It is not surprising that Geoffrey de Say had to sell some of the stores he had bought for the fleet in 1336.[3] Nor is it surprising that a quantity of the large supplies accumulated under Kelleseye's directions in 1346,

---

[1] Yaxley is in Huntingdonshire. In the Middle Ages, goods from various Midland counties were brought to Yaxley and shipped down the old course of the Nene through Whittlesey Mere, Upwell, Outwell to Lynn. See *Cartularium Monasterii de Rameseia*, III, 139–55.

[2] C 76/22, m. 9.   [3] E 372/184, m. 4 dors.

became unfit for consumption and were sent back to England to be sold at the best prices obtainable. He explained that the grain had been unloaded and re-loaded at Portsmouth, at 'Hogges' in Normandy and again in London. He had had the grain spread in granaries at Hull and turned over once or twice a day with a view to drying it. Some of the beans and peas had 'deteriorated by their long detention at sea'; some had been covered by sea water and were rotten. Oats, mutton and cheese were in the same state. Kelleseye duly disposed of the goods in Hull and Lynn.[1]

Another instance of surplus stock and deterioration occurred in 1360 as the English army withdrew from Chartres after the agreement at Bretigny. Roger de Bromley, the receiver of victuals, had quantities of victuals in store at Honfleur. These he was authorized to sell at the best price he could get. Some of his goods rotted; others had to be sold below cost price.[2]

In summary then, the operation consists of the purveyance of authorized quantities of victuals in specified counties, the grinding of the wheat, the conveyance of the accumulated goods to a seaport and their transfer to the ships in the port. At this point, they are deemed to have been delivered to the king's agent, the receiver of victuals. Some small waste or loss there may be through excessive purchasing, long storage or deterioration in transit.

And inevitably complaints will be made, for so large an operation cannot be carried through without causing inconvenience, hardship or even injustice to some of the king's subjects; but a distinction must be made between orders and their execution. When the men of Rutland send 'trustworthy persons' to show the king and council that their county cannot raise the full total of victuals asked for in the operation of 1346, their representations are accepted and the quantity of wheat demanded of them is halved.[3] On the other hand, the conduct of the sheriffs and their agents in the same operation drives the men of Gloucester, Hereford, Worcester, Oxford and Berkshire to complain that in their counties, the rich have been altogether

[1] E 101/25/15 (warrant indentures as to sale of victuals), E 101/24/16 (account of William de Kelleseye), C. Close R., 1346–9, 99; C. Fine R., 1337–47, 486.
[2] E 101/27/17. C. Close R., 1360–64, 186.
[3] Ibid., 1346–9, 44.

spared and the poor compelled to supply corn and victuals. An enquiry is ordered into these allegations.[1] And complaints in Huntingdon lead to an extremely detailed investigation of vendors, goods supplied and prices paid during the purchases and purveyances of 1338.[2]

Discrimination between the rich and the poor was only one of the charges brought against purveyors. Two others were common during the period under consideration, namely that they bought grain ostensibly for the king and sold it at a profit for their own advantage; and that no payment was made for goods taken. Both complaints were voiced in the Commons and a number of statutes were framed to deal with dates of payment for goods purveyed. By the 1350's it was held that small purveyances should be paid for 'at the time of taking' and large ones within a fixed period—in 1354, a quarter of a year, in 1360, within a month or six weeks.[3] The whole field of purveyors' malpractices is revealed in the detailed prohibitions of a statute of 1362 with which we deal in a later chapter. (The French government had to deal with similar difficulties. The *droit de prise* led inevitably to abuses, and there were complaints over fair prices and the date of payment for goods taken.)[4]

But the complaints must not divert attention from the achievements of 1346–7. The shipping and victuals of England had afforded Edward's army a favourable start on the French coast in July. The same shipping and supply of victuals came to his aid when, after Crécy, he returned to the coast in September and began the siege of Calais. In this undertaking, organization in England made success possible in France. Militarily speaking, the capture of Calais was indispensable, but the capture itself was an exercise in starvation by blockade rather than a military exploit, and the exercise was based on the delivery to the besieging army of huge quantities of English food. Once captured, the town's retention was an object of national policy which could be achieved only by the shipment of further supplies from England. When the Commons in 1350–1 drew the king's attention to the shortage and dearness of corn in England and the quantities that had been taken to Calais without their

[1] *C. Pat. R.*, 1345–8, 113.
[2] E 101/21/39 (County of Huntingdon: writ and inquisition).
[3] *The Statutes at Large*, I, 487; II, 103, 136–7.
[4] *Registres*, 86–103.

consent, the king replied that it was imperative to victual Calais.[1] In his grasp of ends and means, Edward was both soldier and statesman.

For fourteen years after the capture, supplies were poured into Calais. The town, emptied of its former citizens and 'colonized' by English people, had but the smallest of hinterlands and was wholly dependent during war, and very largely dependent during truces, on English sources for its maintenance. Detachments of English troops were stationed at several points some little distance outside the walls, and the total garrison, including masons, carpenters and other workers, amounted to a thousand men. For them and for the new, civilian population of the port, it was necessary to send food, money, munitions and material for fortification. The ships linking this country with the newly acquired port conveyed, therefore, not only springalds, crossbows, saltpetre, engines of war and stones for those engines, but also naval tackle, cords, boats, pitch, tar, canvas, thread and also lime, bricks, timber and nails.

As regards victuals, between the arrangements for provisioning the start of an expeditionary force and those for maintaining a fortress, there were three differences:

1. the needs of the fortress had to be met not by one great operation, but by a continuous stream of goods.
2. the stream could be supplied by a combination of purveyance and controlled merchant-enterprise.
3. Since Calais had mills, it was not necessary to grind all the wheat before it was shipped.

These circumstances and the general conditions of the times governed the broad movements of commodities down to 1361.[2]

The town had been captured in August 1347. Grants of shops, inns and tenements to the incoming English 'colonists' were made in early October. As a large part of the army was gradually withdrawn and the English townsfolk entered, the body of people (civilians and the resident garrison) for whom it was necessary to provide, took shape.[3] From September 1347, when instructions were sent out for English wheat to be purveyed and

[1] *R.P.*, II, 225.
[2] Burley, S. J., 'The Victualling of Calais', *Bulletin I.H.R.*, XXXI, 1958, 49–57.
[3] *C. Pat. R.*, 1345–8, 549, 561–8.

forwarded, down to 1361, when ale was among the supplies conveyed, there were many orders for victuals. Parallel with the purveyances there were ordinary business transactions. Though the export of corn from England was periodically prohibited, Calais was always excepted, and licences for the shipment of authorized quantities to that town were issued to merchant applicants.

One crisis in supplies is known to have occurred. In the summer of 1355, when war was resumed and ships and victuals for the expeditionary forces of Henry of Lancaster and the Black Prince were in great demand, there was a grave shortage of corn, especially of oats, in Calais. Proclamations were made in the seaports from Newcastle upon Tyne to Southampton urging merchants who had corn for sale to take it to Calais immediately. Buyers, the proclamations said, would be numerous and payment prompt.[1]

There must also have been a very heavy demand for food in the late summer and autumn of 1359 when large numbers of English troops, with allies and volunteers from several states, assembled at Calais for the great campaign which the king conducted towards Rheims.

The following table shows the total receipts of food at Calais between 1347 and 1361 and the importance of purveyance as a source of food:

Quantities received	Wheat	Malt	Oats	Beans and Peas	Meat (Beef and Bacon Carcases)
	Qrs.	Qrs.	Qrs.	Qrs.	
Total	14,188	4,164	8,072	2,412	3,168
From purveyance	13,138	3,964	6,726	2,211	2,814

It has been calculated that the defence of the town (including the cost of the garrison) amounted to over 14,400*l* a year.[2]

For two other parts of the king's dominions, namely the Channel Isles and Gascony, supplies had to be maintained. The former were commonly victualled from the resources of Hampshire. Gascony presented a complex problem. Famed for its

[1] *C. Close R.*, 1354–60, 223.

[2] Burley, op. cit., 53, 57. See also Greaves, D., 'Calais under Edward III' in Unwin, G. (ed.), *Finance and Trade under Edward III*, 313–50, and an unpublished thesis, 'The Colonization of Calais under Edward III, 1347–1377', by Linton S. Thorn in the Bodleian Library.

great exports of wine, it was already well known to be deficient in grain—even in peace time. English rule was seen in the existence of bastides, in the presence of some small garrisons strategically placed, and in a body of officials in charge of the administration. But increasing French determination to gain more and more English territory led to a more active policy on England's part—that is to say to the successive campaigns of the earl of Derby (1345–6), the earl of Stafford (1352), and the prince of Wales (1355–7); and to an increase in the size and number of garrisons maintained between the campaigns and after their ending. Some part of the victuals required for troops in winter quarters and, at times, some part of those needed by the civil population had to be obtained from England.

It is significant that during the periods in which the export of corn from England was prohibited, Gascony was usually coupled with Calais; they were the only destinations to which merchants might send English corn. Additional precautions were, however, taken: surety had to be given that the corn would be carried to Bordeaux only;[1] letters were demanded from the Seneschal of Gascony or the Constable of Bordeaux that the goods sent to Gascony were indeed delivered in Bordeaux[2] and, in view of the dangers from piracy, protection was commonly furnished for ships not sailing in the usual convoys.

As in the victualling of Calais, both purveyance and ordinary business transactions are to be found from the beginning of our period to the end. In 1338, licence was given for the shipment of 1,000 quarters of corn to Gascony; there was an order for 2,000 quarters of wheat to be purveyed, brought to London and stored there in preparation for export to Gascony;[3] arrangements were made for the protection of vessels conveying victuals from Southampton to Bordeaux.[4] As the period advances, further exports are implied in the permission given to the Lord d'Albret to take 300 quarters of wheat and 100 quarters of oats from Sandwich to his castle in Gascony,[5] in the permission for some Gascon merchants to load ships in London and Sandwich

---

[1] *C. Pat. R.*, 1350–4, 318–19, 329, 346.

[2] *C. Close R.*, 1346–9, 116.

[3] *C. Pat. R.*, 1338–40, 81, 84.

[4] Ibid., 164. Further instances of protection for the transport of victuals and money are found in *C. Close R.*, 1343–6, 620 and 675.

[5] Ibid., 1349–54, 331.

with wheat for conveyance to Bordeaux,[1] and in instructions to the Treasurer of Ireland to buy and send to Bordeaux 2,000 quarters of wheat for the maintenance of the king's lieges living there.[2]

Specifically military needs are seen in the forwarding of quantities of wheat, oats and flour to Henry of Derby (Lancaster) and his men (then serving in Gascony),[3] in the chartering of vessels to convey provisions for the earl of Suffolk and for the household of the prince of Wales (both serving in Gascony), and in the transport of quantities of wheat, oats and hay for the prince's troops during the winter of 1356–7.[4]

Supplies for forces serving in Gascony are obtained principally from the southern counties. In 1338, for example, it is in the counties bordering the Channel together with Gloucester, Wiltshire and Surrey that large orders for wheat, oats and fish are to be purveyed for the magnates serving in Gascony.[5] And in 1352, men are occupied for fifteen weeks in getting victuals in Hampshire and Wiltshire for the king's castles in Gascony.[6]

ARMS

Archers and footmen raised for overseas service were, of course, armed with bows, arrows and cutting weapons variously described as knives, lances, spears, swords. These cutting weapons may have been made in the localities from which the troops were drawn or in the iron-producing areas. They formed part of the equipment provided by the county and cannot have been uniform in pattern and size.

[1] Ibid., 1346–9, 116.   [2] Ibid., 1343–6, 284.
[3] Ibid., 1349–54, 131; Rymer, III, i, 64.
[4] Hewitt, *B.P.E.*, 93, 141.   [5] C 61/50, m. 8.
[6] E 101/26/22.

The Kitchen Journal, E 101/390/11. This volume contains a record of kitchen expenses (or the value of goods consumed) in the king's household week by week from April 1344 to November 1346. That is to say it covers the period in which the goods gathered by Kelleseye were delivered. The volume was used by Thompson, E. M., in his edition of *Chronicon Galfridi le Baker*, Oxford, 1889, 252–3, to check chroniclers' statements of the king's itinerary in France in 1346. It might be used to throw light on the circumstances in victualling in France. (There is a large fall in the average expenditure per week after the king's landing.) I have been unable to relate the supplies to the expenditure. In the Fine Rolls the reason for bringing the goods back from Normandy is that 'the king had no need thereof'. *C. Fine R.*, 1337–47, 486.

TABLE VI

Some orders for bows and arrows

	Bows					Sheaves of Arrows					
Columns Year:	A 1341	B 1346	C 1356	D 1359	E 1359	F 1341	G 1346	H 1356	I 1359	J 1359	K 1359
Bedford and Bucks	100			300		300		600	100	300	500
Cambs and Hunts	200	150					250			400	600
Cornwall and Devon											400
Essex and Herts	300	160		300		1,000	400		200	300	500
Gloucester		300	500	500	600		500	600	200	300	700
Hants	500	100				1,000	300			200	
Hereford								1,000			400
Kent	300	100	400	400		1,000	300	700	200	500	700
Lancs	100					1,000					
Lincoln	1,000		1,500	800	200	300		600	500	500	1,000
London	2,500	300				1,000	1,000				
Midd'x		100					300				
Norfolk and Suffolk	200	200	600			300	400	700		400	900
Northants	200	100	400	300		300	200	600	200	300	600
Notts and Derby	200					500				400	800
Oxford and Berks	100	200		200		1,000	400		100	300	400
Rutland	100	50				200	100				
Salop						1,000		1,000		300	500
Somerset and Dorset	300	200	300			300	500	400		300	400
Stafford							500	500		500	400
Surrey and Sussex	500	100				2,000	500		200	300	800
Warwick and Leics	300	120	200	500		600	200	1,000	200	400	600
Wilts	100					200				500	300
Worcs	200	100	400			500	200	1,000		300	600
Yorks	500					500				500	600

All the above figures are taken from big orders sent to many counties at the same time. None of the goods shown in Columns E and K was delivered, and in various other places deliveries fell short of orders.

References: Columns A and F, Rymer, II, ii, 157; Columns B and G, ibid., III, 8, 87, 68; Columns C and H, *C. Close R.*, 1354–60, 244; Columns D and I, Rymer, III, i, 414; Columns E and K, *C. Close R.*, 1354–60, 601–2; Column J, Rymer, App. E, 36.

Counties: Gloucester sometimes included, sometimes excluded, Bristol. In 1341, 1,000 bows and 300 sheaves were demanded of Bristol while Gloucester-except-Bristol had to find 2,000 arrow heads and 500 dozen bowstrings. Cheshire was called on to provide comparable quantities (e.g. in 1341, 300 bows and 100 sheaves) but orders usually came from the earl of Chester (the prince of Wales).

Column K: Sheriffs were directed to send the quantities stated or the cash value of those quantities. See p. 69.

Bows and arrows, on the other hand, were standard articles, needed in large quantities and stored in the Tower of London or sent direct to a seaport for carriage to a campaign area. Bows were white or painted and bought in units. Their length is seldom mentioned. Arrows, an ell in length and in some instances steel-headed, were bought in sheaves of twenty-four. Prices tended to be uniform and, at times, they were fixed in advance by the king.

Orders great and small for the purchase of bows and arrows were sent out on many occasions during our period. Though the records throw little light on the bowyers and fletchers themselves, it is clear that their products were obtainable—as would of course be expected—in every county, and the general course of the transactions can often be followed in some detail. The sheriff receives a writ directing him to obtain within his bailiwick a certain quantity of bows, arrows, (occasionally) bowstrings and (much less frequently) arrow-heads. A few weeks may elapse before he has accumulated the required quantities, and occasionally he reveals the sources from which his purchases are drawn. The sheriff of Somerset and Dorset,[1] for example, in 1346 gathers together at Bristol supplies which his men have brought in, thus:

				bought at	miles
120 bows				Wells	15
40 sheaves of arrows				Somerton	25
60	,,	,,	,,	Bridgewater	30
100	,,	,,	,,	Taunton	38
50	,,	,,	,,	Sherborne	30
153	,,	,,	,,	Bristol	
53	,,	,,	,,	Fleetbridge	

The goods having been assembled at one point, the bows are packed in canvas and the sheaves of arrows corded. Where empty tuns are available, they may be used to hold the corded arrows. In some instances small quantities are carried by sumpters, but usually wagons and horses are hired for transport and a mounted clerk accompanies the convoy. It is his duty to ensure that the goods not only reach the Tower of London, but also that delivery is fully acknowledged. The general movement may be illustrated in the execution of orders issued early in 1356. On

[1] E 372/191, m. xi. Some of the goods ordered in 1346 can be followed from county town to London in m. ix dors.

this occasion the sheriff of Somerset and Dorset[1] assembles his supplies at Dorchester and explains his expenses thus:

300 white bows at 18d.	22l 0s. 0d.
400 sheaves of arrows at 16d.	26l 13s. 4d.
Collection of goods to Dorchester ⎫ Carriage of goods to London ⎬ Wages of clerk ⎭	3l 14s. 0d.

52 17 4

The sheriff of Bedfordshire and Buckinghamshire loads his sheaves at Woburn Chapel and charges for four days' transport (going, staying and returning). From Nottingham and Derby, 117 white bows and 202 sheaves of arrows are sent in a wagon with six horses at a cost of 2s. 8d. per day on the outward journey and 2s. a day on the return. From Stafford, the sheriff sends 113 white bows and 186 sheaves of arrows in three carts with eighteen horses, delivery and return taking eight days. And the sheriffs of Kent, Hereford, Worcester and other counties forward their quotas similarly. William de Rothwell, clerk of the wardrobe at the Tower, formally acknowledges receipt of the goods delivered.[2]

When orders for large quantities of bows and arrows are sent out, it is realized that they cannot be immediately executed. On such occasions, sheriffs may be directed to forward half the required quantities by a certain date (e.g. Easter) and the remainder by another (e.g. Whitsuntide), or the instructions read 'as soon as possible' or 'as many as possible up to——'.

The quantities asked for are by no means always delivered. In the instances quoted above, for example, the sheriff of Somerset and Dorset carries out the order in full, but the county of Hereford from which 1,000 sheaves were asked, supplies only 363, while Bedford and Buckingham, commanded to provide 600 sheaves, sends only 260.[3]

During the truces, orders for bows and arrows were naturally fewer. The resumption of hostilities renewed the demand, and the early months of 1356 (when the arms mentioned above were being forwarded) were a period of great scarcity. 'No arrows can be obtained from England', the chamberlain of Chester was informed, 'because the king has . . . taken for his use all the arrows

---

[1] E 372/201.   [2] Ibid.   [3] Ibid.

TABLE VII

*Quantities of bows and arrows received at the Tower**
May 1355–June 1360

| County | Date | Bows | | Sheaves of Arrows |
		Painted	White	
Lincs	1355 Jun. 8	217	555	—
	Jul. 1	141	280	—
	Oct. 8	—	—	334
	1356 May 5	96	550	—
	Aug. 6	—	832	—
	1357 May 16	—	139	133
	1359 May 11	—	—	416
	1360 Feb. 14	—	—	499
Gloucester	1355 Oct. 8	—	—	116
	1356 Jun. 26	230	—	446
	1359 Aug. 3	—	—	300
Kent	1356 May 5	—	—	112
	Aug. 23	—	—	120
	1359 May 15	—	—	346
	Jun. 16	—	—	300
Norfolk	1356 May 19	66	164	—
and	1359 Jul. 11	—	—	400
Suffolk	1360 Feb. 11	—	—	900
Stafford	1356 Jun. 21	—	113	186
	1359 Aug. 28	—	—	240
Notts and	1356 Jul. 6	—	118	202
Derby	1359 Aug. 19	—	—	428
Hereford	1356 Oct. 16	—	—	363
Bedford	1356 Oct. 13	—	—	260
and	1359 Jul. 11	—	—	300
Bucks	Aug. 19	—	—	200
Worcs	1357 Feb. 23	—	50	—
Somerset	1357 Feb. 6	300	—	400
and Dorset	1359 Jul. 24	—	—	300

(Similar quantities were received from other counties.)

* E 101/392/14 (Account of William de Rothwell).

that can be found anywhere there.'[1] The chamberlain was instructed to help an agent sent from Gascony by the Black Prince
to obtain 1,000 bows, 2,000 sheaves of arrows and 400 gross of
bowstrings. The agent was to requisition all the available
stocks in the county of Chester and to ensure that the fletchers
continued production till the prince's needs were satisfied.

[1] *B.P.R.*, III, 23.

Supplies were also to be obtained in Lincolnshire and in London and steps taken for the transport of the goods from all three sources direct to Plymouth and thence to Bordeaux.[1]

In accordance with military needs, quantities of arms were sent direct to various other ports: to Orwell (1341) for example, to Sandwich (1359), to Southampton (1360) and to the Scottish border. And the prince of Wales had large stores made to be 'held in readiness' without indicating a depot or port.[2] But most of the quantities produced in the Midlands and southern counties were taken to the Tower of London.

That great and complex establishment contained an arms department the activities of which fall into four classes:

1. The manufacture of arms.
2. The purchase of arms.
3. The storage of arms purveyed by the sheriffs or purchased, or transferred from other quarters (for example, the Scottish border when they were no longer required), or arrested in the port of London, or made on the premises.
4. The provision of arms for expeditionary forces.

Within the department there were armourers, carpenters, smiths, bowyers, fletchers and artillers (*attilatores*), men possessed of skill in making arms in general. There was a senior or king's artiller who was provided with a house in the Tower (and towards the end of our period with an annual robe), and sometimes entrusted with the supervision of artillers elsewhere. The number of men employed in the production of arms probably varied inversely with the skill and diligence of the sheriffs in supplying bows and arrows from their counties. If the store fell low at a time when arms were urgently needed, then they had to be bought, or made in the Tower.

In 1338 (while the king was overseas with his army), Nicholas Corand, the king's artiller, was directed to buy with all speed 1,000 bows and 4,000 sheaves of arrows with steel heads. If, however, he should be unable to get the full number of these goods, then he was to buy timber, feathers and steel and to employ men to produce them as quickly as possible. When ready they were to be handed over to John de Flete for shipment to the king.[3]

[1] Hewitt, *B.P.E.*, 92.   [2] *B.P.R.*, II, 155.
[3] *C. Pat. R.*, 1338–40, 124–5.

John de Flete, who was the keeper of the king's armour and keeper of the wardrobe in the Tower, was also concerned in the purchase of arms. For the fortification of Southampton and the equipping of its garrison after the disaster which befell the town in 1338, he was ordered to buy springalds, quarrels, breast-plates, lances, arbalests, bows and arrows.[1]

During the long truce which followed the Black Death, the demand for arms fell. In May 1353 William de Rothwell took over his predecessor's stock in the Tower, which included 3,300 arrow heads, quantities of bows and arrows (with some arrows of ash wood) and bowstrings. Rothwell's detailed account for the years 1353–60 throws light on the activities of his depart-ment. John de Brakelond, who was in charge of the production of bows, was sent to Lincolnshire (which was well known for the making of arms) to get additional staff; and Rothwell was able to show that, by purchase and manufacture, he had added to the stock 4,062 painted bows, 11,303 white bows, 4,000 bow-staves, 23,643 sheaves of arrows, 341 gross of bowstrings.[2]

But the king's great expedition of 1359 called for very great supplies both from the Tower and from the sheriffs. In July, Rothwell was ordered to send his entire stock of bows, arrows, bowstrings and winches (for crossbows) to Sandwich, duly packed in chests, quivers, pipes and barrels.[3] Moreover, he bought 4,000 bowstaves in July and paid over 560*l* in August for bows and arrows 'for the king's passage'.[4] Still further de-mands were made in November when the sheriffs were con-fronted with the grave alternative of delivering immediately at the Tower large specified quantities of bows and arrows or forwarding the purchase price of the full number demanded to the receipt of the exchequer.[5] The sheriffs failed[6]—as was probably expected. Rothwell was therefore empowered to take additional staff and additional material for the production of arms, and also to buy 1,000 bows, 10,000 sheaves of arrows, 1,000 sheaves of well-steeled arrows, 100 gross of bowstrings, and feathers from goose wings. Storage space in the Tower was

---

[1] *C. Close R.*, 1339–41, 83, 135, 163, 185, 189, 191.
[2] E 101/392/14.
[3] *C. Close R.*, 1354–60, 574.
[4] E 101/392/14.
[5] *C. Close R.*, 1354–60, 601.
[6] Ibid., 1361–4, 10.

provided.[1] His successor, Henry de Snayth, had similar powers but as peace came in 1360, the need for arms declined.[2]

The fourth activity of the department, namely the provision of arms for the expeditionary forces, has been illustrated in the preceding paragraph. We offer for contrast a smaller instance: the furnishing in 1358 of 500 bows (200 painted, 300 white), 100 sheaves of arrows and 1,500 bowstrings for the archers of Oliver de Clisson who was about to leave for service in Brittany.[3] This order was probably executed in London with little or no expense; but Rothwell had had to pay more than 25*l* for the transport and unloading of the arms and armour he had sent from the Tower to the ports.[4]

Material for the manufacture of arms is often mentioned. The artiller is provided with the necessary timber, iron and fuel, or he is authorized to buy wood, iron and steel, or he is allowed to fell yew trees in certain of the king's manors. There are orders for bowstrings—generally in dozens or grosses—and (infrequently) for horses' manes of which 100 stones were asked for from five counties in 1340.[5] Hemp also is needed for making canvas and various kinds of thread, string and rope for packing arms. (Parenthetically, it may be added that ropes of many kinds and large quantities of sail cloth were obtained, chiefly in Dorset, collected at Bridport and forwarded in wagons to the naval stores section of the Tower.)[6]

Though iron was necessarily used in all parts of England, arrow heads in large quantities could be obtained only in those counties where iron was worked, namely in Gloucester, Salop, Stafford, Yorkshire and in the Weald. It is therefore from these areas that iron- or steel-headed arrows were ordered. They were made in various places, gathered together in the chief towns and sent to the Tower in wagons, except those of Yorkshire which were shipped down the Ouse for carriage by sea. Sometimes the heads only were sent. These might cost as much as 2*s*. 6*d*. a hundred. In 1359 a fletcher was appointed to get smiths in Kent

[1] *C. Pat. R.*, 1358–61, 323.   [2] Ibid., 422.
[3] *C. Close R.*, 1354–60, 481.
[4] E 101/392/14.   [5] C 61/50, m. 13.
[6] See, for example, E 101/26/29, mm. 1–6 (indentures of receipts by Matthew de Torksey, clerk of the king's ships), E 372/200 last membrane, E 372/201, m. 42 dors (accounts of the sheriffs of Somerset and Dorset). And see R. Lane-Poole, 'A Medieval Cordage Account', *Mariners' Mirror*, XLII, 67–73, and *V.C.H. Dorset*, II, 344–53.

and Sussex for the forging of 500 steel arrow-heads, and some months later iron, steel and charcoal were ordered for the work of the smiths in the Tower.[1] Finally, bows and arrows were needed for the 'munition' of the king's and the prince of Wales' castles. Whenever invasion was believed to be threatened, orders were sent out for a review of the arms and victuals in stock and for additions to be made if necessary. The year 1359 was exceptional but the measures taken at Chester in that year will give an idea of the quantities bought in an emergency.[2] The chamberlain of Chester provided for three castles—those of Chester, Flint and Rhuddlan. His account for the year 1359–60, contains the following expenses:

					l.	*s.*	*d.*
Arrows without heads, 355 sheaves					19	4	7
Arrow heads, 4,000 for the above					2	12	5
Bows	33	2	4	0			
	25	1	11	3			
	36	1	19	0			
	42	2	5	6			
					7	19	0
Bowstrings	5,624				5	8	2
Lance heads	24				1	0	0
Hemp, 16 stone						16	0
Wages: 2 men 56 days at Chester Castle			12	3			
2 ,, ,, ,, ,, Flint ,,			12	3			
					1	4	6
Carriage: stones from the river Clwyd to Rhuddlan Castle					1	0	
24 bows, 24 sheaves of headed arrows and 4 stones of hemp, Chester to Rhuddlan Castle					1	0	
24 bows and 24 sheaves of headed arrows, Chester to Flint Castle						6	
					38	7	2

(The bowstrings are 36 gross plus 8 at 3*s.* per gross containing 13 dozen.)

Beyond these well-known weapons and their accessories, there remain the 'engines', contrivances which the more ingenious minds were constructing for attack or defence. Illuminated manuscripts provide pictures of various devices—chiefly for flinging great stones—and Froissart refers to 'great engines casting day and night against the castle' and adds 'they within

[1] *C. Pat. R.*, 1358–61, 222, 304; Schubert, H. R., *History of the British Iron and Steel Industry*, London, 1957, chapter VII.

[2] *Cheshire Chamberlains' Accounts*, 273. There are instructions respecting the castles of Conway, Rhuddlan and Flint in *B.P.R.*, III, 377–9.

F

had also great engines which broke down all the engines without'.[1] Some such devices may have been made by John Crabbe who supervised the construction of certain engines for the siege of Dunbar castle.[2] He was later employed on repairing the king's engines in the Tower and on making engines and hoardings for the war.[3] The word often occurs in lists—'springalds, arbalests and other engines', 'engines, springalds and other things', 'cross bows, springalds and other engines'—and there are references to stones for 'engines' at Folkestone to be sent to Calais.[4] The most that can be said with certainty is that those made in England in the 1340's were large, built mainly of timber, and they were not cannon. Their structure and mode of operation is not revealed in the records.

Cannons were, however, among English arms by 1346 (and, of course, gunpowder). Robert de Mildenhall (keeper of the privy wardrobe in the Tower, October 1344–September 1351) was ordered in 1345 to repair and forward guns and 'pellets' for the king's projected expedition of that year and later to make one hundred 'ribalds' (tiny cannons grouped together and mounted on a single carriage). In September 1346, all the guns and engines in the Tower together with 'pellets', saltpetre and gunpowder were required at Calais, and, for some time, quantities of sulphur and saltpetre were being bought for gunpowder in the Tower. William de Rothwell, the next keeper, purchased four 'gunnes' of copper.[5]

During the period of this study, the artiller was concerned with both the older and the newer types of engines, all missile weapons and military machines being comprehensively classed as *artilleria*. He was employed not only in casting the cannons but also—as craftsman rather than soldier—in using them.[6]

There remain the ancillary crafts carried on in the Tower or mentioned among the purchases in the keeper's accounts—the making of covers for crossbows, of corslets for archers, of boxes covered with leather for containing arrows, of quivers covered with leather for use by mounted troops, of boxes with, and boxes

[1] Froissart (Macaulay), 92.
[2] C. Close R., 1339–41, 11. The timber was supplied by the sheriff of York. E 372/190, m. ix.
[3] C. Close R., 1341–3, 27, 295.   [4] C 76/33, m. 1.
[5] Tout, T. F., Chapters in Admin. Hist., IV, 469–71.
[6] Idem., in E.H.R., XXVI (1911), 666–702.

without, double locks for conveyance of arrows, of bowstaves bound with iron to carry the king's banners. And there is the painting of the king's ships and of shields for those ships.[1]

In addition to the supplies of victuals and arms we have described, many miscellaneous goods, more or less obviously needed, had to be taken overseas. These include parchment,[2] tools and implements (axes, scythes, sickles, spades, miners' tools), arms not mentioned above (falchions), harness (especially for 'draught horses), horse-shoes, nails, carts, and occasionally drinking vessels.

While all the above-mentioned goods may be regarded as supplies and equipment essential to the expeditionary forces and therefore demanding cargo space in the ships, there remain personal goods—the knights' armour, arms and clothing, for example—of which no mention commonly appears in chronicles or records, and the great quantity of impedimenta taken to Calais in 1359 for which shipping had to be found. According to Froissart, English lords on that occasion had hundreds of tents, and very many forges, stoves and aids to cookery.[3]

Were any medical stores taken? It is very likely that the leaders had some available for their own use. Apothecaries had accompanied both Edward I and Edward II on some of their expeditions and their accounts for medicaments have survived. As already stated, Edward III took his physician to France in 1346 and the Black Prince's physician was with him in Gascony in 1355–7. Some of the Welsh units were accompanied by physicians. During the siege of Rennes, Henry of Lancaster had a physician and this Henry was the author of a devotional treatise in which he mentions ointment, plasters and 'fine, white bandages'.[4] A wound must be dressed, he says, with clean bandages and kept free from air and dust. The bandages are to hold the plaster and ointment in place and to prevent flies from defiling

[1] E 101/392/14 (account of William de Rothwell). E 101/392/1 mm. 1, 3 (Book of Payments of the Chamber).
[2] The king granted a large number of pardons during his campaign of 1346–7 and needed a small secretariat wherever he went.
[3] Froissart (Lettenhove), VI, 216–25.
[4] *Le livre de seyntz medicines*, ed. Arnold, E. J., 128, 159–60, 198, 202, 207–8.

it and making the wound worse. Such a man, it would be inferred, would take medical stores among his personal goods. The
only clear reference to the matter that I have found is in an
order of 1359 to 'deliver all the drugs made for the king's present
passage to parts beyond the sea to the clerk of the king's spicery',
stating the number and price of the drugs.[1] (Froissart implies
the use of medical stores in stating that after the battle of
Cocherel, 1364, each man 'took heed to his prisoners and dressing them that were hurt',[2] and Chaucer in his Knight's Tale
mentions 'narcotykes and opie', salves, charms and 'drugges of
herbes'.[3])

*   *   *   *

Military power does not consist solely in the size, skill, courage
and equipment of armies. It derives also from the efforts of non-
combatants gathering from a score or more of counties hundreds
of small purchases—here a few bushels of corn, there a few
sheaves of arrows, elsewhere a side of salt pork—amounting in
the aggregate to supplies for an army. The organization of
these purchases and of their carriage to the ports is discharged
efficiently, if at times ruthlessly, by men who contribute to
England's military success equally with the military staffs.

We turn to the organization of shipping for the transport of
these supplies and of the men and the horses.

[1] C. Close R., 1354–61, 594.
[2] Froissart (Macaulay), 151.
[3] Canterbury Tales (Everyman), 35, 64.

CHAPTER IV

Shipping and the Movement of Troops

T H E small size and draught of fourteenth-century ships enabled their masters to find shelter in creeks, inlets and river mouths which have long ceased to be serviceable for shipping. The silting of harbours,[1] changes in the land level and changes in the location of industry have gradually altered the pattern of trade and commerce. Sea-fishing was widely practised. Coastal trade flourished: the transport of carts from Cornwall to Southampton, Sandwich and even to London,[2] of slates from Anglesey to Chester,[3] of corn from Winchester to the Dee estuary,[4] of victuals from King's Lynn to Berwick[5] was effected by sea.

The busiest ports were those which afforded easy access to the Continent. Kingston upon Hull, King's Lynn, Yarmouth, London, Dover were in constant communication with the ports of Flanders. Sandwich was often used for the embarkation of troops for war. Southampton grew in importance from the wine trade with Gascony, Plymouth from the military expeditions which sailed to Bordeaux or to Brittany. Dartmouth had a considerable miscellaneous trade and was often associated with piracy.

The extent to which man had aided nature in providing facilities for handling cargoes cannot be followed in detail. Occasional references to pilotage,[6] to quays,[7] to windlasses,[8] to a dock,[9] to the prohibition of dumping ballast in a harbour,[10] point to interesting developments. Against these aids—and in

---

[1] Cf. *C. Inqn. Misc.*, III, 5, 6, 7.

[2] *B.P.R.*, III, I, 16, II, 160, 161, 165.

[3] Hewitt, *Medieval Cheshire*, 94.   [4] Ibid., 40.

[5] *C. Close R.*, 1339–41, 384.

[6] *C. Pat. R.*, 1358–61, 114. In 1338, Nicholas Pyk was directed to choose six lodemen to 'conduct' six ships from Sandwich to Gascony. Gascon Roll, C 61/50 m. 2; A 'lodeman' steered the *George* into Sandwich in 1345, E 101/25/7.

[7] *C. Pat. R.*, 1338–41, 212 (Bristol), 346 (Lyme, Drogheda).

[8] In the payment of *windagium*.

[9] *C. Pat. R.*, 1358–61, 26.

[10] *C. Close R.*, 1354–8, 84.

75

the fourteenth century they were very far from general—must be set the absence of lighthouses, the lack of charts, the rudimentary state of the compass (or what served as a compass) and, in most ports, the apparent absence of warehouses. Bordeaux and the major ports of the Mediterranean were better equipped than any English port except perhaps London.

Ships of the period are known as cogs, crayers, ballingers, carracks, hakebots, pickers, barges, doggers, lodships and galleys. Representations of them (in one form or another) are mainly inaccurate: those on coins and those in seals had to be fitted into circular frames; the beautifully executed illustrations of the chronicles are largely the work of artists of the following century. It is, however, clear that typical ships had one large mast and one large, squarish sail.[1] On many, but not on all, there was a fixed rudder. Almost all these ships bore Christian names; some had saints' names; some were called *Trinity* and quite commonly two or more ships from one port bore the same name.

Ships of up to 100 tons were common. A few approached 200 tons, but many of no more than 30 to 50 tons were engaged in trade in the Channel and even sailed to Bordeaux. Gear, tackle, equipment in general and even the crew may be included comprehensively under the word *eskippamentum*.[2] Canvas for sails and ropes of many kinds were produced in Dorset, especially at Bridport.[3] Some ships were fitted out at Bordeaux with masts, anchors and cables of up to 30 fathoms and hawsers of up to 35 fathoms.[4]

Crews were (by modern standards) large. Their pay when in the king's service was a uniform 3*d*. a day without distinction

[1] Contemporary representations of ships may be seen in (i) the gold noble of Edward III, (ii) Pedrick, G., *Borough Seals of the Gothic Period*, London, 1904. See also Clowes, G. S. L., *Sailing Ships*, London, 1932, 10; Robinson, G., 'The Medieval Artist', *The Mariners' Mirror*, III, 353, and Quennell, M. and C. H., *A History of Everyday Things*, 3rd edn., London, 1950, I, 135.

[2] '. . . men for the equipment of the said ships refuse to set out . . .' *C. Close R.*, 1333–7, 593.

[3] References in the accounts of the sheriffs of Somerset and Dorset are numerous, e.g. account of John de St Laud, E 372/200 last membrane, account of John de Palton, E 372/201 m. 42d. See also *V.C.H. Dorset*, II, 344–53.

[4] E 372/207 m. 17, (account of John de Stretele) constable of Bordeaux. Some of the ships are mentioned below (p. 79).

of function, but fairly often there were boys or apprentices employed at lower wages.

Over the whole body of shipping the government exercised very wide powers, 'arresting' ships for national purposes in peace as well as in time of war. For the transport of victuals to Calais, to Scotland, to certain castles in Gascony, for the conveyance of ministers and staffs appointed to offices in Ireland and in Gascony, for the journeys of envoys to foreign countries and the papal court, and for many other purposes, the king's serjeants-at-arms were directed to requisition ships. During wars, their powers were enlarged and 'admirals' were appointed to take charge of all ports 'from the Thames northwards' and 'from the Thames westwards'. These officers not only arrested ships and had charge of convoys; they also impressed mariners, administered the embryonic maritime law and had wide, disciplinary powers over men serving in the fleets.

The arresting of ships was a very serious hindrance to trade and commerce[1] as well as to the continuance of personal relations. For a cargo of wine from Libourne, destined for Kingston-upon-Hull, might have to be unloaded at Dover; and secondly, the vessel and crew might be diverted to Southampton or Plymouth for a journey to Brittany, Spain or Gascony.[2] Instances occurred of suits for breach of contract-to-deliver between merchants and masters[3] and even of the arrest and use of a Spanish ship to serve English purposes.[4]

Ships arrested by the admiral or his agents became the troop-carriers for the war in France (or sometimes for military service in Ireland) and, as war stores differed little from ordinary

[1] Cf. a complaint of Great Yarmouth that the arrest of ships deprives the owners of profit. *C. Inqn. Misc.*, III, No. 14, and a complaint from Sandwich, *C. Close R.*, 1349–54, 550–1.

[2] Examples of compulsory unloading: Rymer, III, i, 174, 478–9.

[3] In 1347, the *Plentee of la Hoke*, laden in London with wheat for Bordeaux, was seized for the king's service, unloaded and sent to Calais 'whereby the ship did not take the wheat to Bordeaux according to the contract'. *C. Pat. R.*, 1345–8, 270.

[4] 'To the king of Castile '. . . we kept Martin de Gyteria, your subject and master of the *St Antoyne* to help us in our urgent journey at sea . . .' Gascon Roll, C 61/67, m. 6 (date 1355). The French authorities appear to have acted similarly: in 1340, the *Maudelayne of Lescluses* was captured and utilized to send messages and victuals from France to Scotland. It was however taken by men of Berwick. *C. Close R.*, 1339–41, 560–1.

cargoes and the voyage across the Channel was short, they probably proved satisfactory without adaptation.

Ships could be adapted to meet hostility at sea by an extension of their structure or by the addition of archers to the crew. By raising the body of a ship at stem and stern and, on the parts so raised, laying beams across, castles were made from which archers could shoot with greater advantage than from ordinary deck level. Alternatively ships were 'prepared for war' by the provision of 'double equipment' (*duplex eskippamentum*). A ship needed to be adequately fitted out (*sufficienter de guerra munitus*) and the men on board had to be enough for sailing her (*gubernacio*) and also for combat (*defensio*). Only large vessels had *duplex eskippamentum* or *double eskipison*.[1] Their crews were large and there were also on board armed men or archers.

A third class of vessel was made expressly for war (though it might at times be used for the transport of goods). These vessels were constructed with castles fore and aft, with crow's nests placed high on the masts, and were generally large. They formed the nucleus of the royal navy and were known as 'the king's ships'.

The movements, crews and equipment of several of the king's ships can be followed in the 1340's. The *George*, for example, lying near Southampton with a total crew of twelve, is taken in March 1345 to Sandwich where the crew is enlarged to eighty for the king's passage to Sluys. After his return, she lies in the Thames for 153 days with a mere maintenance crew. Purchases for her equipment and stores are set out in detail. She provides canvas for half a dozen of the ships' boats belonging to the vessels which transported the king's army to Normandy in 1346, and a cabin on the *Isabelle* for Sir Guy de Brian.[2] Misfortune befalls her in the summer of 1346. She is sailed to a spot near Winchelsea and gradually breaks up.[3] Others in the same category are the *Isabelle*, the *Edward* and the cog *Thomas*. There is a good deal of information about the painting of these vessels and the

---

[1] In the account of Robert de Wembury of naval expenses (33 Edward III), Lynn supplies 5 ships, Blakeney 17, Great Yarmouth 26, Orford 4, and the largest vessel from each port has *double eskippamentum* (or *double eskipison*). Ipswich supplies 11 and the second largest is thus fitted. E 101/27/25. The term *simplex eskippamentum* is rarely used. An instance occurs in Rymer, III, i, 15.

[2] E 101/25/7 (account of Thomas de Snetesham).

[3] *C. Pat. R.*, 1345–8, 95, 102, 149, 151, 164, 197.

painting of flags bearing the arms of St George for use on the masts.[1]

At least two of these ships survived into the 1350's and enable us to consider a group of seven: the *Faucon* (crew 30), the *Rodecog* (crew 35), the *Isabelle* (crew 30), the *Mariote* (crew 25), the *Alice* (crew 45), the *Edward* (crew 60), the *Gabriel of the Tower*. All these ships were supplied with new ropes at Bordeaux[2] in 1354. The first six sailed in the large convoy that took the Prince of Wales to Gascony in the following year (and John Clerk of Southampton who had commanded the *Isabelle* in 1346, was captain of the *Christopher* in which the prince[3] sailed). The last three were also used in the transport of the king's army to Calais in 1359.[4]

For the movement of large numbers of horses, two steps had to be taken. That the horses might be conveniently got on board special gangways were made, broader and longer than would ordinarily be in use. That they might be tied up, separated and fed, hurdles, boards, racks, ropes, canvas, rings, nails and empty tuns were brought to the port of embarkation and fitted into the ships. Commonly gangways measured from 15 to 20 feet and hurdles 7 to $7\frac{1}{2}$ feet by 4 or $4\frac{1}{2}$ feet. Occasionally the former were as much as 30 feet by 5 feet. The provision of both gangways and hurdles became the duty of the sheriffs of the neighbouring counties. The construction, conveyance and delivery of large numbers of hurdles, and the fitting of the hurdles inside the ships, must have involved a great deal of labour.

Such then are the conditions of the period: crews familiar with the dangers arising from widespread piracy and from war, sailing in small, ill-equipped vessels which are liable to arrest and to use, immediately or after adaptation, as troop carriers or horse transports, while a few ships are constructed directly for purposes of combat.

We turn to the dispatch of the expeditionary forces. In the choice of the port of embarkation, two factors had to be considered, namely the length of the journey to the point of disembarkation and the need of a suitable roadstead. The second was the more important. Dover was inferior to Sandwich, for its harbour was

---

[1] E 101/391/1 (book of payments of the chamber), pp. 1, 3, 6.
[2] See page 76, note 4, above.
[3] Hewitt, *B.P.E.*, 42.
[4] Rymer, III, i, 428.

tiny, whereas Sandwich[1] had spacious waters in which the slowly gathering fleets could ride—vessels anchored in the 'Downs'
—and it was as near to London as Dover by road, and nearer
to London by sea. London itself was seldom used.[2] Southampton
and Portsmouth had merits for a descent on the north of France.
Plymouth became the usual port for expeditions to Gascony and
was sometimes used by troops setting out for Brittany. After the
capture of Calais, Dover gained importance and a dock was
made at Sandwich. Of the harbour installations in the other
ports little is known, but by the middle of the fourteenth century
Plymouth appears to have had a quay.[3]

Next, in order that the arrival of the troops and the assembly
of the ships may be co-ordinated, it is necessary to decide on a
date for the departure of the expedition. The admirals are then
empowered to arrest ships 'in all the ports towards the west' (or
'towards the north' or in both directions). In some instances,
their judgement of the suitability of shipping for the required
purpose may be sufficient; in others, the minimum burden is
stated ('all ships of 30 tons and upwards', for example). The
admirals are also empowered to direct that the ships shall be
sailed to the selected port and to impress mariners for that purpose.
A comprehensive formula commonly used states that ships will
be 'prepared for war and furnished with men, victuals and other
necessaries and brought to the port of — by (the chosen date)'.

Some of the difficulties of medieval administrators now become
evident. The admiral may send his agents to every port between
Margate and Penzance or even Bristol, but the slowness of communications renders impossible a quick assessment of the ships
immediately available. The weather makes prediction of the date
at which vessels still at sea will put into port, impossible. The
incoming vessels have cargoes to discharge before they are

[1] On the history of Sandwich, see Gardener, D., *Historic Haven*, Derby,
1954. Williamson, J. A., *The English Channel*, London, 1959, 111 shows a
conjectural map of the surroundings.

[2] Ships for the expedition of Henry of Lancaster were assembled in the
Thames in 1355.

[3] The dock at Sandwich was constructed for the *George. C. Pat. R.*, 1358–
1361, 26. In a very detailed statement of the expenses of John de Padbury,
a nuntius taking a large sum in gold from London via Plymouth to Bordeaux,
there are charges for 'batellage' and 'wyndage' at Plymouth. In this
instance, I think that wyndage implies that a windlass stood on a quay.
E 101/313/29.

available for other uses; enough victuals for the crew for at least a few days must be got and put on board; and a favourable wind is needed to move the vessels up or down the Channel to the chosen port.

Some of the consequences also are apparent: the progress of assembling the fleet will be slow; many weeks' notice must be given of the proposed date of sailing of the expeditionary force; there will be a great waste of man power in the idle ships and a serious loss to trade and commerce; the fleet seldom, if ever, sails on the appointed date. Frequently its departure is delayed for several weeks; troops and mariners consume all the victuals in the port and the neighbouring region; morale declines; the campaign starts later than was intended; spies may easily gain useful information.

These consequences may be illustrated by brief summaries of events in the preparations for four of the expeditions. We begin with the king's first great, overseas undertaking. During 1337, some ships were being adapted for the transport of horses.[1] On 24 February 1338, the two admirals were instructed to have fleets assembled at Orwell and Great Yarmouth by 26 April.[2] On 15 April, the king was surprised and angry that the ships provided were insufficient for his purpose.[3] It was not till 16 July that he sailed.[4] In the meantime some of the troops who were stationed in, or near, Norwich awaiting embarkation, had mutinied—'conspiring to withdraw from the army without licence, dishonouring us and hindering our business'—and an officer had been sent to pacify them.[5]

The preparations for the king's expedition of 1346 suffered similar delays. Late in 1345 and at the beginning of 1346, orders were given for ships to be assembled at Portsmouth by 14 February.[6] Later orders fixed mid-Lent for the arrival of the ships and the troops,[7] but a storm necessitated a delay in the assembly of the fleet[8] and, in view of the great consumption of victuals by an army waiting in one place for a long period, the king deferred the date both for ships and for troops till a fortnight after Easter.[9] In April the date for the arrival of troops was put back another

[1] C. Close R., 1337–9, 189.
[2] Rymer, II, ii, 1015.
[3] Ibid., 1027.
[4] C. Close R., 1337–9, 522.
[5] Rymer, II, ii, 1045.
[6] Ibid., III, i, 65–7.
[7] C. Close R., 1346–9, 44.
[8] Rymer, III, i, 67.
[9] Ibid., 67, 76.

fortnight.[1] Preparations were completed by the end of May but, owing to adverse winds, the fleet did not leave Portsmouth until 5 July.[2] It paused for several days off the Isle of Wight and, before it finally left English waters, messages were sent—probably with spies in view—to London, Dover, Winchelsea and Sandwich directing the port authorities to allow no one to leave England for eight days.[3]

For the prince of Wales' expedition to Gascony in 1355, almost every step in the complex preparations has been worked out.[4] Briefly, many ships prepared for another expedition were already waiting in the port of Southampton when orders were given for all the necessary transports to be at Plymouth by 14 June, and for the troops to arrive by mid-July, but the prince did not sail till 9 September. The long delay led to very grave difficulties in feeding the waiting troops.[5] A general prohibition of men going overseas, proclaimed in June—no doubt to prevent the sending of military information—was made absolute on 15 September. Port authorities were 'not to permit any ship great or small or boat or man' to leave before 29 September.[6]

The king's expedition of 1359 had so short a sea passage (from Sandwich to Calais) that it was possible to use ships for more than one journey.[7] On the other hand, a great deal of miscellaneous apparatus (carts, wagons, tools, forges, hand mills, cooking utensils) was made or collected and shipped to France for the use or comfort of the army.[8] The first date given for the assembly of ships was 6 July, but a few were allowed to leave English ports with cargoes for Flanders on their masters' giving security that the ships would be at Sandwich and available for the king's use by 15 August.[9] Archers were to be ready to march

---

[1] Rymer, III, i, 79.

[2] Baker, 79. Baker uses the same words 'waiting for a favourable wind' to explain the prince of Wales' delay at Plymouth in 1355. As this chapter shows, wind was by no means the only factor causing delay.

[3] Rymer, III, i, 85.   [4] Hewitt, B.P.E., 36–42.

[5] Ibid., 26. Moreover, the debts incurred in purchasing provisions led to further trouble. Vide infra, p. 170.

[6] C. Close R., 1354–60, 209, 226.

[7] But Gray states that the expedition was 'delayed for want of ships'. Scalacronica, 145. According to Avesbury, the army of Henry of Lancaster was moved in 1356 by two journeys of the same ships. Chronica, 462.

[8] Froissart, VI, 216–25.

[9] Rymer, III, i, 428; C. Close R., 1354–60, 574, and see Rymer, Appendix E, 49.

to the port by 15 July, and orders were given on 4 August for commissioners of array to have their men at Sandwich by 30 August.[1] Some of the army sailed for Calais at the beginning of October; the king sailed on 28 October.[2] (A spy hunt in London had been ordered in August.)[3]

Delays in setting out from the port of embarkation overshadowed all the major overseas enterprises or business of the period: the many expeditions to Brittany, to Flanders, to Ireland, the transport of reinforcements or supplies for these expeditions, the conveyance of new seneschals to Gascony. There were assemblies of ships also for expeditions which were cancelled and assemblies at one port which were moved to another port before finally sailing.

The delays were deplorable, but they sprang, as we have suggested, mainly from the circumstances of the time rather than from incompetence in administration, though in some instances the time allowed for the assembly of ships was quite insufficient.[4] Minor causes fall into perspective. A few men of course deserted[5] but the majority appear to have reached the port long before the ships were ready. There may have been difficulties in getting victuals, forage and arms to the port, and in delivering hurdles. In some instances, the needs of one expedition were competing with those of another,[6] or the option of taking out horses or buying them overseas may have made impossible an assessment of the requirements for horse transports.[7] In other instances, masters disobeyed the orders to sail their vessels to the chosen port,[8] and there were rumours that, in return for gifts, agents appointed to arrest ships were prepared to spare towns which should have contributed their due share.[9] Basically, however,

[1] Rymer, Appendix E, 37, 41; Rymer, III, i, 440.
[2] C. Close R., 1354–60, 599, 657.　　[3] C. Pat. R., 1358–61, 284–5.
[4] Letters dated 16 March 1347 directed sheriffs of western counties to have ships sent to Sandwich by 2 April, and a letter dated 25 March ordered the mayor and bailiffs of Exeter to send ships to the same assembly. Rymer, III, i, 112.
[5] Hewitt, B.P.E., 18, 21. Sometimes sailors also deserted. In C. Pat. R., 1345–8, 109, fifteen are said to be 'roaming about London'.
[6] In the summer of 1355, the expeditionary forces of Henry of Lancaster and of the prince of Wales were being assembled at the same time.
[7] Hewitt, B.P.E., 33.
[8] C. Pat. R., 1338–40, 71; ibid. 1340–3, 585–6; ibid., 1343–5, 81, 258, 404.
[9] Ibid., 1340–43, 592.

the cause of delay lay in the absence of accurate knowledge of the location of ships at a given time, the slowness of communications and man's inability to move ships without nature's aid.

Of necessity, very many soldiers and sailors had little direct employment during these long pauses. Whether the soldiers practised archery or engaged in contests or had any kind of drill or instruction, it is not possible to say. If they were not kept active in some way, a decline in morale would seem to have been inevitable. As already stated, a mutiny occurred at Norwich in 1338.

Two operations no doubt absorbed the time of some of the men. The first was the unloading of supplies from wagons and their transfer to the holds of the ships. Victuals, forage, arms, harness and tools were ordered in considerable quantities and, although the figures do not necessarily afford an accurate indication of the quantities obtained, they show the scale on which purveyors were expected to work, and shipmen to store the bulk of goods brought into the port from many miles around by land and, in some instances, from distant ports by water. We cite some examples:

Victuals: from East Anglia and the east Midlands to Great Yarmouth or to Orwell in March–April 1338, 3,600 quarters of wheat, 200 quarters of peas and beans, 4,100 quarters of barley, 500 quarters of salt, 1,340 salt pigs, 490 carcases of beef, 4,100 carcases of mutton, 80 lasts of herrings, 5,900 stones of cheese.

At the same time, smaller quantities of the above commodities (except peas, beans and salt) were ordered to be sent to the same ports from the southern counties together with 86,500 stockfish and 80,000 horse shoes with the necessary nails.[1]

Forage: from Essex to Orwell in May 1340, 30 wagon loads of hay, 120 quarters of oats, 20 wagon loads of litter and 20 tuns for carrying water.[2]

Arms: from 'the realm' to the king (who was in Flanders) in August 1338, 1,000 bows, 4,000 bowstrings, 4,000 sheaves of arrows with steel heads.[3]

Harness: from the counties stated to 'beyond the sea' in February 1339: from Yorkshire, 500 whips for great horses, 200 leather

---

[1] Rymer, II, ii, 1021.   [2] *C. Close R.*, 1339–41, 391.
[3] *C. Pat. R.*, 1338–40, 124–5.

halters, 400 trammels and pasterns, 200 leather collars for cart-horses, 200 hooks, 200 pairs of traces, 20 tanned horse shoes. From Nottingham, 10,000 horse shoes and 60,000 nails. From Kent, 30 falchions, 300 sickles, 100 small axes.[1]
Tools: from Ireland to Scotland in July 1340, 100 shovels, 100 axes, 100 spades, 24 kettles.[2]

For the gathering together of goods and commodities on such a scale, it was necessary to 'take carriage', that is to say, to requisition carts, wagons and horses. In some instances this was effected by the sheriffs; in others, men were appointed for the work and empowered to take vehicles according to their own judgement, bailiffs being warned of their powers and directed to give assistance. (It is likely that monastic granges were a source of much of the transport.)[3] We have therefore to visualize the conveyance in the spring of 1346, for example, of victuals along the roads and rivers of very many counties to the ports —Hull, King's Lynn, Ipswich, London, Bristol—while Ports-mouth becomes not only a centre for the assembly of ships drawn from almost every port in England and a centre on which troops converge from Wales and most parts of England, but also a centre of inland transport as wagons conveying hurdles, gangways, harness, arms and food are brought in from neigh-bouring counties.[4]

By the autumn of 1346, Sandwich has become the chief port for the movement of both men and goods, and as siege appara-tus—including specially constructed long ladders[5]—has to be transported for the assault on Calais, quite large vehicles are needed. From the moment Calais is captured, Sandwich is the principal port for the forwarding of supplies not only to Calais itself, but to the army operating around Calais and later to the expedition of 1359–60.

---

[1] *C. Close R.*, 1339–41, 28.   [2] Ibid., 518.

[3] This was fairly common. Cf. *Literae Cantuarienses* (Rolls Series), II, 190, 374, 378.

[4] Gascon Rolls, C 76/22, mm. 5, 17, 19; Rymer, III, i, 70–1, 79.

[5] Concerning cannons, springalds, engines see p. 72. (Later, stones obtained at Folkestone are used in the defence of Calais, C 76/33, m. 1.) In respect of long ladders, in 1346, the sheriff of Surrey and Sussex sent twenty ladders 25 feet long to Shoreham and the sheriff of Essex sent eight ladders 40 feet long to Manningtree for the assault on Calais. E 372/191, mm. 11, 7 dors.

The other operation was the preparation of some of the ships for the transport of horses. The fittings needed for this purpose

TABLE VIII

Hurdles and gangways

Year	Transport		Hurdles	Gangways
	From	To		
1338	Surrey and Sussex	Winchelsea	For 600 horses[a]	
1340	Essex	Harwich	418	4[b]
1340	Kent	Orwell via Sandwich	1,000	12[c]
1346	Hampshire	Portsmouth	1,000	20[d]
1346	Surrey and Sussex	Portsmouth	1,000	20[e]
1354	Hampshire	Southampton	For 1000 horses[f]	
1355	Hampshire	Southampton	2,500	15[g]
1355	Devon	Plymouth	2,500	15[g]
1355	Cornwall	Plymouth	2,500	15[g]
1356	Devon	Plymouth	400[h]	
1356	Hampshire	Southampton	800[i]	
1356	Hampshire	Southampton	700[i]	
1356	Hampshire	Southampton	200[i]	
1358	Hampshire	Southampton	For 400 horses[j]	
1359	Kent, Sussex, Essex	Sandwich	3,000	90[k]

[a] *C. Close R.*, 1337–9, 400. (The P.R.O. officials agree that the word 'helm' in this entry (and elsewhere) should be 'hurdle'.)

[b] E 372/185, m. 5.   [c] *C. Close R.*, 1339–41, 505.

[d] E 372/191, m. 11 dors.   [e] Ibid., m. 11.

[f] *C. Close R.*, 1354–60, 3.

[g] Hewitt, *B.P.E.*, 38. The order is in Gascon Roll, C 61/67, m. 14. The execution may be followed in E 372/201, m. 4 (Cornwall).

[h] *C. Close R.*, 1354–60, 256.

[i] E 372/201, m. 42d. The quantities are for shipping the horses of Henry of Lancaster to Brittany, of Philip of Navarre to Normandy and of Philip de la Vache to Normandy respectively. The same matter is set out in the account of John de Stretele, E 372/207, m. 2.

[j] *C. Close R.*, 1354–60, 256.

[k] Ibid., 1354–60, 564. This records the orders to the three sheriffs for 1,000 hurdles from each county and for 30 gangways from Kent. The sheriff of Kent supplied the full number of gangways but only 942 hurdles. E 392/204, m. 11.

have already been mentioned. Hurdles were made and taken to the chosen ports by land or/and by water, and gangways were usually ordered at the same time.[1] The accompanying table shows examples of the quantities sheriffs were directed to provide and forward (or in some instances, forwarded).

The exact manner in which the hurdles were fixed remains a matter for conjecture. It might be surmised that when horses were waiting near a port for some weeks, paddocks would be needed and that hurdles would serve for temporary fencing, were it not that hurdles are always treated as part of the *eskippamentum*, the equipment of the vessels.[2] There can be no doubt that the hurdles were intended to separate the horses—and rings, staples and nails were usually provided—but how they were suspended or maintained in position is not to be inferred from the evidence.

Before the horses were led on board, they were valued— usually by two men, a military leader and an official appointed by the king who noted down for each horse its owner's name, its colour and distinctive marks, and its estimated value. Of the appraisal lists for the expeditions to France, very few appear to have survived, but examples from the lists for the wars in Scotland and Ireland are available. Some are very brief: 'Peter de Wyndsore, one sorrel-grey horse, value 10 marks.' Often, however, there is something more distinctive: 'Nicholas Lonnor, a bay horse with a star on its forehead', 'a grey horse with one left foot white', '. . . with a cross on the left shoulder . . .', '. . . a black destrier with a white muzzle and left hind foot white . . .'[3]

---

[1] Some of the sheriff's accounts provide very detailed statements of the costs of construction and carriage. See Appendix I.

[2] During the Boer War, horses shipped to South Africa were separated by planks suspended from the ceiling. For the Crimean War (see *The Times*, 3 April 1854, quoted 3 April 1954) those conveyed in sailing ships were 'berthed in padded stalls 7 feet long by 2 feet 2 inches wide in the clear' and had 'loose slings constantly round them'.

[3] E 101/Bundle 28, No. 11, m. 4; *Cal. Doc. Scotland*, III, 409. The horses were also commonly branded. The usual instructions run '*juxta morem guerrae appreciare certoque signo ut est moris signare faciatis ut sic haberi possit notitia eorum*'.

Though appraisal lists are scarce, payments in compensation for horses lost in the king's service (*restauro equorum*) may be readily traced. E 101/172/4, for example, contains instances (stating colours and values—from 8 marks to 10 pounds sterling) of horses lost in the war in Gascony between 1354 and

At this point, however, organization sometimes broke down. Horses and fodder require a good deal of shipping space. For a cross-Channel passage difficulties are not insurmountable. For that from Southampton or Plymouth to Bordeaux, it may be impossible to find enough space (or impracticable since the ships would not return to port for a month). When the earl of Stafford went out in 1352, it was necessary for some of his men to send their horses back from the port 'for lack of shipping'. Horses therefore had to be bought for their use in Gascony.[1] When the Black Prince's army was being assembled in 1355, notice was given that knights and men at arms might buy horses on their arrival at Bordeaux and arrangements were made for their appraisal there.[2]

Concerning the actual numbers of horses transported, useful figures are available in some instances (see Table IX).

Finally, wages had to be paid to both soldiers and sailors. Arrayed archers received payment from their counties for the estimated number of days' march between their county boundaries and the port of embarkation. On reaching the port, they

TABLE IX

Shipment of horses: expedition of 1359

For	To Calais	From Calais
Prince of Wales	1369	2114
Earl of Ulster	126	164
Edmund of Langley	—	145
Earl of Richmond	741	787
Duke of Lancaster	—	1611
Earl of Suffolk	134	214
Earl of Stafford	414	486
Earl of Warwick	—	203
Edward Ledespens	100	150
Walter Manny	100	112
Reginald Cobham	149	157
William la Zouche	112	170

(and many smaller numbers)[a]

[a] E 101/393/11 (Wardrobe Accounts), pp. 80–7.

1360. Issue Roll, E 403/379, m. 7 contains payments for horses lost in Brittany. Cott MS. Caligula D III, 30 contains a list of horses belonging to William Trussel (with colours and values) lost in the service of the prince of Wales.

[1] E 101/26/25.   [2] Hewitt, *B.P.E.*, 33.

were 'at the king's wages'. For mariners the starting date is seldom quite clear because they may have been several weeks in harbour and the date of the previous payment may not be known. Clerks came from London bringing the necessary cash and drew up statements of disbursements in this form:

Ship	Port	Master	Crew	Days	Total
Thomas	Plymouth	Edward Bondy	1 constable and 29 mariners	7	57s. 9d.
Margaret	,,	John de Burnford	and 26 ,,	,,	52s. 6d.
Seintspirit	,,	Robert West	and 26 ,,	,,	52s. 6d.
Seinte-mariecog	,,	Robert Ashtone	and 26 ,,	,,	52s. 6d.
Seinte-mariecog	,,	Robert Clerk	and 16 ,,	,,	35s. –d.
Fluve Edward	,,	John Fayrman	and 57 ,,	,,	108s. 6d.

(From payments at Plymouth, November–December 1344)*

Port	Ship	Tons	Master	Crew		Days	Total
				Men	Boys		
Newcastle	Blithe of Newland	26	John Ward	10	1	31	4l 9s. 0d.
,,	Thomas	80	Robert Cotum	16	1	29	6l 14s. 1½d.
	Godier	30	William Harness	12	1	33	5l 19s. 7½d.

(From some payments at Southampton, July 1355)†

* Part of a fleet assembled for the passage of the earl of Gloucester to Brittany. E 101/23/22.

† E 101/26/38. For such disbursements, the coins were packed in canvas bags and borne by horses. Very large sums sent to Gascony were packed in barrels which were placed on wagons.

I have found no reference to payments to owners for the use of their ships, but there is evidence of payments in compensation for damage sustained by ships 'while in the king's fleet' in Brittany in 1345. Exchequer Various Accounts, E 101/24/8, E 101/24/9.

Not all ships of course were used for the transport of troops. Horses, victuals, siege material and miscellaneous goods had to be carried. A very large number of ships were needed in 1347 for the siege of Calais. Part of the cost of these ships was levied on east coast ports, and masters and crews received wages in the same way as those carrying troops. Exchequer Various Accounts, E 101/25/23, E 101/25/24.

With money in hand, the men are momentarily gratified, but as soldiers and sailors outnumber the whole population of the port, scarcely anything remains for sale: whoever could make or repair clothes, footwear, harness, armour has thriven. Whoever had victuals available has sold them at a profit.

If the king himself is about to leave the realm, there is an 'act

of state' during the waiting period: the seals are solemnly transferred in the presence of witnesses and a memorandum of the
event is made. In 1346, the ceremony takes place before the high
altar in the church of Fareham; in 1359, it is held in the king's
lodging at Stonor near Sandwich.[1] (A final act for the officers
waiting on the king is the dispatch from Sandwich to London
under armed guard of the valuable vessels of gold and silver and
other goods used by the household during the king's stay in the
neighbourhood of the port.)[2]

At last, it is believed that sufficient shipping has arrived to
transport the men and stores. Of the eighty, hundred or even
hundred and fifty vessels crowded into the harbour, one is
chosen for the Commander.[3] The remainder are allotted to the
various leaders for their men.[4] Victuals, forage and arms are
taken on board. If (or when) the wind blows in the right direction, the great tuns are filled with water and the final act begins.
It calls for skilled organization, good discipline and speed, for
from the great fleet, vessels must be brought a few at a time to
the quayside or the water's edge, held there while the horses
and men pass along the gangways, and then moved quickly into
mid-stream or down the harbour in order that other ships may
take their places. In the departure from Portsmouth in 1346,
the king's ship was among the first to leave.[5] In that of 1359
from Sandwich, it may have been the last.[6]

Departures are described by chroniclers: 'the king entered
into his ship and the prince of Wales . . . and all other lords,
earls, barons, knights with all their companies. . . . Thus they
sailed forth that day.' 'At last with a thousand ships and smaller
vessels, they began to sail wonderfully . . . the masters of the
ships did not know which way they were to steer, but followed
the admiral as they were bidden.' 'The king bid them hasten
into the ships assigned to them and set an example by going
aboard his ship and sailing to the Isle of Wight.' The prince

[1] C. Close R., 1346–9, 137; ibid., 1354–60, 656.
[2] E 372/204, m. 11 dors.
[3] The Chroniclers quote large numbers, but for some of the expeditions,
official lists exist or can be compiled. In 1355, for example, the prince of
Wales had more than 75 ships (Hewitt, B.P.E., 40–42). In 1345, Henry of
Lancaster had 152 ships. E 101/Bundle 25, No. 9. See Appendix II.
[4] Avesbury, 164, 198.
[5] Ibid., 198.
[6] Henry of Lancaster and others had sailed four weeks earlier.

PLATE II. English troops embarking for France

'anon embarked all the noble knights. There might one see the flower of chivalry and of right good bachelry who were very eager and desirous to acquit themselves well.'[1] Official records run thus: 'The king set sail between the hour of prime and the hour of none with his magnates and others and with the fleet gathered at Great Yarmouth in which . . . (others) were assembled, which joined the king's fleet to go to parts beyond the sea.'[2] 'Between dawn and sunrise, the king embarked in a ship called *la Philip of Dartmouth* in the port of Sandwich and having set sail, passed thence to Calais with the lords and other magnates, and arrived there about the hour of vespers.'[3]

Of the disembarkation of the men and the unloading of the ships the chroniclers give no clear description. It is evident that some little time had to elapse between the arrival at a port (or on a foreign shore) and the beginning of a campaign. One chronicler says of the king's landing in Normandy in 1346 that he 'discharged the ships of the horses and other baggage'; others show that there was a pause of five days for this operation.[4] And the prince, notwithstanding the vexatious delay at Plymouth in 1355, did not set out from Bordeaux 'until he had made his preparations and well rested his horses',[5] the 'rest' being an indispensable period for recuperation after the debilitating effects of ten or twelve days spent on board the ships.

Clear directions had been given for the assembly of ships at chosen ports. Concerning their disposition after their function had been performed, directions are less clear. A tendency to return without licence to England is not surprising. A large number of the ships which went with the king to Brittany in 1343, left the port of Brest notwithstanding orders to stay there.[6] There was equally flagrant disobedience shortly after the king landed in Normandy in 1346. Edward himself sent back the earl of Huntingdon with some prisoners, but the return of the ships laden with spoils, which the chroniclers proudly record,

---

[1] Froissart (Macaulay), 93; Baker, 79; Avesbury, 198; *Life of the Black Prince* (Chandos Herald), 140.

[2] *C. Close R.*, 1337–9, 522.

[3] Ibid., 1354–60, 657.

[4] Froissart (Macaulay), 94; a Cottonian MS. quoted in Baker, 253, 255; Moisant, 159.

[5] *Life of the Black Prince*, 140.

[6] *C. Close R.*, 1343–6, 128 *et seq.*; *C. Pat. R.*, 1348–50, 72, 448.

was contrary to orders. Lords, masters and mariners had been commanded to stay on the coast 'for the succour and safety of ourselves and our army and to hold themselves available for the fight against our enemies'. Nevertheless, having gained the loot, 'without our permission or command, they had slyly gone back to England, leaving us and our army in the midst of enemies in very great danger'.[1] It is not surprising therefore that in 1355, the indenture of the earl of Northampton contained a clause that a third of the ships which conveyed him and his army to Brittany should be ordered to remain with him as long as he was in those parts.[2]

No invasion of France could take place without adequate shipping, and shipping could not have transported and maintained armies in Flanders and France had French naval power been strong enough to gain the mastery in the Channel. During the period under consideration, the French managed to capture and, for a period, to hold some of the Channel Islands, to make savage but quite infrequent attacks on south-coast towns, to harass English ships in the narrow seas, to threaten or seem to threaten invasion of England. But expedition after expedition sailed safely from English ports to ports in Gascony, Brittany, Normandy, to Calais and to Flanders. The movement of English troops in fact suffered very little hindrance. Hundreds of vessels and thousands of sailors played their parts in the various enterprises and they were drawn from almost every port in England.[3]

But the withdrawal from mercantile life and use—not for weeks only, but often for months—of such large numbers of mariners and ships on so many occasions, must have had a seriously adverse effect on the economic life of the country.[4]

[1] French Roll, C 76/23, m. 21.

[2] E 101/68/4, m. 72.

[3] Wrottesley. G. (*Crecy and Calais*, 204), states that for the siege of Calais 700 English ships and 8,151 mariners were used while ships from Bayonne, Spain, Ireland, Flanders and Gelderland numbered 38 and their crews 1,204.

[4] Postan, M., in *Past and Present*, number 27, 39, touches this aspect, and cf. p. 77, nn. 1–4 *supra*.

CHAPTER V

War

THE men who landed in France were shortly to spend much of
their time and energy in the destruction of property, in the
forcible seizure of food and forage, and in plundering. These
three operations were of course illegal in their own country.
They were, however, normal and purposeful accompaniments
of war; they were diametrically opposed to the lives and interests of the people of the invaded regions; and they could be
carried to lengths which exceeded military necessity, military
advantage or even good sense. At times, therefore, it would fall
to a commander to set limits to his soldiers' activities and enforce his orders—if he had sufficient control over the men to do
so. Before dealing with these activities in detail, it is appropriate
to consider briefly the background to the discipline of the
armies.

Recruits were animated, as would be expected, by such
divers motives as the honourable pursuit of the profession of
arms, the attainment of fame, the desire for adventure or for
the spoils of war, and the need to gain pardon for crime. There
were also men raised by the commissions of array. And in most,
if not all, of the *chevauchées*, they were joined by non-English
elements—Gascon subjects or Flemish allies or miscellaneous
volunteers—attracted largely by hopes of plunder. But the
differing motives could not alter the nature of war which at
that period consisted very largely of military pressure involving
the destruction of the means by which life is maintained.

The men carrying out this work had to act corporately and
needed therefore principles of conduct for battle, for the march,
for the camp and for relations with civilians in the invaded
areas. It was—as always—necessary to gain both obedience to
commands for action and compliance with prohibitions.

With the discipline of the battle and the march we are not
here directly concerned. As for the discipline of the camp, the
arrival of the army at a given town meant the diversion from the
local population of as much food as the commander decided to
take. Since the economical use of food might govern the length

of the stay—if a stay was desired—maladministration or misuse of victuals was a serious breach of camp discipline.[1] But it is with conduct in relation to the civil population and especially with restraints on conduct that we are chiefly concerned.

The morale of a modern army is the fruit of months and even years of training of officers and men. Now it might be maintained that fourteenth-century armies had neither training nor instruction. Archers, for example, were chosen, tested and arrayed, and leaders were appointed, but between the issuing of orders for the array and the date by which the men were expected to be available for the journey to the port of embarkation, the period was often no more than two months. Training, if any, could hardly have lasted more than one month. It must usually have been much less than that and more probably spent in archery than in cultivating that trained submission to Authority which ensures prompt compliance with orders or prohibitions. It is true that there was commonly a delay at the port which might have been used for training, but there is no evidence that it was so spent.

English soldiers, therefore, crossed the seas and were soon on the march in a foreign land. That they were engaged day after day in looting, destruction and burning, the chroniclers both English and French make certain. That in some—probably very many—instances there was maltreatment of non-combatants there can be no doubt.

For a considered judgement on their conduct, the following factors must be borne in mind. The slowly evolving general practices which would gradually develop into a system and become known as international law, did not yet distinguish between combatants and non-combatants. Customs of war were gathering round such recurrent events as the siege and surrender of towns, and the capture, treatment and ransoming of prisoners.[2] Humanity to civilians was not yet a prevailing principle though, as we shall see, it was sometimes commanded.

Moreover, the obligation to take food for man and horse at one stroke regularized theft, while the ordained destruction of villages and towns led to disregard of the sanctity of 'enemy'

[1] Moisant, App. I, 162.

[2] Audinet, E., *Les Lois et Coutumes de la Guerre* (*Mémoires de la Société des Antiquaires de l'Ouest*, t. IX), Poitiers, 1917; Nys, E., *Les Origines du droit international*, Paris, 1894.

property of any kind. The remoteness of the enemy's force for days, and even at times for weeks, rendered strict discipline unnecessary. There may occasionally have been some unclearness in men's minds respecting the chain of authority when they were enrolled, paid by, and answerable to, knights who were subcontractors of an earl who had raised his quota of men by agreement with the king.

Further, though Froissart's narrative affords so many pictures of knights rejoicing in the business of war, the greater part of the armies were not knights. The men-at-arms, archers and foot soldiers included, as we have seen, many men who had been indicted of murder and no doubt others termed in the Patent Rolls 'evildoers'. Desertion before embarkation was not uncommon. Even from the king's army in Normandy, there were deserters.[1] Wellington knew the effect of wine-drinking on English soldiers.[2] In the fourteenth century, they used their opportunities in France.[3] Finally, in all campaigns there were a few men of the kind Froissart described as 'rascal and other followers of the host'.

We are not therefore considering solely the practices of knights pledged traditionally to certain standards of behaviour, but the conduct of ordinary men—good, bad and indifferent— loosed from their domestic moorings, temporarily following the trade of war in a foreign land, ignorant of its language, not subject to its laws, and probably at first contemptuous of its people. 'Dog of a Frenchman,' a French poet puts into an English soldier's mouth, 'you do naught but drink wine.'[4]

For the maintenance of discipline during a voyage, the admirals were authorized to chastise mariners. During campaigns on land, effective punishment was notoriously difficult to impose. Froissart records the king's resort to hanging for disregard of orders.[5] Between that ultimate expedient and mere reprimand, there were few practicable deterrents. In the armies, strict discipline must have been difficult to maintain.

[1] *C. Pat. R.*, 1345–8, 187, 239, 308.

[2] Stanhope, P., *Conversations with Wellington*, Oxford, 1947, 9, 9 n. 2.

[3] Deschamps, E., *Oeuvres inédits*, Paris, 1869, II, 207, *Les Grandes Chroniques*, Paris, 1836–8, V, 445: Le Normante chante, l'Angloissi boit et l'Allemante margue.

[4] Deschamps, op. cit., 24.

[5] Froissart (Macaulay), 99. Edward I had also resorted to hanging. Knighton, I, 370–1.

A few instances of success and of failure are revealed in the narratives of the *chevauchées*. Routine operations, as we shall see, were fourfold: marching, getting food, pillaging and destroying. The first two were necessary; the second two were not necessary, but commonly permitted or even ordered. It was over these latter activities that crises in discipline might occur, for pillage was profitable to the soldier, and destruction sanctioned unlimited licence. Yet they took time, lowered morale and might be contrary to the overriding interests of the campaign. For reasons of military necessity or diplomatic prudence or respect for the church or respect for non-combatants, a commander might prohibit pillage or/and destruction. The first ground needs no elaboration; the others can be illustrated. Pauses in destruction for prudential reasons occurred in the Black Prince's campaign in Gascony, the most important being when he journeyed westward through the lands of the influential count of Foix who had neither helped nor opposed him. A meeting between the prince and the count was arranged. On the preceding and succeeding days, the usual operations were carried out, but on the day of the prince's visit there was no burning.[1]

More frequently it was respect for the church that led to a prohibition. This was not uncommon before the period we are studying. During his campaigns in Scotland, Edward had destroyed Dunfermline but spared the abbey (1333); he had devastated lands in Elgin but avoided burning the town of Elgin 'because of the Trinity in whose honour stood a pleasing church'.[2] When Bassoue in Gascony surrendered to the prince, he allowed only the victualling officers to enter, because it belonged to the church.[3] In 1339, the king directed that no harm should befall the abbey of Mount Saint Martin;[4] in 1346, as he burnt and ravaged within sight of Paris, he issued an order that on the feast of the Assumption there should be neither spoiling nor firing;[5] in 1359 at Pontigny, the burial place of a former archbishop of Canterbury, he commanded the whole host on pain of life and limb and forfeiture of goods, to spare the abbey.[6] In each case his orders were observed.

[1] Hewitt, *B.P.E.*, 64.
[2] Froissart (Macaulay), 36; Lettenhove, XVIII, 29.
[3] Hewitt, *B.P.E.*, 64.   [4] Froissart (Macaulay), 50.
[5] Moisant, App. I, 171.   [6] *Anonimalle Chronicle*, 45–6.

And at times, he is represented as a humane commander keeping a tight hold on the discipline of his troops when they were in contact with civilians. 'In kindly consideration of the deficiencies of (Normandy)', says a chronicler, 'he made an order for his army that no man should presume to burn towns or manors, despoil churches or holy places, harm little children or women in his kingdom or France; such as attacked other persons—men excepted—or did evil of any kind would do so under pain of life and limb. He ordered also that if anyone violating this order were brought to him, a reward of forty shillings would be paid.'[1] At Caen says the same chronicler, he 'had it proclaimed throughout his army that no one should imprison women, children, nuns, monks, or harm their churches or houses'.[2]

Edward was not as kindly as these orders might suggest. In practice, he was stern both with opponents and with his men, but there were times when his orders were disregarded. At Carentan in 1346, much of the town was burnt in spite of his commands, and he was not able to prevent the burning of a religious house at Messien near Beauvais, but he showed his determination to ensure respect for the church by having a score of men hanged.[3] The Black Prince also saw his orders violated. In his campaign of 1355, against his will, Seissan was fired and could not be saved; in several places church property was destroyed and conspicuously at Carcassone where he had given explicit instructions that it should be preserved.[4] Whether punishment followed is not stated. It must of course be allowed that once a block of wooden buildings had been set alight, a whole town was likely to burn in spite of intentions to save some parts. As for humanity to non-combatants, the chroniclers offer practically no evidence—for this period.

The broad conclusions are that the troops were unaccustomed to restraint imposed by authority; that they were often acting— as we shall see—under circumstances in which restraint would be very unnatural; that while the army was on the march, punishment short of death could not readily be imposed; that discipline could be, and probably often was, strong enough to prevent attacks on church property; that some destruction by burning may have resulted from mischance rather than design.

[1] Moisant, App. I, 160. [2] Ibid., 166.
[3] Froissart, IV, 430. [4] Baker, 130, 133.

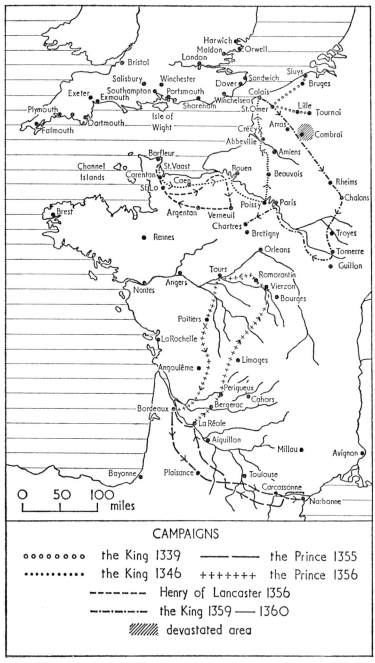

Harwich
Maldon
London
Orwell
Bristol
Salisbury
Winchester
Dover
Sandwich
Sluys
Southampton
Portsmouth
Bruges
Exeter
Exmouth
Winchelsea
Calais
Plymouth
Shoreham
St. Omer
Lille
Tournai
Isle of
Crécy
Arras
Dartmouth
Wight
Abbeville
Cambrai
Falmouth
Barfleur
Amiens
Channel
St. Vaast
Rouen
Beauvais
Islands
Carentan
Rheims
St. Lo
Caen
Chalons
Poissy
Paris
Brest
Argentan
Verneuil
Chartres
Bretigny
Troyes
Rennes
Orleans
Tonnerre
Guillon
Tours
Romorantin
Angers
Vierzon
Nantes
Bourges
Poitiers
La Rochelle
Limoges
Angoulême
Perigueux
Cahors
Bordeaux
Bergerac
La Réole
Aiguillon
Millau
Avignon
Bayonne
Plaisance
Toulouse
Carcassonne
Narbonne

O   50   100
| | | miles

CAMPAIGNS

o o o o o o o o   the King 1339   —— ——   the Prince 1355

• • • • • • • • • •   the King 1346   + + + + + +   the Prince 1356

— — — — — —   Henry of Lancaster 1356

—·—·—·—·—   the King 1359 —— 1360

▨▨▨▨ devastated area

MAP 2. France: the principal campaigns, 1338–62

But on very many occasions, no orders for restraint appear to have been given and the terrible work of war proceeded in the customary way. That the French, the Scots and the Flemings, when occasion offered, sped the work by the same means is evident to any student of the chronicles.

That they and the English regarded themselves as engaged in war none of them would have disputed, but the word used for a campaign of this kind was usually *chevauchée*, that is to say a ride. The increased use of horses was rendering armies more mobile. Not only knights and men-at-arms but also archers were often mounted. *Chevaucher* became ambiguous. Sometimes it was clarified by adding *à l'aventure* to describe the activities of the *routier*, or by adding *de guerre* to describe a specifically military operation. But in certain contexts it could be used alone meaning to ride out to war—usually with a relatively small force. In 1359, when king John of France announced the extension of the truce between the French and the English, he stated that men on both sides would continue in their existing positions till 24 June *sans faire guerre ou chevaucher*.[1] The distinction need not be laboured for, by the fourteenth century, *chevaucher* covered not only simple fighting and the pillaging already associated with it, but also the destruction which had become an important part of campaigning. It follows that the modern English use of 'raid' as a translation of *chevauchée* is not wholly satisfactory. The *chevauchée* moved swiftly and might include the driving away of cattle, but the concept is wider than that of 'raid'.

We proceed to the army's typical activities. Having brought an armed force to the Anglo-Scottish border, or having landed on the coast of France, or led an army from Sluys or Bordeaux to the French frontier, what was the commander's aim?

It was not, as might have been supposed, to seek out the enemy and bring him to decisive combat. Notwithstanding the ideals of chivalry, the Orders of the Garter and of the Star, the romance of the Round Table, the Fight of the Thirty; notwithstanding the laudable desire of young knights to display prowess, the king, the prince and Henry of Lancaster were not —or not usually—bent on that critical conflict of arms, nor

[1] Rymer, III, i, 422.

did they refer to such an aim in their reports, nor did adulatory chroniclers attribute that aim to them.

The commander's purpose was to work havoc, to inflict damage or loss or ruin or destruction on the enemy and his subjects by devastation. Commonly the word used was *damnum* (usually spelt *dampnum*) or *damnificare*. In 1346, king Philip pointed out to the king of Scotland that he had a favourable opportunity for inflicting on England very great damage (*maximum damnum*). He offered Edward a place and date for a battle and asked him in the meantime not to commit further havoc (*damna*), burning and looting.[1] A few years later, the seneschal of Gascony reported that John of Claremont, marshal of France, had ridden into the English dominions working havoc (*damnificando*).[2] The town of Millau placed on record that the king of England was about to work havoc (*damnificare*) in the land of France.[3] The Black Prince decided in 1355 that his army should proceed to inflict damage (*demolicionem*) on the county of Armagnac, and Delachenal regarded the prince's campaigns of 1355 and 1366 as aimed solely at the pillage, devastation and ruin of the lands through which he passed.[4] Eustache Deschamps summed up a sad little poem with '*La guerre est damnation*'.[5]

Exerting pressure by devastation is, however, only one of the army's activities. It has to live on the country, that is to say it has to gather from the invaded region enough food and forage to sustain man and horse. It has also to move forward at quite short intervals. It will often be more profitable to seize cattle, poultry and bags of corn than to destroy them. It will also be more congenial to the soldier to seize certain goods than to destroy them. These circumstances do not alter the fundamental aim of working havoc; but they complicate the procedure for, although the army may often find villages from which the inhabitants have fled in terror,[6] it will also arrive at towns

[1] Heminburgh, II, 422, 424.   [2] *Ancient Correspondence*, LXVIII, 32.
[3] *Documents sur la ville de Millau* (Archives historiques du Rouergue, VII, (1930), 115).
[4] Baker; 128, *Histoire de Charles V*, 126, 189.
[5] Pernoud, R., ed. *La Poésie médiévale française*, 81. 'Guerre mener n'est que damnation.'
[6] Fugientibus incolis pre timore. Baker, 65, and see ibid., 131. 'They fled away as soon as they heard the Englishmen's coming spoken of', Froissart (Macaulay), 96.

where the people offer furious resistance not only to the
soldiers' entry to the town, but also to every act of appro-
priation or destruction. Victualling, looting and destroying,
though routine activities in principle, are not invariably carried
out with quiet efficiency by well disciplined troops. On the
contrary, between hungry, thirsty, weary or drunken soldiers
on the one side and desperate 'civilians' on the other, there will
be scenes of high drama and great violence.

For the sake of clarity, it is necessary to consider the three
concurrent activities separately. We begin with the accumulation of food. The provisioning of English armies serving overseas is a subject large enough for a study in itself. The general
principle that an army had to 'live on the country' must, of
course, be qualified since armies varied in size and speed of
movement, and countries varied very much in the wealth of
their resources. Of few campaigns was the principle wholly
true. Edward I had lightened the task of conquering North
Wales by having supplies sent by sea to the Dee estuary, and for
some of his campaigns in Scotland food was transported from
England.[1] When Edward III proceeded to Scotland or to
Flanders, vessels carrying stores—as we have seen—augmented
local resources. For many years, Stirling, the port of Calais and
the region round Bordeaux needed victuals from English sources.[2]
And no army could prudently land on a hostile shore or cross
a frontier without food or forage for a few days' subsistence.[3]

Broadly, however, the principle is true. The maintenance of a
line of communications from a distant base to the theatre of
operations was quite impracticable. A small quantity of food
was carried to meet emergencies. Day-to-day supplies had to be
gathered wherever they could be found—in national territory
by payment, in invaded territory by seizure.[4] Under dire

[1] Hewitt, *Medieval Cheshire*, 58, 79–80, 113. *C. Pat. R.*, 1307–13, 81.
[2] References in the *Calendars of Close Rolls and Patent Rolls* are very
numerous, e.g.,
   Gascony: *C. Pat. R.*, 1350–54, 318, 319, 329, 346.
   Scotland: Ibid., 1338–40, 199.
   Calais: *C. Close R.*, 1349–54, 274, 290, 291. See also 'The Victualling of
Calais, 1347–65' in *Bulletin of the Institute of Historical Research*, vol. 31, 1958.
[3] Henry V's army leaving Harfleur in 1415 took food for eight days.
[4] For example, as the Black Prince journeyed from Bordeaux to Narbonne
and back in 1355. Hewitt, *B.P.E.*, 50 (purchases made), 52 (purchases
cease), 68 (purchases recommence).

compulsion, owners of victuals might sometimes deliver their goods. Far more frequently, they had fled. The army had therefore to organize a body of men to seek out and transport some kinds of victuals to the columns.

The means of transport—not all of them being required for food[1]—were classified by one chronicler as 'sumpter horses, vehicles and carriers of victuals'.[2] Others refer to the 'carts bearing victuals'[3] and to 'carts and heavily laden wagons'.[4] The army started with many such carts and wagons and seized others according to its needs. For the expedition of 1359, a large number were made in England. The position of the 'baggage train' in the column of march grew important when quick movement was necessary. It might, for example, be necessary to start it on the evening preceding the march of the main body lest it should impede progress at a bridge.[5]

Of the men at their work, ransacking farm buildings and other stores, no chronicler gives any description nor have I found any pictorial illustration.[6] They must have ranged very far from the column or columns, for an army often moved along more or less parallel routes and was divided among two or more villages at nights. (Indeed the repeated emphasis on the width of the track devastated probably implies the carrying off of stores before the destruction of buildings.) They would collect not only corn and flour, but also cheese, bacon, salted meat, salted and fresh fish, butter, eggs and fruit.

They would also round up cattle and sheep and drive them to suitable places for slaughter. Scottish forces raiding Northumberland, Cumberland and Durham almost invariably carried off cattle[7] not solely for their immediate needs but also

---

[1] Some were of course required for arms and miscellaneous stores.
[2] *Eulogium*, III, 222.   [3] Moisant, App. I, 164.
[4] Heminburgh, II, 341.   [5] Hewitt, *B.P.E.*, 108.
[6] Perhaps the nearest approach to description is: 'when they found a fertile area, they stayed three or four days till they had refreshed themselves and their horses, then rode ahead sending their scouts out to strip the land of food, often for 10 leagues on both sides and, if it was well stocked, they stayed two or three days bringing back to the army very many cattle; and they found much wine—more than they needed and they wasted very much of it.' Froissart, V, 378. The illustrations that embellish the Froissart MSS. of the fifteenth century were made for rich patrons who wished to see scenes quite other than merely collecting victuals.
[7] *Anonimalle Chronicle*, 19, 24; *Chronicle of Lanercost*, 216, 219, 346.

for the sustenance of their countrymen north of the border. Some indication of the extent of Scottish raiding may be seen in an official warning in 1345 that a Scottish invasion was imminent and that men of the northern counties should drive their cattle to the forests of Knaresborough and Galtres.[1]

When an army was stationary—for example the king's during the siege of Calais, and subsequently the English garrison within that city, and the prince's in winter quarters in 1355— bold raids into French territory procured numbers of live cattle for the troops. Henxteworth's account shows a large payment to Sir John Chandos and his fellows early in 1356 for 215 head of cattle they had gained as booty.[2]

By one means or another, then, an army usually contrived to 'live on the country', and there are occasional glimpses of the soldiers' satisfaction at the amount of victuals available. A raid on St Amand (1340) produced a great quantity of provisions.[3] At Carentan, at St Lo, at Caen[4] and at le Crotoy[5] (1346), food and drink were in good supply. Carcassonne (1355) was well stocked with wine and food.[6] At Tonnerre (1360) the army found a great quantity of good wine which 'was of great service' to them, and at Flamingy (1360) and in the surrounding region, the supply of provisions enabled the army to stay in one place for an unusually long time.[7]

But the stores accumulated in any one place were quickly consumed and, quite apart from the aim of inflicting further damage, the army was obliged to move forward to obtain supplies. The *chevauchée* could not afford luxurious living for the troops. Conditions during the king's march of 1346 are reflected in a letter from Calais at the beginning of September: 'the king hath sent to you for victuals and that too as quickly as you can send; for from the time that we departed from Caen, we have lived on the country to the great travail and harm of our people, but thanks be to God, we have no loss. But now we are in such plight that we must in part be refreshed by victuals' (that is victuals from England).[8] In contrast with the ample plenty of

[1] Rymer, III, i, 62. The character and consequences of Scots' raids are treated in Miller, E., *War in the North,* University of Hull Publications, 1960.

[2] Hewitt, *B.P.E.,* 90.   [3] Baker, 71.

[4] Moisant, App. I, 162, 163, 165. Avesbury, 204.

[5] Avesbury, 368.   [6] Baker, 132.

[7] Froissart, VI, 254.   [8] Avesbury, 371.

some districts in Languedoc were the poverty and discomfort of others through which the prince's men passed in November 1355, districts in which they had no water for the horses or for cooking, where food was scarce and nights were wet and cold, and swollen rivers had to be crossed without the aid of bridges.[1] And the king's armies during the winter of 1359–60, notwithstanding the provisions brought from England and those found in Burgundy, endured 'the grievous labours of this campaign . . . subsisting all the time upon the [resources] of the country, sometimes in plenty, at other times according to what they could find in a country wasted and raided before their coming by the above-mentioned English . . .'[2]

Forage also was necessary. During summer campaigns no doubt the horses ate the grass at night and, in the winter, wherever it was practicable, they consumed the stores of provender accumulated in the ricks and barns of the monasteries. But scarcity of food influenced army movements. The king himself, for example, as the siege of Cambrai dragged on with slight prospect of success, was prevailed on to push forward into France where both forage and provisions would be more abundant.[3] And in 1360, on the memorable day when the worst storm in living memory wrought such damage on his army, the reason for marching in such weather was the lack of fodder.[4]

The general situation may be illustrated and summarized by two contrasting sentences taken from Froissart. 'They found the country plentiful for there had been no war of a long season.' 'The country was so wasted that they wist not whither to go for forage.'[5] In a region that had not been invaded, a commander might be able to sustain his men for a quite short period, but though their stay might be no more than a single night, the stores accumulated for a whole winter were consumed, carried off or destroyed. When the soldiers had also stolen his treasures and set fire to his house, the 'civilian' had lost his all.

We turn to plundering. The practice of seizing goods belonging to the enemy is, of course, very old and must have been universal. The Old Testament abounds in references to spoils;

[1] Hewitt, *B.P.E.*, 63, 65, 67.   [2] Gray, *Scalacronica*, 161–2.
[3] Froissart (Macaulay), 49.   [4] Gray, op. cit., 158.
[5] Froissart (Macaulay), 80, 50.

the Romans made much of booty; Villehardouin and Joinville deal at length with plunder gained by the Crusaders; and, in the French plan, drawn up in 1339, for an invasion of England, arrangements were made for the collection and division of the booty to be taken by the sailors manning the transports.[1]

As with victualling, so here with plunder, we are treating separately one of three concurrent activities. So closely related were these activities that cattle might be seized for victuals, driven away as plunder or simply destroyed. Goods similarly might be looted or destroyed.

Now while the main aim of the *chevauchée*, havoc, could not be attained without the forcible seizure of cattle, corn and forage, it could, in theory at least, be achieved without plunderings of household goods and money.[2] Yet plundering of this kind was very widely practised by all armies. It may be regarded as enlarging the havoc since it increased impoverishment and sadness among the enemy. On the soldier the effect was threefold: the lure of booty (as well as good pay) aided recruitment; the prospect of treasure helped to maintain cheerfulness on a dreary march; but just as the desire to capture prisoners for ransom, even during an encounter, diverted men from the supreme aim of battle, so the search for private booty might hinder the work of destruction and even the progress of the march. A further effect was evident in some wars. When soldiers' pay was greatly in arrears, plunder became a substitute for wages.[3] In all wars of the period, in the absence of specific prohibition, leave to plunder was probably taken for granted.

The scope for such work varied greatly. The towns of France were more attractive than the march of Scotland but a large town might prove disappointing. At Carcassonne, for example, and at Narbonne—both flourishing cities—the inhabitants fled

[1] *Black Book of the Admiralty*, London, 1871–6, I, 426–7.
[2] Rights of seizure, marauding, expropriation and pillage with their legal and moral implications are discussed, for example, under 'Guerre' in Larousse, *Dictionnaire universel du dix-neuvième siècle*.
[3] '. . . the foot soldiers did not receive their [wages], wherefore they ranged the countryside, plundering the inhabitants for food. All were astonished that the king did not satisfy the infantry, since they could not live properly without wages . . .', *Vita Edwardi Secundi*, ed. N. Denholm-Young, London, 1957, 136. And cf. the first of 'Bentley's petitions' (1352): the soldiers have made 'outrageouses prises et estortions en defaute de leurs gages . . .', printed in Froissart, XVIII, 339.

to their great citadels before the prince's troops arrived. With them, it is clear, they took their money and much of their portable valuables. As conditions at each place were unfavourable for a siege, the army had to move on without the rich spoils that might have been expected.[1] Many smaller towns, however, were easily denuded of valuables. Occasionally a religious house was despoiled. Panic-stricken people might leave their goods anywhere. The Black Prince himself is reported to have alluded to the 'splendid spoils' Englishmen had gathered in France.[2]

For the chroniclers, plundering of goods was so common that they usually record it in a single word. The illuminators of manuscripts ignore it. From Froissart, however, we may quote a few descriptions of scenes:

The French in 1339:

. . . knights and soldiers on the French side desired nothing but that they might pass in Hainault to pillage and profit . . . so the French went in and found the people, men and women, in their homes; they took them as they would and all their goods, gold and silver, cloth, jewels and cattle; then they set fire to the town and burnt it so clean that nothing remained but the walls. Within the town was a priory . . . The Frenchmen robbed the place and burnt it to the ground and with their pillage returned to Cambrai.[3]

The English in Normandy in 1346. A general picture a few days after the landing:

. . . the country [was] plentiful of everything, the granges full of corn, the houses full of riches, rich burgesses, carts and chariots, horses, swine, muttons and other beasts: they took what them list and brought it into the king's host; but the soldiers made no count to the king nor to none of his officers of the gold and silver that they did get; they kept that to themselves.[4]

At Barfleur:

. . . there was found so much riches that the boys and villains of the host set nothing by good furred gowns.[5]

A specific industry:

. . . the king came to St Lo, a rich town of drapery and many rich burgesses. . . . Anon the town was taken and clean robbed. It was hard to think the great riches that there was won, in clothes especi-

[1] Hewitt, *B.P.E.*, 58, 61.   [2] Baker, 146.
[3] Froissart (Macaulay), 57.   [4] Ibid., 59.   [5] Ibid., 95.

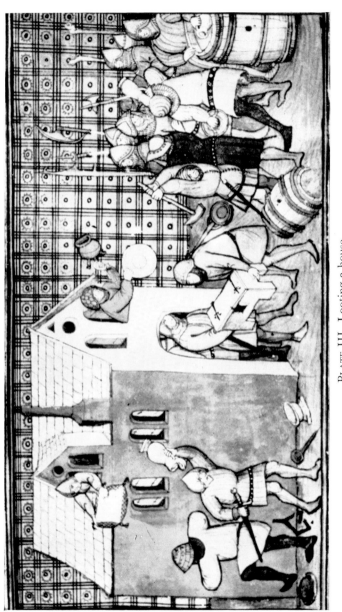

PLATE III. Looting a house

ally; cloth would have been sold good cheap, if there had been any buyers.[1]

An anonymous chronicler describing the sack of Caen says:

The English desiring spoils brought back to the ships only jewelled clothing or very valuable ornaments.[2]

The Anglo-Gascon force in Languedoc in 1355:

The wanton:

they took what they liked and burnt the rest.

The discriminating:

they disregarded clothing and went only for silver plate and cash.

The indiscriminate:

nothing of value remained. They carried off everything, especially the Gascons who are very grasping.[3]

Just one pictorial illustration of looting has been found. It shows soldiers removing valuables from a house, carrying out the money coffer, drinking wine and smashing the wine vats. (See Plate III.)

No such detailed sketches, verbal or pictorial, are available for the looting by Scots in the north of England. The chroniclers say tersely that they took much booty. But there are instances of Englishmen paying the Scots sums of money as an alternative to suffering spoliation.[4]

It would be interesting to know how the material booty (as distinct from the cattle) was shared among the troops. The individual soldier needed answers to two questions—'How soon may I begin (to gather goods)'? and 'May I keep all I can gain?' Answers to these questions had been provided long before the fourteenth century. They were indeed hardening into customs but they were not yet invariable, for the share which commanders might expect in the light of custom, or insist on as a right, or wish in practice to take, was not fixed; and even if a system had been universally accepted, its operation would depend on the state of discipline prevailing in any given unit at a given date.

---

[1] Ibid., 96. [2] Moisant, App. I, 167.
[3] Froissart, V, 346–7.
[4] Baker, 87; *Anonimalle Chronicle*, 24; Miller, op. cit., 6–7.

Light is thrown by Villehardouin and Joinville on the principles underlying the sharing of booty in the later Crusades. They refer to strict orders to bring every article seized to a central place, to the guarding of the accumulated treasure, to the equal or proportionate distribution of the spoils and to the strong tendency among the soldiers to dishonest concealment of their finds. Stern penalties were visited on defrauders.[1] Oliver de la Marche, in the fifteenth century, describes the taking of a town which had not offered resistance: the control of the soldiers till a given moment, then the rush for booty, the order to bring everything—gold, silver, copper, cloth, leather work—to the booty officers, the well-conducted public auction of the goods and the rumour that the booty officers made a profit for themselves.[2]

It is, of course, necessary to distinguish between single episodes, common practices, military regulations and jurists' declarations. There was evidently a general trend towards a controlled, equitable and pre-determined distribution of spoils. In the French plan of 1339 for the invasion of England, the sailors transporting the French army were to share the booty:

No armed man shall go out to plunder, but there shall be chosen in each ship a certain number of the men at arms and they shall pillage and get booty and bring away the beasts. Also in each ship shall be chosen two men [who] shall receive all the booty and profit and it shall be parted as well among the men of arms as among those which shall abide in the ships, and those which shall part it, according to the condition of the persons.[3]

This appears to be the clearest statement of principle on the French side for the brief period under consideration.

A pre-determined but less controlled plan is recorded of a French attack on Roche Derrien when held by the English:

The lord of Craon (sent by the French king) offered a purse of fifty écus d'or to the first man who should enter the town. It was won by a Genoan . . . and then any who would, entered . . . for it had been laid down in advance by the captains that the goods in the town should be common and abandoned to all those of the army who should be able to gain them.[4]

[1] *Memoirs of the Crusades* (Everyman), 66, 119, 176–8.
[2] *Les chroniqueurs français du moyen âge* (extraits), Paris, n.d., II, 95–6.
[3] *Black Book of the Admiralty*, I, 426–7.
[4] *Les Grandes Chroniques*, V, 479–80.

Other references, for example, 'The French ... went to Auberton and there divided their booty',[1] are too brief for guidance. On the English side also the evidence is not abundant. At Newcastle-upon-Tyne in 1319, as he prepared for an expedition into Scotland, Edward II had 'granted to each man as much of the enemies' goods as he could seize up to a hundred pounds'[2] without the risk of restitution being negotiated in a truce. It is, however, clear that in campaigns on the Continent, the leader had a share of the booty. In 1340, when Edward III returned from Flanders he 'distributed the spoils among his earls'.[3] Walsingham says of Henry of Lancaster's campaign of 1345 that his 'liberality and munificence attracted recruits. They found it pleasant to go to war under his command for when he took a town, he kept very little or nothing for himself but let the army have it all.'[4] Of the earliest phase of the campaign of 1346, we have the illuminating statement already quoted: vehicles and cattle were brought into the common fund; gold and silver were kept by individual soldiers. But in recording that 'they made no account to the king nor to none of his officers ...', Froissart probably implies that the soldiers' conduct was contrary to current practice or in disobedience of an order. From then onward, though the chroniclers refer many times to pillage, they have little or nothing to say about the division of spoils.

Honoré Bonet (born c. 1340) says 'the law on the matter is involved and by no means clear'. He insists on the right to take plunder, allows that men may have to 'hand it over to the duke of the battle', and adds that 'the duke should share the spoils out among his men, to each according to his valour'.[5]

When allowance has been made for some picturesque exaggeration, the quantity of goods taken by English invaders from French towns must have been very considerable. Froissart says of the prince's campaign of 1355 that the baggage train returned to the base loaded with plunder, and the *chevauchée*

[1] Froissart (Macaulay), 56.
[2] *Vita Edwardi Secundi*, 94.   [3] Baker, 70.
[4] Walsingham, 284. He was prodigal in society also, Froissart, V, 117.
[5] Bonet, 150. Other aspects of plundering are treated in Treue, Wilhelm, *Art and Plunder*, London, 1960; Hay, Denis, 'The Division of the Spoils of War in Fourteenth Century England', *Trans. R.H.S.*, 5th series, vol. 4, 1954; Redlich, F., *De Praeda Militari*, Wiesbaden, 1956. *Vide* also p. 105, n. 2 *supra*.

brought 'much profit'; and he records that in 1356 the prince's army came back to Bordeaux 'laded with gold, silver and prisoners'.[1] There is moreover other evidence of valuables found in the French tents near the battlefield of Poitiers.[2]

As for the ultimate end of the riches seized, Froissart, ever mindful of cash values, has a comment on the prince's men in winter quarters near Bordeaux in 1355: they 'spent foolishly the gold and silver they had won'.[3] No doubt for one reason or another, a good deal of the looted material remained in France. But in 1346 large quantities were brought from Normandy to England.[4] Baker says that the spoils seized were transferred to the ships which followed the army along the coast.[5] Froissart says the ships were 'charged with clothes, jewels, vessels of gold and silver . . . and prisoners'.[6] And Walsingham adds that by 1348 much of it had been dispersed in England; 'there were few women who did not possess something from Caen, Calais or other overseas towns, such as clothing, furs, cushions. Table clothes and linen were seen in everybody's houses. Married women were decked in the trimmings of French matrons and if the latter sorrowed over their loss, the former rejoiced in their gain.'[7]

Scarcely anyone, says a guide for priests, was prepared to admit (to a priest) the sin of plundering, but if one did, then 'modern confessors and especially those of the mendicant orders... having altogether no power to absolve such a sinner in this case, if some part of the plunder or something else is given to them, absolve *de facto* the plunderer and his adherents . . .'[8]

We turn to the third regular activity of the invading forces and the main purpose of the expeditions, namely devastation. The leaders' own reports relate their achievements to that aim. In 1339, the king sent word to his son Edward that he had begun operations near Cambrai on the appointed day and that there had been much destruction.[9] A fortnight after his landing in

[1] Froissart, V, 353.   [2] Hewitt, *B.P.E.*, 134–5.
[3] Froissart (Macaulay), 133.
[4] *Les Grandes Chroniques*, V, 451 *et seq.*   [5] Baker, 80.
[6] Froissart (Macaulay), 98.   [7] Walsingham, 292.
[8] From 'Memoriale Presbiterorum' printed in Pantin, W. A., *The English Church in the Fourteenth Century*, 209.
[9] Rymer, II, 1094.

Normandy in 1346, he informed the archbishop of Canterbury of the destruction he had caused, and when the long march ended, it was officially summarized in these words: 'He passed through France to Calais, wasting and destroying.'[1] Henry of Lancaster briefly described his campaign of 1345 and summed it up as a 'fine chevauchée'.[2] 'We took our road,' the Black Prince reported of his campaign of 1355, 'through the land of Toulouse where were many goodly towns and strongholds burnt and destroyed,' and Wengfeld, his chief secretary, commented: 'Since this war began, there was never such loss nor destruction as hath been in this raid.'[3] Such reports might be regarded as claims intended to justify the various expeditions but, as will be seen, in many places the damage done was very great.

We have stressed the aim of the invader, for, although it is a commonplace to all who study the chronicles and records, it receives slight recognition in the military histories, and still less in the political and other studies, of the period. Oman dismisses the prince's autumn campaign of 1355 in two sentences. Of the king's work in Normandy in 1346, Lot has not one word on destruction. And A. H. Burne finds difficulty in explaining the purpose of the devastation near Cambrai in 1338, but adds 'it was a very usual custom for an invading army not only to pillage but to burn a hostile country'.[4] Writers who exclude devastation from the study of medieval campaigns, or regard it only as a 'custom', may deal adequately with the *art* of war. They cannot portray the *practice* of war.

For medieval war did not consist wholly or mainly in battles and sieges with the marches necessary to effect encounters. It consisted very largely in the exertion of pressure on the civil population, and this pressure took the form of destruction, of working havoc. The ends sought in twentieth century-warfare by blockade and aerial bombardment had to be sought in the fourteenth century by operations on the ground. That in recent periods civilians suffered in mind, body and estate and were intended to suffer, is universally allowed. The circumstances of the fourteenth century, though not wholly parallel, are

[1] *Chronicon de Lanercost*, 343; Rymer, III, i, 187.
[2] Avesbury, 372–4.   [3] Ibid., 437, 443.
[4] Burne, A. H., *The Crecy War*, 45. (But some years later in an article in *History Today* (February 1959) he found reasons for devastation.)

sufficiently similar to enable us to infer the purpose and the effect of the devastation carried out in that period.

In such phrases as 'utterly destroyed', 'wholly devastated', the terse narratives state comprehensively the result without referring to the means employed. Devastation called for neither skill nor courage nor strength. It afforded no opportunity for personal distinction. Much of it was no more than arson. City walls, castles, armour, weapons remain to this day as evidence of the apparatus of war. Devastation by its nature has left no material evidence. It needed no detailed description in the chronicles and no entry in the administrative or financial records of the attacker. Unfortunately also, it is extremely rare to find it portrayed in illuminated manuscripts.

The principal agent was, of course, fire, but several other means of working havoc were available. The trampling of growing corn, the damaging of vines, the slaughter of unwanted cattle and the smashing of vats of wine are occasionally, but not frequently, mentioned. The manual destruction of buildings is perhaps reflected in such contemporary verse as

> And by assaut he won the citee after,
> And rente adoun both wall and sparre and rafter.[1]

But the breaking of bridges is frequently recorded—usually not as devastation, but as a defensive measure. When the king approached the Seine in 1346, he found the bridges down, and was driven to march many miles in search of a crossing. The destruction (by the French) and repair (by the English) of the bridge at Poissy form an important incident in his march. As the Black Prince moved toward the great curve of the Garonne in 1355, Jean d'Armagnac had all the bridges destroyed except the one in the city itself; and on his westward journey a few weeks later, the prince found the bridges over the tributaries of the Garonne had also been cut.[2] That the English also broke bridges is extremely likely. Whether the work was done by one side or the other, the economic effect would be serious.

The most useful means of destruction was fire, for it was all-consuming, and its ravages in France at this period have formed the subject of vivid pictures and strong comment by writers of

---

[1] Chaucer, *Knight's Tale* (Globe edn.), lines 989–90.
[2] Hewitt, *B.P.E.*, 55, 65–7. And Baker mentions the French king's breaking bridges in 1339. *Chronicon*, 66.

later centuries. It must, however, be seen in the perspective of history. Fire was not an extraordinary means of destruction, nor was its use peculiar to the fourteenth century, nor was it used solely by the English. Fire had been an agent and accompaniment of war almost since the dawn of recorded history. Troy had been reduced to ashes. Burning was sufficiently common in the inter-state wars of Greece for Plato to question the propriety of burning homesteads. Carthage and Jerusalem had been destroyed by fire. If it be objected that these were great, walled cities whose resistance infuriated the besiegers, whereas the English fired quite small towns and even villages, it may be replied that the Romans burned villages in Palestine; the Danes burnt houses and corn; William the Conqueror used fire extensively in France as well as in England; the Crusaders used it; and the Scots burned buildings wherever they could reach south of the Cheviots.

It was certain therefore that fire would be used in the Hundred Years' War. It had two obvious limitations. In the first place, since its property is to destroy combustible matter, it was an instrument of attack rather than of defence. Denifle's dictum[1] that 'fire was the constant ally of the English' needs qualification, for fire was the ally of any army that could use it to advantage. On French soil, the English were almost always the attackers and their use of fire is the more conspicuous. When on the other hand, the French attacked the southern ports of England, they too invariably used fire. And occasionally they applied the policy subsequently known as 'scorched earth', burning their own towns on the coast of northern France that the English might not with advantage land there.[2]

A second limitation lay in the need for the attackers to get very near combustible material in order to start a conflagration. A captured town could be set alight from within, but the high stone walls of a city or a castle usually afforded an effective defence against fire from without. The English 'brent clean hard to the gates all the suburbs' of Beauvais, says Froissart, but the city itself escaped major damage.[3] It was in the unwalled towns and the villages that havoc was wrought most easily.

[1] Denifle, H. S., *La désolation des églises, monastères et hopitaux en France*, Paris, 1897-9.
[2] Baker, 125-6. *Chronicle of John of Reading*, 122.
[3] Froissart (Macaulay), 99.

A third aspect of fire, though it did not limit its use, led to contemporary blame and subsequent condemnation. It is an undiscriminating agent and may get out of control, destroying —as we have seen—property a leader intended to preserve.

Concerning the methods used to start or spread a conflagration, most of the chroniclers are completely silent. Since fire was needed and probably maintained for cooking (and at times for shoeing horses), it would be inferred that burning material could be carried away for destructive purposes. In towns of any size, the operation would need to be organized. Two writers throw a little light on the means employed. Of Narbonne, Baker says the town was set alight by 'burning carts'[1] and of Caen, an anonymous chronicler says the 'burners' (*combustores*) 'scatter' (*spargunt* (without an object)) 'all around them as they do their work'.[2]

The effect would be speedy. Where houses, churches, shops, stables, barns, granaries, mills, windmills and storehouses of every kind were built wholly or largely of wood, where wood was stacked for fuel, for building purposes, for the making of barrels, dairy and domestic utensils and agricultural implements and carts, where most of the roofs were of thatch, where hay and straw were stacked, where ripe corn was standing in the fields—in all such places, once a fire had been started, it would be impossible to extinguish it. Ships in harbour with their tackle and cargoes were fired.[3] So were carts and wagons conveying weapons and victuals.[4]

For the most part, the chroniclers treat the matter in the same laconic way as they treat pillaging. They merely record events which needed no description for their contemporaries. Typical formulae are 'burning and pillaging', 'laying waste and burning', 'destroying and burning', 'burning and exiling the country'. A distinction could be made between route-burning in which the army destroys as it proceeds, and region-burning in which destruction is spread systematically over a limited area —the devastation near Cambrai was a full week's work—but the methods and results differ only slightly. Baker reveals his

[1] *Chronicon*, 80.
[2] Moisant, App. I, 164, or 'practise their craft' or 'exercise their skill' (*suis ministeriis utentes*).
[3] Ibid., 159.
[4] Baker, 81, 114.

satisfaction in the thoroughness of the work done by his fellow countrymen especially in Languedoc. In his narrative, this or that town, he says, was 'burnt', 'consumed by fire', 'reduced to ashes', 'burnt out', 'given to the flames'.[1] *The Anonimalle Chronicle* shows that in the march of Scotland, the work was of the tit-for-tat order. Froissart associates Scots' burning with its current evidence: the English 'followed the Scots by the sight of the smoke they made with burning'. On another occasion, the smoke from burning hamlets came into the town of Newcastle-upon-Tyne. Still later, 'tidings came in that the Scots were abroad and that they might well see by the smoke abroad in the country'.[2]

The most vivid impressions however are those experienced in darkness. Baker describes the scene near Cambrai one very dark night in 1339 when Geoffrey le Scrope took a French cardinal to the top of a lofty tower. The whole countryside was lit up for miles with the fires still burning from king Edward's work. 'Your Eminence,' Scrope said, 'does it not seem that the silken thread which girdles France is broken?' The cardinal is said to have been so overcome that he fainted.[3] Our anonymous chronicler, dealing with English fires near Caen, says 'the sky appeared to the eyes of onlookers as if it were of fire', and a few nights later, 'they set alight the homes so that whichever way a man turned his eyes, his face was lit up by the brightness of the fire'.[4]

Smoke by day, glowing lights by night marked the route of the *chevauchée*. For many months—in some instances for years—across the countryside lay a track several miles wide without habitation for man or beast and (except for grass and fruit) without food for either. This was the 'desolation', the achievement of the leader's aim. Great material damage had been inflicted and the consequences were inescapable. Homeless people crowded into other localities; the carrying off and destruction of food raised prices; for lack of means, rents were not paid; and, directly or indirectly, public revenues were diminished.

Devastation is the typical military operation of the period and, in some campaigns, almost the only significant one. War

---

[1] Ibid., 131–5.   [2] Froissart (Macaulay), 18, 110, 370.
[3] Baker, 65.
[4] Moisant, App. I, 160, 164.

consists in military pressure applied at those points, that is to say in those regions, where it may be most effective. The regions chosen are those in which provincial loyalties are as strong as or stronger than national loyalties, or in which other particularist forces are working against the consolidation of the French kingdom. The two kings are competing for provincial allegiances, and the theatres chosen by Edward for military operations are designed to impress provincial opinion.[1]

But what impression is it intended to make? On the one hand, we have the general circumstances of the period and the events set in motion by design—all incompletely known, of course. On the other hand, we have to try to divine the motives of the English king, the state of mind of the not wholly loyal provincials, the hopes, fears, capacity and temperament of the French king. And we seek to define the function of devastation —the destruction of the means by which life is maintained—as understood by king Edward and his army leaders.

A few Englishmen—perhaps rationalizing or seeking to justify what in their hearts they deplored—offered their own explanation: the aim, they said, was to provoke the French king to fight.[2] That probably seemed plausible to many people, but in the light of all the circumstances, it is inadequate. Devastation was not a new feature in war requiring justification to rational minds. It was a very old accompaniment of war, feared but expected, in the marchlands of most states. Further, in most wars—as was well understood at the time—fast-moving raiders operating at selected points could inflict damage with slight risk to themselves. The aim was damage itself,[3] independently

[1] Le Patourel, J., 'Edward III and the Kingdom of France', *History*, XLIII, no. 149, October 1958, 188.

[2] Richard Wynkeley writes that notwithstanding the extensive devastation, the French king would not or dared not cross the Seine to defend his people and realm. Avesbury (date 1346), 363; King Edward's purpose: that he might the more sharply provoke the people of France to fight, *Chronicle of John of Reading*, 122 (date 1355); that he might sting Philip into fighting, *Chronica de Melsa*, III, 41 and 50 (dates 1339, 1341).

[3] Devastation is 'doing harm' and some instances of it call for no more explanation than animosity, revenge, contempt. Cf. 'the earl's intent was to go and bren the lands of the lord of Vervins'. Froissart (Macaulay), 58. There are also—as would be expected—threats to do harm. Cf. 'Je lui porterai tel damage qu'il ne l'amendera jamais' (Charles, king of Navarre, in a letter printed in Froissart, XVIII, 355) and the use of the phrase 'porter damage' three times in letters. Ibid., 351–3.

of provocation. Finally, though common reasoning would suggest that on grounds of political prudence there was a degree of endurance beyond which a king would be compelled to fight, experience was showing that such reasoning was not necessarily valid. The prince of Wales' march through some 600 miles of French territory in 1355 and the king's march of some 500 miles in 1359–60 amounted to provocation indeed. Yet French forces had not opposed them. On the two occasions when French kings had been provoked to fight—at Crécy and Poitiers—the results were so disastrous to the French that their government resolved to endure rather than to fight.

Some further explanation is called for. Edward may at times have believed that the French king would be provoked to give battle. Tentatively, however, we suggest two other lines of thought. The campaigns, particularly those of 1345, 1346, 1355, 1356, 1359, were demonstrations of English might. This might was not directed against the knight or his warhorse, the archer, the castle or the engine of war. Its weight, its ruinous effect fell on the people whom a later generation would call 'civilians'. That fact was perfectly understood by the leaders of the invading forces. For the sufferers—the French people at large, including the rich—the only conceivable reaction proper in a king was defence or retribution in kind. Where defence was effectively organized (as it was against the Scots in 1346) or retributory devastation was promptly inflicted (as the Scots discovered in 1355–6), a king was respected. Where there was neither defence nor retaliation, loyalty might be very seriously undermined. The ultimate aim was of course political. The means for the attainment of that end (that is to say the military commander's immediate aim) was devastation. It demonstrated the power of the English king and the feebleness of the French king.

Secondly, since it was impracticable to occupy France, the war was becoming one of attrition: the enemy was to be weakened by the destruction of his resources. Devastation was a negative, economic means for the attainment of the ultimate, political end.

Thus devastation, which the military historians find so difficult to fit into the art of war, takes its place in the practice of war. King Edward could 'cry "Havoc!" and let slip the dogs of war'. Knights and men, when the occasion arose, would acquit themselves well. If however the occasion did not arise, their march would not have been in vain, for havoc was itself an important means to his end.

At least three kinds of attempt were made to arrest or escape the terrible destruction. In the first place, papal envoys not only urged peace on both the English and the French kings and promoted every possible meeting for the arrangement and extension of truces; they also went to interview king Edward near Lisieux as he wasted the land of Normandy (1346), and the prince when he was engaged in equally destructive work near Narbonne (1355), and at Montbazon (1356).[1] Neither father nor son was deflected from his purpose.

Secondly, there were efforts at Carcassonne in 1355, and at Perigueux in 1356, to negotiate with the prince for the payment of large sums of money in return for promises that these towns should not be destroyed.[2] The offers were rejected.

Thirdly, in some places, the inhabitants were protected— temporarily, at any rate—against all three of the routine operations by the strength of their fortifications. The construction of defensive works, varying from earth mounds to massive, crenellated walls, had been governed in France (as elsewhere) as much by strategic as by commercial considerations, some small towns such as Roche Derrien being well walled, while growing centres of industry remained undefended. If a city had satisfactory stores of food, it might withstand attack for many weeks and, by a sortie at a well-chosen moment, the garrison might gain enough additional victuals to prolong its resistance. Commanders tended to avoid sieges; they were costly in time and, if assaults were seriously made, in lives also.

For the citizens within the walls, the difficulties were three-fold: slow starvation as the food supplies diminished; injury or sudden death from big stones or burning material projected into the city from 'engines', 'balistae' or 'belfries'; and weakening morale since, if the city should be taken, the besiegers would destroy mercilessly.

In several instances the besieged escaped this terrible fate. Cambrai was surrounded in 1339 by Edward and his allies but,

---

[1] For a detailed account of papal efforts at this time, see Zacour, N. P., 'Talleyrand: the Cardinal of Perigord (1301–64)', *Transactions of the American Philosophical Society*, N.S., vol. 50, part 7, 1960.

[2] Hewitt, *B.P.E.*, 59, 89.

as winter approached, it became evident that the citizens could hold out longer than the allies could afford to wait. The siege was raised.[1] In 1340, Tournai underwent a siege which lasted for nine (summer) weeks. It was ended by a truce concluded between the English and the French.[2] In 1346, an English force was besieged in Aiguillon by French troops under the command of John, duke of Normandy, the heir of the French king. John was, however, called to the north to oppose Edward III, and the defenders, after holding out from April to August, found themselves free.[3] Rennes was surrounded in October 1356 by Henry of Lancaster. The siege (prolonged irregularly in violation of the truce concluded at Bordeaux in March 1357) was lifted in July 1357.[4] Finally, Rheims, well stocked with provisions, was besieged from December 1359 to January 1360 when king Edward marched away his men without taking the town.

On the other hand, La Réole, St John d'Angely and other towns in Gascony had to surrender during Lancaster's campaigns of 1345–6; and Perigueux, for which a large sum was offered that it might remain immune, fell to the Captal de Buch in 1356.[5] But the most notable surrender was that of Calais after some eleven months of siege (September 1346–August 1347). Though the townspeople took steps to protect their houses against stones projected over the walls by engines, Edward realized that the low-lying land and the water-courses rendered the use of siege artillery impracticable. He decided to starve the town into surrender—and succeeded. The inhabitants underwent terrible privation; many died and, but for the queen's urgent entreaty, the remainder would have met a frightful end. As it was, those who survived lost their homes and businesses, for the town was re-peopled with English folk.[6]

An act of surrender was not a mere acknowledgement of inability to resist any longer. Messengers might be appointed by either side to invite the other side to parley. The besieged

[1] Baker, 65–6.   [2] Froissart (Macaulay), 68.
[3] Ibid., 91–3, 108; Baker, 78, 249.
[4] *Grandes Chroniques*, VI, 59.   [5] Hewitt, *B.P.E.*, 89.
[6] The fullest accounts of the siege of Calais are in Froissart (Macaulay), 107–9, 114–16 and Baker, 89–92. There is an account of the re-peopling in an unpublished thesis, 'The Colonization of Calais under Edward III, 1347–1377', by Linton S. Thorn, in the Bodleian Library.

naturally prayed for mercy and sought to make some kind of terms. If they succeeded, the opposing commander might give leave for the besieged to quit their town 'with their lives and goods' (meaning of course portable goods) or 'with their lives' only. In some instances, the townsfolk negotiated the surrender of their town, while the garrison within the citadel continued to resist. (This occurred at La Réole. The earl of Derby was able to take his engines and miners into the town and attack the citadel itself till the captain and garrison yielded and were allowed to depart 'with their lives'.) The surrender of a town was marked by the public, ceremonial handing-over of the keys.[1]

But some towns, for example Auberoche, Bergerac and Poitiers, were taken by force. The circumstances of course differed from place to place. Auberoche underwent two sieges—first by the English who gained possession, then by the French who were taken by surprise by a relieving force. At Poitiers, which was taken after a very short siege, the earl of Derby stopped the burning and destruction because he wished to stay in the town for a period. In such instances, there could be no question of terms. Nobles, or men rich enough to be worth ransoming, might be spared. All others might perish as the excited besiegers rushed in to loot and then to burn.

Limoges suffered this fate in 1370. The date is a few years after our period but the episode is described in sufficient detail for study. Miners tunnelled till they reached the walls. These they supported with props and, at a moment when the English army was ready, the props were fired. Part of the wall fell. Immediately footmen rushed through the gap and opened a gate through which the army entered 'to pill and rob the city and to slay men, women and children' . . . 'Thus the city . . . was pilled, robbed and clean brent and brought to destruction.' Non-combatants, 'such as were nothing culpable', without distinction of age or sex, perished with the fighting men.[2]

Since the episode has been cited as an example of butchery in medieval warfare and of the Black Prince's cruelty (for

---

[1] The ceremony of handing over the keys was also a prominent feature of the transfers of territory in Aquitaine. *Vide infra,* pp. 146, 149.

[2] Froissart (Macaulay), 199–202. Walsingham (I, 311–12) says that the inhabitants were given full warning that the town and people would be destroyed unless they surrendered.

PLATE IV. Surrender of a town
Burgesses offer the keys to the Commander of the besiegers

according to Froissart, he commanded the killing), it deserves consideration. There are no grounds for regarding the prince as more humane than the men of his generation. He was at the time so ill that he had to be carried to the siege on a horse litter. He had troubles enough—political, military and financial—to disturb the balance of mind of any ruler; and—crowning provocation of all—the city of Limoges had not only changed sides, but it was his trusted friend, the bishop of Limoges, who had been the chief agent in bringing about the change. Soured in temper, thwarted, very angry, he may have determined to visit condign punishment on such treachery. On the other hand, it has been shown that Froissart overpainted the scene and exaggerated the numbers of the killed. 'More then three thousand' is his figure.[1] Though his general picture of his age is indispensable, his figures are always to be treated with reserve.

Nevertheless, the fate of a town taken by storm must usually have followed the general lines of that of Limoges. The three routine activities of the *chevauchée* must be seen combined in a triple operation, conforming to the customary practices of the period and linked with the degree of discipline a commander could maintain on a given day. Though the death of noncombatants who had no connection whatever with the quarrels of princes was coming to be regarded as undeserved and even regrettable,[2] no widely accepted code protected their lives. (Still less was there protection for their goods.) In some instances, butchery may have been ordered. In far more instances, the absence of orders left the soldier free to hack his way against all opposition to the goods he wished to possess for himself or his company. In general, the fighting men behaved as men tend to behave when excited by lust, rapacity or revenge, and unrestrained by law or custom. *Vae victis* was not confined to Roman times, nor indeed to medieval times. The wars of later, and supposedly more humane, centuries have produced scores of episodes equally repugnant to moral sentiment. Whatever the state of discipline may have been in fourteenth-century armies, some atrocities must be reckoned as more or less inevitable accompaniments of war.

Moreover, with the passage of time, the conception of atrocity has been enlarged. An incident which writers of later

[1] Burne, A. H., *The Agincourt War*, 20–2, 28.
[2] *Vide infra*, pp. 137–8.

centuries would discreetly conceal or mention only with reasoned justification or extenuation or shame, can be related with
relish by a chronicler provided it is the nation's enemies who are
killed. Two examples may be cited in illustration. The operations for the capture of Caen in 1346 included an attack on a
very solidly built bridge which the French sought for long to
break down:

> In the course of the attack, as the English grew more numerous, the
> French turned and fled to their homes. The earls and others fol-
> lowed them, killing on all sides. The remaining [Frenchmen] wishing
> to flee, left their ships. The English crossed the water in little boats
> and all they caught they killed with the sword. Those who had fled
> to their houses, the able bodied and grown up . . . seeing nothing
> but death awaiting them, surrendered to their pursuers, but the
> English footmen refused ransoms and cut them to pieces.

That passage is from an English source.[1]

After the battle of Roche Derrien (1347), the English commander, Dagworth, went to England and the French sought to
regain the town. They overcame the defence and, as already
stated, looted freely. Then

> they killed men and women without distinction of age and even
> babies sucking at the breast. . . . They attacked the castle in which
> about two hundred and forty English soldiers were stationed.
> [These men surrendered and] were conducted some two leagues
> away by two Breton knights who could hardly protect them, for all
> who could get near killed them with sticks and stones like dogs. . . .
> The two knights did their best till near Chateauneuf de Quintin,
> butchers, carpenters and others came out and put them to death
> like sheep. . . . The two knights fled with the captain of the English.
> The people of Chateauneuf de Quintin had the corpses carried away
> to quarries and great ditches outside the town where they were eaten
> by dogs and birds.

That passage is from a French source.[2]

Probably both incidents have been exaggerated by the
writers, but the fact that such accounts could be written is
evidence that when a town was taken by force, its inhabitants
or occupants might have short shrift. Here also, in all prob-

---

[1] Moisant, App. I, 166; Baker, 80 and Froissart, IV, 411–13, refer to the
slaughter at Caen.

[2] *Grandes Chroniques*, V, 480–1.

ability, amid the carnage and excitement, occurred the more shocking scenes in the churches for, notwithstanding the general principle that church property and churches should be exempt from looting and destruction, in practice some of them suffered damage of both kinds.

Aspects of soldiers' conduct—good, bad or indifferent—unrelated to the war effort, seldom receive mention. Froissart cites some instances of attempts to mitigate the worst excesses. During the fierce fighting at Caen (1346), Sir Thomas Holland, he says, 'mounted his horse and rode into the streets and saved many lives of ladies, damosels and cloisterers from defoiling, for the soldiers were without mercy'. Godfrey de Harcourt is said to have reasoned with the king about further slaughter and, having gained acceptance of his view, to have ridden from street to street commanding 'in the king's name that none be so hardy to put fire in any house, to slay any person, nor to violate any woman'. 'But', Froissart adds, 'there were done in the town many evil deeds, murders and robberies', for 'in a host such as the king of England was leading, there must needs be some bad fellows and evildoers and men of little feeling'.[1]

The evidence is not at variance with that quoted earlier concerning discipline. Orders for the army were proclaimed in the king's name. They did not necessarily arise from his initiative, for there was a hard side to his character, an indifference to the more cruel and more wanton effects of war.

We have quoted the commanders' claims to have wrought havoc on the enemy, and traced in a broad way the activities by which an invading army effected damage while 'living on the country'. That the havoc was very serious is clear. It may, however, be felt that the chroniclers exaggerated the ravages as their imagination or pity moved them. This is not the place for a detailed analysis of the accuracy of their evidence, but it may be allowed that the terse narratives necessarily lack precision. Sweeping statements such as 'he devastated the whole district' occur fairly often. Some kind of quantitative or qualitative check is needed.

At first sight, Denifle's massive compilation might appear to

[1] Froissart, IV, 412–13. The quotations are taken from Macaulay's edition, 97–98, except the passage 'in a host such as the king of England . . .' which is significantly omitted.

afford the precision we seek: it throws light on the geographical extent of the damage. On its origin and on the economic and social effects, it is less valuable. Moreover, the evidence comes from the sufferers themselves, and from sufferers who hoped to gain by proclaiming their losses.[1] Further, again and again, the causes assigned for losses are twofold or threefold, namely war, the companies and the pestilence.[2] Finally, Denifle himself states that the French were responsible for some of the damage. 'Many towns like Evreux', he says, 'were taken and retaken and there was ruin even when they were regained for the French power, for whether the French entered as victors or were driven out by the enemy, they set about pillage and devastation in the same way as the English and the Navarrais.'[3] That non-combatants, lay and ecclesiastic, suffered severely the compilation amply demonstrates, but it reveals also that by no means all the suffering was due to war and, of that due to war, not all arose from the work of the English invaders.

Granted a certain imprecision in the evidence provided by the chroniclers and in that compiled by Denifle, we still have valuable means of assessing the effects of the *chevauchée* for several areas. The first campaign of the war took place at, and near, Cambrai in 1339. In compassion for the folk reduced to misery and even beggary by fire, rapine, pillage and mourning, Benedict XII made a grant of 6,000 gold florins, not in the modern sense as 'war damage', but for the immediate relief of the suffering.[4] The sum was transferred to Paris by the Bonaccorsi, changed at current rates into 9,020 livres tournois and handed in two instalments to Bertrand Carit, archdeacon of Eu, for distribution in the devastated areas. The work appears to have been well carried out: careful investigation distinguishing the regular poor from the victims of war, was followed by prompt

---

[1] This aspect was noted as soon as the work appeared. See *E.H.R.*, vol. 17, 1902, 155.

[2] 'propter guerras . . . occasione guerrarum . . . propter guerras et pestilencias', Denifle, II, 281nn. 3 and 55, 282n.7, 280n.1, 278n.3, 301n.6. The Companies are treated in 376–8.

[3] Ibid., I, 299 and see II, 344, for French pillage of monastic property, 30–31 for native evildoers seizing their opportunity to rob, and 283 for monks committing more terrible crimes than the laity had done.

[4] Carolus-Barré, M. L., 'Benoit XII et la Mission Charitable de Bertrand Carit dans les pays dévastés du Nord de la France', *Mélanges d'Archéologie et d'Histoire*, t. LXII, 1950 (Ecole française de Rome), 165–232.

payments based on individual circumstances. A very full report on the work has survived.

For the purpose of our present study, the important aspects are the light the report throws on the extent of the devastated areas and on the circumstances of the sufferers. Baker's description runs '. . . except the walled towns, churches and castles, they destroyed the whole countryside (region) of Cambrai, Tournai, Vermond and Laon . . .'[1] This broad summary may be checked by the detailed statements of the report, for the devastation extended to no less than 174 parishes in four adjoining dioceses, and every parish can be identified today.[2] For many of them, there is a note: 'burnt', 'entirely burnt except part of the castle,' 'for the most part burnt', 'partly burnt', 'the middle of the town burnt'. In many places, the parish churches were burnt, and in some the abbeys also. No mode of destruction except by fire appears to be mentioned.

Concerning depredation, the losses of the parishes are described by such phrases as 'many goods plundered', 'movable goods carried off', 'peoples' goods carried off and burnt', 'much goods carried off'; and there is a precise, monetary estimate of the value of goods lost by individual families.

As for the human results of the devastation, the report names hundreds of people, their estimated losses and the sums awarded to them. In general, they are classed as reduced to poverty; many are in deep need; others, though not beggars, are in very grave need; many are now beggars; there are widows whose husbands have recently been killed; there are people who have fled from their possessions and dare not return because of the war; 'many tilled the soil and lived decently on their own lands but dare not go back to them because all the houses are burnt and they lost both their goods and their cattle which provided food and wherewith they tilled their lands. They are neighbours of the lord John Anonie and from his castle men at arms come from day to day, snatching up whatever they find and burning it. Only last Thursday they took two men and, unless God sends peace, they will have to die of hunger or beg.'[3] 'The five Caufiniaul children whose father was killed by the English, are now beggars; they lost with their father about 30 l.'[4] 'Maria,

[1] Baker, 65.
[2] Carolus-Barré, 172. See also Map 4 at the end of the book.
[3] Carolus-Barré, 224–5.   [4] Ibid., 226.

widow of Peter Chapiaul and her daughter whose husband was killed by the English, lost about 50 *l.*'[1] 'Thomas Maurays, an old man formerly of good standing, though he does not beg, is very poor and needy and goes here and there seeking food.'[2] 'Collard's widow and children in dire poverty have to live with friends.'[3]

Not a few of the victims are described as nobles; there are many curés and a few monks who have fled their religious houses and are stranded elsewhere. The total number of beneficiaries runs into thousands.[4]

None of the chroniclers mentions this well-organized relief work. The English ones may have been unaware of it, but it was carried out in an area Froissart knew very well (and four men bearing his name occur among the recipients of alms).[5] As for the writers and historians of later centuries, the bulky manuscript seems to have escaped their notice till parts of it were published in 1950. It may well prove a source for other forms of research. For our purpose, it gives precision to a devastated area hitherto not clearly defined; it affords detailed and convincing evidence that devastation had the effects one would have inferred; it confirms the chroniclers' statements, and greatly enlarges their significance.

Confirmation and deeper significance also accrue from a closer study of some of the Scottish incursions into northern England. As would be inferred, the economic and social effects are felt immediately. Deprived of houses, of animals, goods and accumulated stores of food, the inhabitants of the devastated areas lack the means to cultivate their lands and support themselves. Taxes are nevertheless demanded. The people point to their plight and protest that they cannot pay. Commissions therefore are appointed to investigate their condition, and in the light of the commissioners' reports, decisions are given. 'Out of compassion for their estate', the king may remit payment to individuals, to communities, to the inhabitants of larger areas.

We take for an example an incursion made soon after Michaelmas 1345 and described by Knighton thus: 'the Scots then grew bold, entered the region of Carlisle, laid waste the country and set fire everywhere in the surrounding district.'[6]

[1] Carolus-Barré, 225.   [2] Ibid., 224.   [3] Ibid., 225.
[4] Ibid., 221.   [5] Ibid., 182.   [6] Knighton, II, 33.

In the following spring, a commission reported on the effects of this invasion. No list of victims is known to have survived, but the plight of the inhabitants is acknowledged, the habitations are allowed to have been 'totally burnt and destroyed', and a long list of manors, towns, and hamlets that had suffered devastation enables us to define the area with precision.[1]

In the following autumn, king David's army was busy on the other side of the Pennines and a commission investigated the losses sustained by Robert Herle and his tenants in Northumberland. On Sunday 15 October—it was two days before the battle of Neville's Cross—the following vills, their report states, were totally destroyed and laid waste: Styford, Newbiggin juxta le Blaunchelande, Bromhalgh, Rydyng, Merchemley, Shildeford, Shotteley and Slaveley; the houses and crops burned; and the tenants plundered of 70 oxen, 83 cows, 142 bullocks and queys, 32 avers, 316 sheep and muttons and other goods.[2]

We turn to the region through which the Black Prince passed in 1355 as he journeyed toward Narbonne and returned to English territory. Here again (according to Breuils), an area can be defined containing no less than five hundred '*localités*' which the prince's troops had devastated.[3] But, for the country east of Toulouse, there is evidence of another kind which confirms and complements that obtained from English sources and from Froissart. From the one side, we have descriptions of the destruction of flourishing towns and small fortresses, from the other side instructions for rebuilding and repair. And the promptitude and urgency of the measures taken, form evidence of the calamitous extent of the damage.

The great fire at Carcassonne was started on 6 November. On 22 November, king John sent a letter of sympathy to the citizens, and on the same day, an order to the count of Armagnac directing him to take immediate steps to rebuild the town and put it in a state of defence against future attack. In order to raise funds for the work, the count authorized the levying of

---

[1] *C. Close R.*, 1346–9, 30. See ibid., 448, 449, 462, and Map 3 *infra*.

[2] *Cal. Docs. Scotland*, III, No. 1501.

[3] Breuils, A., 'Jean Ier, Comte d'Armagnac', *Revue des Questions Historiques*, LIX, 1896, 55 and 55n.3. Breuils mentions nineteen place names and states that the document from which they are taken is among the Gascon Rolls. Unfortunately the officials at the Public Record Office cannot trace it.

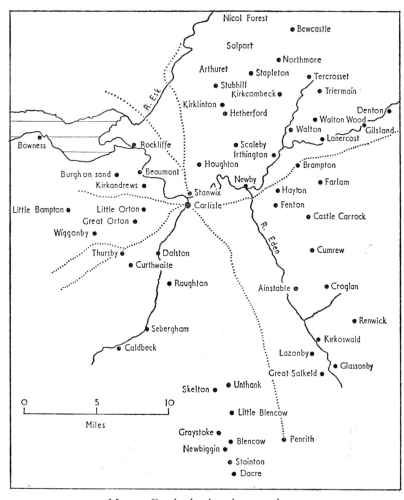

MAP 3. Cumberland: a devastated area

Devastation in Cumberland
Place Names (C. Close Rolls, 1346–9, p. 30)

Modern Forms	
Seburgham	'. . . it is found that Seburgham in liberty of pr of Carlisle in parish of that town
Great Salkeld	Salkeld in same liberty in parish of Addyngham
Dalston	Dalston with manor of Rosa in parish of Dalston
Kirkandrews	Kirkandres . . .
Newby	Newby which is a fourth part of Caldecote in parish of St Mary, Carlisle
Rockliffe	Rouclif with parish of that town
Beaumont / Little Bampton	Beaumond, Bampton with the parishes of these towns
Wiggonby	Wyganby in the parish of Ayketon
Little Orton / Great Orton	Orreton with the parishes of that town
Curthwaite	Kirkethwayt
	Lynthwayt
	Scarthwayt
	Haugholm in the parish of St Mary, Carlisle
Raughton	Raughton in parish of Dalston
Thursby	Thoresby with the parishes of that town
Burgh on Sands	Burgh upon Sands in the parish of that town
Caldbek	Caldebek with the parish of that town
Bowness	Bowenes with that parish
Stainton	the parish of Staynton in parish of Dacre
	Katerlen in parish of Penrith
Unthank	Unthank in parish of Skelton
	Edenhale in parish of priory of St Mary, Carlisle
	Heigheved in parish of same prior
	Hoton in the forest with the parish of that town
Lazonby	the town of Laysyngby with the parish
Newbiggin / Graystoke	Newbygging in the parish of Graystok
Skelton	town of Skelton in parish of that town
Ainstable	Hamelton in Aynstapelyth called le Dale in parish of that town
Kirkoswald	town of Kirkosewald in parish of that town
Renwick	Ravenwyk
Blencow	Blencowe in parish of Dacre
Croglyn	Crigelyn
Glassonby	Glassanby in parish of Addyngham
Bewcastle?	Bothecastre
	Foulwode
Walton	Walton
Lanercost	Lanercost
Arthuret*	Artureth with Randolf
	Levyngton
Stubhill	Stubhille
Hetherford	Hedresford
Solport*	Solperd with Eston in parish of same
Fenton	Fenton in parish of Hayton
Kirklinton	Westlevyngton in parish of Kirklevyngton
	Liddel in parish of Artureth

Brampton	Brampton in parish of same town
Northmore	Northmore
Walton Wood	Waltonwode in parish of Walton
Irthington	Irthyngton with parish of that town
Triermain	Trevermane in parish of Lanercost
Hayton	Hayton in Gilleslonde
Tercrosset	Torcrossok in parish of Lanercost
Cumrew Castle Carrock	} Cumrewe and Castelcayrok in parish of Cumrewe
Farlam	Farlham with parish of that town
Scaleby	Scaleby (in parish of ?) Kirklevyngton
Stanwix Nicol Forest	} Hoghton in Staynwygges, forest of Nicholas in parish of Artureth
Kirkcombeck near Canbok?	} Askerton with parish of Cambok
Denton†	Denton in parish of that town
Stapleton	Stapleton and Cambok . . . were all totally burnt and destroyed by the Scots after the said Michaelmas . . .

* Arthuret and Solport appear to be districts rather than towns or villages today.

† This is Denton east of Lanercost. There is a Denton Holme now in Carlisle.

tolls on goods brought into the town and the task was completed by April 1359.[1]

By the summer of 1356, similar measures were in hand for the rebuilding of Castelnaudary, Alzonne, Limoux, Narbonne, Avignonet and Carbonne. Among the measures taken to raise money, to ease burdens and to facilitate the work, were the allocation of fines to the expenses of building, the exemption of the inhabitants for a period from the payment of debts, the impressment of carpenters and masons, and the right to take timber in the royal forests for the building of churches and hospitals. There is specific reference to the rebuilding of mills and to the drafting of documents intended to replace those destroyed in the fire. The need for all this constructive activity points to the great material damage these towns and their inhabitants had suffered.[2]

A fifth episode, wholly verifiable, may show not the damage done, but a very costly way of escaping havoc twenty years after king Edward's incursions into French territory had begun. In January 1360, the king had decided that Rheims could not be taken without very heavy casualties. He therefore marched south to upper Burgundy where his men 'lived on the country'

[1] Jeanjean, 54.
[2] Ibid., 50–3; Moisant, 35n.2, 55n.3.

for several weeks. Though systematic destruction was apparently limited, the damage to the country and its supplies was very great and as Edward was in no hurry to leave—he was spending some of his time in sport—it might grow even worse if he turned his men seriously to work.

Faced with the appalling prospect, the duke decided to confer with the king on terms for a withdrawal of his forces. Walsingham summed up the conditions: 'provided he would spare Burgundy and refrain from fire and plunder.'[1] Under the agreement reached, the duke promised to pay the king 200,000 *moutons d'or* in return for a three years' truce, and the formal indenture of the truce stated the facts with grim directness:

> The king of England, pursuing his demand for the crown and kingdom of France, is making his way with his army through our country of Burgundy. We, considering the very great evils and damage which could come upon our country if the said king remained in it, and to escape these said evils, and because the said king has granted us a truce . . . we promise to pay . . .[2]

Even the humiliation and expense were preferable to the havoc-working potentiality of Edward and his troops.

Summary accounts of movement of troops and the destruction they achieved cannot have the exactitude of surveys of limited areas or the clauses of a treaty. That chroniclers in some instances exaggerated the ravages of war is possible and indeed likely. But in the five instances examined (and others could be adduced) where the damage implied in the strongly worded phrases can be assessed by evidence from other sources, the chroniclers' statements are confirmed and even illuminated.

We turn from particular episodes to general statements on the nature of war as it appeared to the men who were engaged in it, or men in a very good position to understand the practice (as well as the art) of war.

At a time when idealized knightly conduct coloured the pages of literature, when war and romance might appear to go hand in hand, when new orders of chivalry were being founded, the stark realities of war were known to all men and not disguised

[1] Walsingham, I, 287.
[2] Rymer, III, i, 473-4. Payments are recorded in ibid., 498, and III, ii, 632-3, 696.

by the founders of the Orders of the Garter and the Star. Whether operations are conducted in Scotland, northern England, Brittany or France, the chroniclers (English and French) use the same terms. And the two kings, judged by their official letters, see war in the same light: it consists in destruction and is accompanied by other evils.

In the summer of 1346, king Edward announces with satisfaction the great damage he has done in northern France.[1] Within a very short period, he is made to announce that 'while we are away, the Scots invade our country and commit murders, depredations, burnings and other crimes',[2] and in the following year the Rolls of Parliament record that during the king's absence the Scots invade the land and criminally commit robbery, murder and arson.[3]

King John authorizes du Guesclin to issue to men who have helped the French cause pardons for crimes committed during the war 'whether they were murder, theft, violation of captured women, robbery, pillage, firing'.[4] In a letter explaining the effects of the peace treaty of 1360, in particular the transfer of territory and of people to the obedience of the king of England, he recalls—what, he says, they know well of the recent war— 'the mortal battles, the killing of people, pillaging of churches, destruction of bodies, loss of souls, violation of girls and maidens, foul treatment of married women and widows, the burning of towns, manors and buildings, and the ambushes along the highways'. 'Righteousness', he says, 'has vanished; Christian faith has grown cold; commerce has perished; and so many other evils have followed that they could not be said, numbered or written.'[5]

The Pope equally is under no illusions. In 1345, Clement VI deplores the 'depopulation, the burning and other dreadful evils'.[6] In 1347 he seeks to reason with Edward about the woe produced by war: 'the sadness of the poor, the children, the orphans, the widows, the wretched people who are plundered and enduring hunger, the destruction of churches and monasteries, the sacrilege in the theft of vessels and ornaments of divine worship, the imprisonment and robbery of nuns . . .'[7]

[1] Avesbury, 201; Rymer, III, i, 88.
[2] Rymer, III, i, 88.   [3] *R.P.*, II, 165.
[4] Luce, S., *La Jeunesse de Bertrand*, 559.
[5] Bardonnet, 14–15.   [6] Avesbury, 180.   [7] Ibid., 377.

Later, Innocent VI rebukes Charles the Bad, king of Navarre, for 'conduct conducing to human conflict, to burnings, to violations of maids and other innumerable evils of war'.[1] In April 1356, Innocent VI, in instructing Cardinal Talleyrand to strive for a reconciliation of the kings of England and France, refers to 'bloodshed, devastation, burning, looting, spoiling and the destruction of churches'.[2] In 1360, when peace is declared, he recalls the many instances of devastation, depopulation and burning during the war.[3]

In four writers there are comments on the dangers of ignorance: 'dispirited . . . for they knew not yet what war was' and 'good simple folk who did not know war for they had never had war made upon them' (Froissart); 'fearful, knowing not what to do . . . for never before had war's fury come upon them' (Baker); 'there is ful many a man that crieth "Werre! werre!" that wot ful litel what werre amounteth" (Chaucer); 'no wight knoweth what war is when peace reigneth' (Langland).[4]

Other men give their miscellaneous testimony. Sir Thomas Gray (who had been a prisoner in Scotland) muses: 'Peace in itself is the earthly possession most to be coveted by all reasonable natures as the sovereign blessing of the age . . .'[5] Chaucer (who was a prisoner in France) says nothing directly on the conflict but, in his Tale of Melibeus, stress is laid on the tendency of wars to continue indefinitely. 'Once begun', an old man declares, 'children yet unborn will starve because of that war or live in sorrow and die in wretchedness.'[6] John de Venette (who from the walls of Paris had seen Edward's army in 1346) says that all men rejoiced when peace came, except those who gained from war—profiteers, traitors and thieves.[7]

Mandeville had taken no part in the fighting—he was living elsewhere—but 'since the time of my departure, our two kings . . . have not ceased to wage war with destructions, depredations, ambushes and slaughter . . .'[8] Writing in 1360, Petrarch says 'By fire and sword the English have so ravaged the kingdom of France that in my recent business travels I could hardly

[1] Denifle, 318n.5, 319.
[2] Moisant, 235. [3] Rymer, III, i, 502.
[4] Froissart, V, 345–6; Baker, 131; Chaucer (Globe edn.), 99; Langland (Everyman edn.), 158.
[5] Scalacronica, 164. [6] Works (Globe edn.), 95. [7] Chronicle, 104.
[8] Mandeville's Travels, Hakluyt Society, series II, vol. CI, i, xx.

persuade myself that this was the land I used to know. Outside the walls of cities, there was, so to speak, not a house standing.'[1]

Eustache Deschamps and Honoré Bonet were younger men. The former was about twenty-two years of age when peace came, the latter about twenty. Both were well informed. Their evidence cannot be excluded but, as they lived for many years after the resumption of the war, their views may have been coloured by events subsequent to the short period we are considering.

Deschamps was a poet, often at court and familiar with prominent men. In a 'ballade', after surveying various ways of life, he says, 'The worst occupation is war. It destroys everything. War is nothing but damnation. . . . Prince, henceforth I wish to lead an ordinary life, to leave war aside and live by working. Conducting war is nothing but damnation.'[2] In another poem, he describes the scene at Virtus, where he had been born, a particular place but no doubt typical of many others: 'If you would see great poverty, the countryside destroyed, and town emptied, ruinous walls where the shield has been, poor houses and unhappy people, you will find it at Virtus. You will have a poor bed and no sheets, and poor fare for your horses, so mind where you go, I beg you. The walls are falling. Things go ill and it's dangerous. The English have been burning everywhere . . .'[3]

Bonet had not suffered directly (so far as is known) but he had had much talk with knights in his youth and his great work, the *Tree of Battles*, is a study of war illustrated by scores of instances drawn from the contemporary struggle. He deplores pillaging, especially of the poor:

That way of warfare does not follow ordinances of worthy chivalry or of the ancient custom of noble warriors who upheld justice, the

---

[1] Quoted in slightly different forms by Boutruche, R., 'La dévastation des campagnes', *Mélanges 1945*, III *Etudes historiques*, Paris, 1947, 130; by Collis, M., *The Hurling Time*, London, 1958, 97; and by Tout, T. F., *History of England, 1215–1377*, 402.

[2] Pernoud, R., ed., *La Poésie médiévale française*, 81. A century earlier, Colin Muset had written 'Je ne vueil pas chevaucher', 'I have no wish to ride about setting fire to things, and I detest waging war, and shouting and gathering great booty and robbing people. It is indeed a foolish business to lay waste everything', *Penguin Book of French Verse*, I, 163.

[3] Deschamps, E., *Oeuvres inédits*, 41.

widow, the orphan and the poor. And nowadays it is the opposite that they do everywhere, and the man who does not know how to set places on fire, to rob churches and to usurp their rights and to imprison the priests, is not fit to carry on war. And for these reasons, the knights of today have not the glory and praise of the old champions of former times.[1]

Bonet's evidence is important, for no chronicler of the period explicitly connects the knightly class with the 'evil deeds' of war, though the inference is, of course, inescapable. King Edward, the prince of Wales and many of the nobles were deeply interested in ransoms; all leaders were entitled to a share in the spoils; war was in some respects both a sport and a business. It was also an opportunity for working off primitive urges. But the constant use of the passive voice ('the country was robbed and destroyed') or the summary statement ('he destroyed the countryside') might permit the reader to suppose that the 'flower of chivalry' were bent solely on noble deeds while archers and footmen were allowed to engage in less worthy practices which, in view of the circumstances, it was expedient to tolerate. The knightly class must bear its share of responsibility for the activities it organized and from which it profited.

Members of that class might still in fancy project themselves into chivalrous roles and even, on occasion, remember the code of knightly conduct, or (like king John) act with theatrical bravery, or (like Sir Walter Manny) act with ostentatious daring, or issue challenges to single combat (which seldom materialized). But such posturing—infrequent but well reported because of the social eminence of the persons concerned—had little relation to the daily work of seizing food, looting and devastation. The view that chivalric ideas still profoundly influenced the conduct or results of war at this period springs largely from a confusion of 'war' with 'battle'. Battles were infrequent; they lasted only a few hours. War was military pressure exerted day after day for weeks or months. King Edward in the Cambrésis and Thiérache in 1339, in Normandy in 1346, in Burgundy in 1360, and the prince of Wales in Languedoc in 1355, were conducting war, though no French knight gave them an opportunity for a display of prowess. We

[1] *Tree of Battles*, 189. A tendency to contrast 'the Knights of old' and 'the Knights of today' was common. See Owst, G. R., *Literature and Pulpit in Medieval England*, Oxford, 1961, 331.

K

are not disparaging either side but stating the circumstances. No glory was gained. Much misery was inflicted.

While Bonet (from a safe distance) deplored the decline of chivalry and of knightly reputations, Walter Bentley, living in the midst of turmoil in Brittany, was deeply concerned about the conduct of certain English soldiers who, he said emphatically, were not knights: men who had used their opportunities to grow very rich by squeezing money from the inhabitants of territory recently taken from the Blois party; who dared not apply through regular channels for leave to go home to England by sea, but paid big sums for French safe-conducts through France; who engaged in war for their personal enrichment. When a big army comes along, he wrote, it is very difficult to get these men together, for they are so rich and so softened by easy living that they do not wish to risk their lives. They are not knights, he declared, or squires; they are fellows of low degree.[1]

The years following the battle of Poitiers, though formally marked by a truce (1357), by the resumption of war (1359), by a peace treaty (1360) and by the transfer of fortresses and territory, are years of great confusion and, for France, of great distress. The peace liberated large numbers of soldiers who promptly joined together in the Companies and continued the worst practices of war while the kings were at peace. Breton and Gascon as well as English troops roamed at large pillaging. 'The highways', wrote Jean de Venette, 'were actually less safe at this time than they were when the English were waging war on France.'[2] France was rent by internal violence. Some of her magnates (the counts of Foix and Armagnac) engaged in their private feuds. Heavy taxes and the devaluation of the currency bore on the cost of living, and the plague, with its immediate mortality and prolonged social and economic effects, revisited France.

All classes suffered, but an interesting strain of sympathy may

[1] The third petition in the memoir on the state of Brittany sent to Edward III by Gauthier Bentley, printed in Froissart, XVIII, 339–43. In 'The Division of the Spoils of War in Fourteenth Century England', *Trans. R.H.S.*, 5th series, vol. 4, 1954, 91–109, Denys Hay draws attention to other irregularities of the soldiers in Brittany at this time.

[2] *Chronicle*, 104.

be traced for the non-combatants, the 'little people', especially the poor. A century earlier, St Louis had counselled his son to avoid war against Christians. If it should happen that he had recourse to war, he was directed to 'order that the poor folk who have had no share in the war, should be safeguarded against all damage resulting from burnings and other causes'.[1]

Of the year 1340, the *Grandes Chroniques* note that the kings achieved nothing worth remembering, but the war fell heavily on the poor and burdensome exactions fell on all the common people.[2] The chronicler Jean de Venette is sympathetic toward the poor. Froissart notes that during the siege of Calais, the captain urged 'all poor and mean people to issue out of the town'; that at the sack of Limoges, men who were 'nothing culpable' were killed, and 'there was no pity taken of the poor people who wrought never no manner of treason'; and that in 1369, Charles V, mindful of the past, was reluctant to renew the war because of 'the destruction of the poor people that he thought should ensue thereby'.[3]

Reporting on the condition of Brittany in 1352, Walter Bentley draws attention three times to the position of the poor: the disrepute falling on the English when officers in newly gained strongholds plunder the poor of the region, the foresee-able danger when the poor peasants dare not plough their land because the new officers fail to protect them, and the need to reorganize the system of raising funds for the defence of towns in order that it may not be necessary to take the money of the poor townsfolk.[4]

In a tribute to Bertrand du Guesclin, Eustace Deschamps writes, 'When he came there was desolation, war and tribula-tion in the whole kingdom, but by his foresight he consoled the nation and the lesser folk (*le peuple et la gent menue*) . . .'[5]

The fullest statement, however, is found in the writings of Bonet. In his view, 'war is not an evil thing', but he allows that 'in war many evil things are done', that 'the good have to suffer for the bad', and that the 'humble and innocent suffer harm

---

[1] *Clio: textes et documents d'Histoire*, II, ed. Calmette, J., 159. Similar counsel is quoted by Joinville in *Memoirs of the Crusades* (Everyman edn.), 323.

[2] *Chronicle*, 5.   [3] Froissart (Macaulay), 108, 201, 193.

[4] Froissart, XVIII, 339–42.

[5] Quoted by Joan Evans, *Life in Medieval France*, 136.

and lose their goods'. He proceeds to consider many typical instances of legal and moral problems rising from the practice of war in the mid-fourteenth century: may an English bishop be imprisoned by a Frenchman? If a French soldier captures an English child, should the child be put to ransom? If an English student is living in Paris for purposes of study, can he be imprisoned? If his father or brother come to see him, can either of them be imprisoned?[1]

Bonet's judgements on these and many other current problems of war and statesmanship, throw light on the circumstances of his day. Concerning the poor folk, he is clear and emphatic:

May it please God to put into the hearts of kings to command that in all wars, poor labourers should be left secure and in peace, for in these days, all wars are directed against the poor labouring people and against their goods and chattels. I do not call that war, but it seems to me to be pillage and robbery.[2]

In his observations on ransoms, he commends mercy and moderation:

But [he continues] God well knows that the soldiery of today do the opposite, for they take from their prisoners or cause them to pay, great and excessive payments and ransoms without pity or mercy and this especially from the poor labourers who cultivate lands and vineyards and, under God, give sustenance to all by their toil. And my heart is full of grief to see and hear of the great martyrdom they inflict without pity or mercy on the poor labourers and others who are incapable of ill in word or thought . . .[3]

Later he writes:

No man should incur blame for a business in which he takes no part. But everyone knows that in the matter of deciding on war, of declaring it or of undertaking it, poor men are not concerned at all for they ask nothing more than to live in peace. . . . If I wanted to decide that there was honour or valour in attacking a poor innocent who has nothing more in mind than to eat his dry bread alongside his sheep in the fields or under a thicket, by my soul, I could not do it.[4]

Though, in some instances, he holds, it is inevitable that the innocent suffer, 'valiant men and wise who follow arms should

---

[1] *Tree of Battles*, 125, 154, 184, 180, 181.
[2] Ibid., 189.   [3] Ibid., 153.   [4] Ibid., 153.

take pains, so far as they can, not to bear hard on simple and innocent folk . . .' And in giving judgement on the question 'What people have of right safe-conduct in time of war?' he mentions churchmen (so long as they do not go to war), hermits, pilgrims, and he adds to his list 'ox herds and all husbandmen and ploughmen with their oxen, when they are carrying on their business, and equally when they are going to it and returning from it . . . . They work for all men [and] they have no concern with war or with harming anyone.'[1]

On the ultimate fate of the peasants who had lost their homes and buildings, their crops and their cattle, the evidence is insufficient to bear generalizations. Those who lived in Languedoc suffered only the great raid of 1355, those in Burgundy only in the opening weeks of 1360. But Brittany, Normandy, Picardy, Flanders, the Agenais, Quercy, Saintonge and Poitou suffered the passage of armies several times (and were to endure further passages after the resumption of the war). Moreover, areas which escaped havoc from the English invader might suffer harm from the defender by the destruction of foodstuffs which could sustain the English, by the seizure (under *droit de prise*) of goods and transport needed for the French army,[2] and by the ordinary results of indiscipline among the troops. It is probable that many peasants went back to their fields,[3] did a little work, sowed some seed—if they could get any—and stolidly determined to remain where they had been born.

To sum up, leaving aside the morality of war in general, the justice of Edward's war in particular, and the diplomatic aspects, there are three broad approaches to the study of the struggle, namely the romance of war, the art of war, the practice of war.

In following the third of these courses, we have drawn attention to aspects which are empty of romance and remote from the textbooks of the military art. They are not beautiful; they may even be tedious. Yet for the great mass of the people —especially in France—they were the realities of the conflict, the social and economic effects of the practice of war.

[1] Ibid., 154, 188.
[2] *Registres*, 89–103, 74 nn. 5 and 6 (goods); 81–6 (transport).
[3] Boutruche, 'La dévastation des campagnes', 151.

CHAPTER VI

Transfer of Territory

THE peace which followed the treaties of Bretigny and of Calais enabled the people of England and the people of France to return to their domestic tasks under more or less accustomed conditions. There remained, however, a great population, mainly south of the Loire, which, in fact if not in law, was temporarily in transition from 'the obedience of the king of France' to 'the obedience of the king of England'. These people were victims of the war and, as such, they come within our purview. Some had experienced the *chevauchées* with their looting and burning; all were now to experience the detachment of their provinces from France, and to come under English rule.

Transfers of territory tend to rouse very deep feelings in the inhabitants of the region which changes hands. Liberation from hated rule or the return to a former allegiance may generate profound joy. Cession by the vanquished to the victor rouses dread, for it involves not only the severance of old ties, but also the prospect of permanent, alien domination.

Confronted by such a situation, the new masters have not a simple choice between being loved or feared. They have to demonstrate that the new régime is actually established and intended to last. They have to forestall opposition and treachery by exacting promises of obedience and loyalty to their new régime from the most prominent citizens. These measures, however distasteful to the subjects, are indispensable. But there is scope for statesmanship. It may, for example, be expedient to promise that certain liberties enjoyed under the former rulers, shall remain unimpaired. It may be necessary, in the early stages at least, that key positions in administration and finance should be held by nominees of the new power, but there comes a point when the employment of trusted 'local' or 'native' officers may render the new government less repugnant to the governed. Finally, the extent to which armed force should be paraded at the time of transfer or used to cow subsequent opposition, calls for sound judgement. The victor's aim is to secure, first, submission and, later, such advantages—military, economic, fiscal—as can be gained from the resources of the newly acquired area. With 'outside' opinion regarding his policy, he is not concerned.

Under the terms of the treaty of Bretigny, Ponthieu and a vast area south of the Loire were ceded to the king of England. The evolution of the French state had not only been halted; it had been reversed, for provinces were now detached from it.

But the permanence of the settlement would depend on factors and forces still to be revealed. One such factor would be the attitude of the governors to the people living in the newly acquired territory, for however gratifying to the English king the cession might be and however great the military or economic advantages gained, the transfer of territory was also a transfer of people. It is necessary therefore to consider the manner in which the transfer was effected and the initial form and personnel of the English administration in the newly acquired lands. Both were of vital importance for an enduring English rule. Delachenal dealt exhaustively with the legal and diplomatic features of the settlement but showed little interest in the more human aspects, while English historians[1] have for the most part overlooked or avoided the subject. It is solely with these aspects (the relations between governors and governed) that we propose to deal.

Both in geographical extent and in the number of inhabitants involved, the cession was the greatest that had occurred in western Europe. The mere mechanism of transfer would need to operate for many weeks before the whole of the territory had changed hands, and thousands of people would flock to city walls and market places to see the representatives of the English king. The transfer would not be a military operation but the

[1] Though the treaties of Bretigny and Calais have been very fully investigated by English historians, the execution of the treaties has received little attention. The episode to which this chapter is devoted is not mentioned in McKisack, M., *The Fourteenth Century*. Delachenal treats the matter in his vol. IV. Moisant touches the subject in his chapter III (and prints a valuable appendix 'La Requête de la ville de Cahors'). Perroy refers briefly to it in his *Guerre de Cent Ans*, p. 115 (and in the English version, *The Hundred Years War*, p. 140). Apart from the treaties themselves, the most valuable document is the '*Procès Verbal de délivrance*' printed by Bardonnet. Other documents are in Chaplais, P., ed., 'Some documents regarding the fulfilment and interpretation of the treaty of Bretigny' in *Camden Miscellany*, XIX, Camden 3rd series, vol. LXXX (1952).

substitution of one administrative system for another, with proper safeguards for the effectiveness of the new system. In practice, it might be a change of personnel rather than of system, but hundreds of thousands of men must have regarded the prospective régime with foreboding. Great lords could not avoid an act of submission. Merchants, bankers, craftsmen, labourers looked to the future with uncertainty.

As the evidence bearing on the execution of the treaty is limited and the period of this study also is limited, we shall not provide a long introduction to the problems to be solved by the English king, but suggest that chief among the factors to be considered were formal loyalty, sentimental attachment and self-interest.

Formal loyalty to one king or the other there had to be. Of the many territories to be transferred, some had never formed part of the dominions of any English king; some had been detached from English Aquitaine for five or six generations; some had been taken into France through the systematic nibbling of contrived litigation or open encroachment; some had been gained over by Jean d'Armagnac in quite recent years; and some had 'come into the obedience of the king of England' only since the arrival of the prince of Wales in 1355. From all alike, allegiance to the king of England had to be exacted. Such allegiance might be no more than *de facto* recognition of sovereignty, but it had to be demonstrated publicly and ceremonially.

The existence in some measure of a sentiment of attachment to France and the French monarchy may be admitted, but there is no means of assessing its strength. No doubt it varied from place to place, from family to family, from person to person and even from time to time. It was not yet a patriotic force. In many places it was less powerful than attachment to the province.

Self interest was of great importance. It was not wholly or even mainly a matter of material advantage in the individual but rather the perpetuation of divers advantages gained. Lords differing widely in wealth and circumstance, differed also widely in rights, privileges and duties and were involved in complex relationships with the duke of Aquitaine or with the king of France. The maintenance of these rights was their primary aim. While France lacked unity because of provincial

loyalties, Gascony lacked unity because of seigneurial inde-
pendence. Self interest equally marked the attitude of the
towns. Their charters were—or were believed to be—the bases
of their prosperity, the foundations of their civic life, the sources
of their dignity and status. The protection of their rights was
the dominant interest of the burgesses.

To these three basic factors may be added the circumstances
of the immediately preceding years: the occupation by English
garrisons of certain fortresses, the growth of the Companies, the
renewed invasion of France, the publication of the terms of the
treaty (including the payment of an enormous ransom for king
John). None of these circumstances could ingratiate the English
in Gascon eyes.

We cannot of course attribute to king Edward and his
advisers a modern analysis of the situation with which they had
to deal, but all the above factors and circumstances were well
known; and it is probable that the task, as they saw it, was to
demand of all men in the transferred lands an affirmation of
formal loyalty and, by respect for all such acquired privileges as
were compatible with English rule, to seek to weaken the sentiment of attachment to France and cultivate attachment to
England. Years would be needed for the necessary mental and
moral adjustments to take place. Statesmanship might utilize
the first steps in the interests of reconciliation.

The man chosen by king Edward to execute this part of the
treaty was Sir John Chandos. It was a significant appointment,
for Chandos was not of noble birth. He was one of the group
of men of this period—Calveley, Knolles and du Guesclin are
others—who gained distinction by their abilities. After service
under the king in the campaigns of 1339 and 1346, he accompanied the prince to Gascony in 1355–6. Here his name is constantly coupled with that of Sir James Audley and often with
that of Sir Richard Stafford. At the battle of Poitiers, while the
earls led their respective commands, Chandos and Audley were
posted with the prince till Audley asked leave to join in the fray.
Chandos then remained as the prince's counsellor in the direction of the battle. Among the many rewards the prince gave for
service in Gascony, none was so great as that given to Chandos.
He was a member of the group appointed to draw up the Truce
of Bordeaux, and he remained with Audley for duty in Gascony
when the prince returned with his army to England. After

serving in the campaign of 1359–60, he was one of the negotia-
tors of the peace, was given the lands and castle of Godefroi
d'Harcourt and made Viscount of Saint Sauveur in the
Cotentin peninsula.

If Froissart himself had any hero, it was Chandos; and there
is evidence that the French respected and even admired the
man who was not only their capable opponent in war but also
the agent entrusted with the execution of a humiliating peace.
Modern French historians acknowledge both his military skill—
he twice captured du Guesclin—and his political sagacity.

Under the provisions of the treaty, both sides had to surrender certain fortresses. Chandos had been occupied with the
handing over of those held by the English, while Thomas de
Holland, earl of Kent, was to have taken those held by the
French. Holland, however, had died before beginning his work.
In July 1361, while Chandos was at St Sauveur, he received
news of his appointment as one of seven men commissioned to
'take possession in the king's name of the cities, towns, castles
and lands which the French had to surrender, to take oaths
of fealty, to appoint officers, to confirm privileges[1] (provided
they were not at variance with the terms of the treaty) and
to take all necessary action in execution of this part of the
treaty'.[2]

Chandos went to see king John and, for the next six weeks, he
experienced the evasiveness and calculated delays which were
symptoms in French high places of a natural reluctance to face
a very distasteful situation. The king himself made distinctions
between items in the treaty: this, it was allowed, should be
handed over while that should be delayed. Chandos stood
firmly for the prompt execution of the treaty. The king agreed
therefore to send letters to the towns, castles and regions which
were to be surrendered and to appoint commissioners to act
with the English commissioners.[3]

Chandos waited in vain for several days in Paris, then went

---

[1] The power to confirm privileges was of fundamental importance and—
as this chapter shows—exercised by Chandos. It was in keeping with
Edward's earlier policy at Calais: 'Firstly, the king wills that the ancient
customs and franchises which were held in Calais before it was conquered,
be held and kept there henceforth in all points', Rymer, III, i, 142.

[2] Bardonnet, 132–3; Rymer, App. E, 59.

[3] Bardonnet, 2–9.

to Tours, and, on 7 September, to Chatellerault in order to start his work at Poitiers. Still, the leading French commissioner, Boucicault, had not arrived, and when at last he appeared, he asked that the operation should start in Saintonge! Chandos would endure no further delay. Poitiers stood first on the list of places to be surrendered and at Poitiers they would begin.

The people of Poitiers and Poitou had known the impact of English arms. In 1346, Henry of Derby had taken the city. In an engagement in July 1356, their mayor had been captured and held to ransom, and in September of that year, after the appalling rout of French arms, English soldiers had pursued Frenchmen to the gates of the city and butchered them outside the walls. Many scores of the dead who had fallen in battle and in the subsequent slaughter, had been buried within the city.

The impending transfer must have been well known for the treaty had been made sixteen months earlier, and Michaelmas 1361 had been the date assigned for its completion. John had already absolved the mayor, the chatelain and the principal burgesses of their oaths of allegiance, and directed them earnestly to swear oaths to the king of England.[1] And some kind of private 'feelers', made from Chatellerault to test opinion, had revealed that Poitiers would be quietly surrendered—so it was said—were Boucicault present.[2]

Boucicault was present with the other French commissioners when Chandos and the English commissioners reached Poitiers on the afternoon of 22 September. Their coming had been anticipated. The gates had been closed and the drawbridge raised, but the mayor, the more prominent citizens and churchmen had assembled in a space before the St Ladre gate. The instructions to the English commissioners have already been stated. Those to the French[3] included an order to deliver, or cause the people of Poitiers to deliver, the city and castle to the English king or his deputy, to do homage to the English king, to pay him the revenues and to obey him 'reserving to ourselves' (that is the king of France) 'sovereignty and "darrein ressort"'.

In the presence of the assembled representatives of the city, the French commissioners read a letter from king John addressed to the people of Poitiers and Poitou, recalling the evils

[1] Ibid., 17–19.   [2] Ibid., 9.   [3] Ibid., 12–14.

of war, the conclusion of peace and the promise he had made to hand over for ever to the king of England Poitiers (both city and castle) and Poitou. He bade them therefore to do homage, pay revenues and render obedience to the English king as they had previously done to the French king 'saving to us sovereignty and "darrein ressort" '.

After some discussion between the commissioners, Boucicault stated on behalf of himself and his associates that the English demand was in accordance with the treaty, that he was prepared to carry it out, and that he would obey Chandos as king Edward's representative. He then directed the mayor to hand him the keys of the city. The mayor complied and asked for confirmation of the city's privileges. Chandos promised to secure confirmation from the king. Then Boucicault, in the name of the king of France, placed the keys in the hands of Chandos as representing the king of England, declared formally that the city and castle were handed over and ordered both the mayor and the chatelain's deputy—the chatelain was absent through illness—to obey Chandos. Chandos accepted the keys as a sign of true possession and, when he and Boucicault entered the city, Boucicault handed to him the bolt of the St Ladre gate also to confirm possession.[1]

As they passed through the town, Chandos formally took possession of the castle and of the keys of the Trench gate. He then handed back the keys to the mayor to hold till the following morning.

That evening a proclamation was made throughout the city that at prime on the next day all men—lay and ecclesiastic, nobles and burgesses—were to assemble in the great hall to meet Chandos.

The town-meeting thus convened received an explanation of the proceedings in which they were about to take part: they had left the obedience of the king of France for the obedience of the king of England, and were required to take an oath on the holy gospels, swearing to Chandos, as king Edward's lieutenant, that henceforth they would be good, loyal and obedient subjects of the king of England . . . defend the city of Poitiers . . . recognize no other lord . . . and pay the revenues due. . . . The mayor, echevins and jurats (twenty-six in all) promptly took the oath; the other men took the oath collectively by

[1] Bardonnet, 21.

raising their hands to the gospels, and arrangements were made for still others to take the oath in their parishes. The names of all these men were written down and kept.

As for the administration of the city, the mayor was to remain in office, to hold the keys and exercise the rights he had hitherto enjoyed until the following All Saints' Day, by which time a report on the nature of those rights was to be forwarded for Chandos' consideration. With this clearly stated, Chandos formally handed the keys to the mayor. The ceremonial aspect of the meeting was ended.

The significance of the proceedings must have been understood by every adult. It is probable that the more influential people, well aware of the impending change, had decided to accept the inevitable. Their king had ordered submission: they were victims of war. That they and the inhabitants of the other towns should wish to bargain with the new masters, to make obedience seem to be conditional on the granting of this or that favour, would be natural. But the evidence does not warrant the inference that they opposed the English commissioners, or could have opposed them with any serious effect. Chandos was not 'obliged to calm fears and respect susceptibilities'. He had the perception and good sense requisite for the task. The statement that 'Poitiers insisted on the confirmation of its rights before making its submission' misrepresents the situation.[1] The confirmation of rights (provided they were compatible with the treaty) was, as we have seen, part of the commissioners' instructions.

So far as is known, the proceedings had been smoothly conducted. The *procès verbal* on which our narrative is based is concerned solely with the delivery of the towns, castles and regions which were to be transferred to the English king's dominions. It mentions no disturbance, resistance or demonstration, nor does it purport to describe the sentiments of the people of Poitiers. A disinterested spectator might have predicted that their reactions would be largely determined by the kind of government they experienced, and that that government would be regarded as chiefly the work of the officials appointed to administer English rule.

The first steps towards establishing the new régime were taken on the same day when, in a council consisting of two of

[1] Moisant, 69.

his fellow commissioners and five Frenchmen, Chandos made the following appointments: William Felton (an Englishman, a fellow commissioner and member of the council) to be seneschal of Poitou, and Maurice Raclet to be the seneschal's lieutenant; Walter Spridlington (an Englishman) and William Pechlvoyson to be chatelains of Poitiers and keepers of the rivers and forests of Poitou; Jean le Breton to remain in his office as receiver; Regnaud Poulaillier to remain in his office as provost of Poitiers; Helie Baugis (a French counsellor) to be procureur in Poitou; Jean Bonin to be keeper of the royal seal and Jean Bonneau judge of the seal.[1]

Thus, by the end of the second day, the transfer had been formally carried out, the people made aware of the change, the chief citizens sworn to maintain English rule, and arrangements made for the machinery of government. In that machinery, from the beginning, Frenchmen were to play a considerable, if inferior, part.

The events at Poitiers formed the first of a long series of episodes which were to take the commissioners (both English and French) to many parts of Aquitaine. Through the closing months of 1361 and the opening months of 1362, while Frenchmen in the royal dominions were very hard pressed to raise money for the king's ransom, while on both sides of the boundary pestilence was rife, and here and there the countryside was ravaged by the Companies, the commissioners pursued their task.[2]

There were differences in the rights the towns possessed, in the form in which the oaths were sworn, in the status of the men who took the oath, in the courtesies extended to Chandos. (Millau provided presents.)[3] In some places (Angoulême, Limoges, Perigueux) the attitude of the townsfolk was ascertained before the commissioners' arrival. Towns around Cahors agreed to act jointly respecting their demands. Perigueux had an internal debate which Chandos was asked to settle. And late in November a company of Bretons in Limousin made it necessary for Chandos to employ a large, armed guard.[4]

Basically, however, the commissioners' proceedings were the

---

[1] Bardonnet, 26–7.
[2] The pestilence is mentioned in Chaplais, op. cit., 13, 20.
[3] *Documents sur la ville de Millau*, 128n.1.
[4] Bardonnet, 140.

same in one place as in another. They were designed to achieve one clear end, and the means employed were the holding of a public meeting, the explanation of its purpose, the ceremonial handing over of the keys, and the taking of oaths of loyalty. And they appear to have raised no more open opposition than the formal demand for the protection of their rights which, as we have seen (provided they were not contrary to the terms of the treaty), Chandos was prepared to grant.[1]

In respect of administration also, the pattern set at Poitiers was largely followed. In very many places, Frenchmen were confirmed in their offices. Some Frenchmen were appointed to high office: Elias de Pomiers became seneschal of Perigord and of the Cahorsin; Ammanieu de Fossat was made seneschal of Rouergue. Some Englishmen received office: Felton added to his post of seneschal of Poitou that of seneschal of Limousin; Richard of Totesham became seneschal of Saintonge and of Angoumois, and chatelain of La Rochelle; John Harpenden was made chatelain of Fontenay-le-Comte.[2]

Two places—Cahors and La Rochelle—call for separate mention. While for most of the towns the requests for the protection of their rights are known only in general terms, that made by Cahors is known in detail. It is a very long document running to more than fifty distinct requests, and is remarkable for the light it throws both on the outlook of the Cahorsins and on the attitude of Chandos. It covers of course all aspects of the city's life and activities, and goes far beyond rights already gained into existing circumstances (punishment of the predatory Companies, recompense for losses sustained during the recent war) and even advances boldly to future possibilities (exemption from payments towards costs of war outside Quercy and any war against the king of France).

In his replies to these 'demands', Chandos was frank. 'This I will do willingly,' he says to several. 'I will do that as soon as I can.' 'My lord the king will settle that,' he answers several times. 'Let the [evidence] be produced and I will do what I ought and can.' 'I have no power to do that.' 'This request

---

[1] Perroy agrees with this view and adds 'Perhaps the populations would not have shrunk from changing masters if the king [of France] had remained their supreme suzerain', *La Guerre de Cent Ans*, 115.

[2] Bardonnet, 45, 128–31.

does not seem reasonable to me.' 'I will not and cannot do that.'[1]

The town was formally handed over on 9 January and, at the town-meeting, the consuls argued that by virtue of their office they were not required to take oaths or, if they were, *their* oaths should suffice for all. Chandos however showed why all—churchmen, nobles, burgesses—should swear. The outcome was that not only all twelve consuls, but also ninety-two (male) inhabitants took the oath. Audacity had been met by firmness and firmness had won.[2]

La Rochelle had had to be handed over as a token connected with the liberation of king John long before Chandos began to receive the delivery of French towns and castles. This thriving port had protested to John but, on receiving his instructions to surrender to the English, it had complied. The town's privileges—and they were very considerable—had been formally confirmed and the public proceedings had differed a little from those we have described elsewhere: instead of the ceremonial transfer of the keys, the mayor had taken the hand of the English commissioner (Bertrand de Montferrand) and opened the town's gates for him; instead of the public meeting for taikng the oaths, they had been sworn at a special mass (though arrangements were made for some to be taken elsewhere later).[3]

When therefore Chandos arrived on 5 October, it was not for the usual purpose. But the visit, far from being a passing call, was evidently carefully planned. Other commissioners, including Sir Richard Stafford, seneschal of Gascony, had already arrived, and if there was no need to explain to the Rochellais their relation to the king of England, that relation was made clear when Totesham was made chatelain of La Rochelle and formally invested there as seneschal of Saintonge and Angoumois. He took the oath to execute the duties of his office, rendering justice to rich and poor alike, and the oath to defend the castle for the king of England. Note was taken of those who had already taken the oath of fealty, and five men who had been chosen to go to king John to oppose the transfer

---

[1] Moisant, App. III, 197–207. Cahors had enjoyed great commercial importance but was declining in the fourteenth century. Renourd, Yves, 'Les Cahorsins, hommes d'affaires français', *Trans. R.H.S.*, 1961, 43 *et seq.*

[2] Bardonnet, 85.   [3] Ibid., 143–54.

of La Rochelle, now took the oath of obedience for themselves and for their fellow townsmen.[1]

The last entries in the *procès verbal* are in late March 1362. On 19 July, king Edward created the prince of Wales prince of Aquitaine. In July 1363, the prince landed at La Rochelle and during the following weeks received the homages of the lords and began to rule his principality.

Two aspects of the transfer of territory and obedience call for stress. However harsh the treaty may have been, Edward was less harsh in its execution. For one reason or another, over the payment of the first instalment of the ransom, over the recalcitrance of La Rochelle, over the date on which the transfer of territory began, Edward was lenient. Equally, over the rights of the people in the newly acquired territory, just and prudent consideration was shown. So far as is known, the confirmation of established rights—subject to verification—was nowhere refused.

Secondly, the operation of transfer was carried through without bloodshed and with very little demonstration of opposition. That it was distasteful to the people of the towns need not be doubted, but the closing of the city gates was largely a formality. Cahors received a very discriminating answer to its request but did not keep its gates shut. Only one place actually declined to admit the commissioners. That was the small town of Saint Romain de Tarn. But on the following day, two consuls from Saint Romain duly took the oath at Millau.[2]

La Rochelle has received the publicity which is given to the exceptional or extreme case. Scores of French towns were to be transferred to English rule after a fixed date. La Rochelle was to be transferred months before that date. Thus singled out, it displayed its hot resentment. 'They would obey,' Froissart quotes a citizen as saying, 'with their lips but not with their hearts.' Its people are said to have declared 'that they would rather be taxed half their wealth every year by France than be ruled by England.'[3] (The declaration was however made when there was no risk of their being so taxed.) The attitude of La Rochelle must not be regarded as typical of the towns of Aquitaine. The fact that Chandos or his deputy was able to

---

[1] Ibid., 45–6, 46n.1.   [2] Ibid., 110–11.
[3] Froissart, VI, 325–6.

L

proceed from place to place with so little delay, taking the oaths of hundreds of men, is evidence that opposition to his mission among the burgesses was slight.

The civilians who had experienced the evils of war had now to adjust their outlook to the immediate problems of peace. War had impoverished them (Chandos himself admitted that); the pestilence, the Companies, the disorganized currency, the need to raise ransoms for lords taken captive to England, the repair of walls, houses, bridges damaged by war—all had economic repercussions.

On the other hand, no town had lost the trading rights it valued. Over markets and tolls, the position was unchanged. Over distant trade the treaty imposed no new obstacles. When the merchants of Cahors expressed their hope that they might trade in France without the hindrance of new tolls, Chandos promised to help them.[1] The Rochellais retained their rights of trading with merchants of the Low Countries. King John promised them special protection for their goods in France, and king Edward gave them leave to trade anywhere in England.[2]

Nor had the towns suffered changes in the control of such internal affairs as the appointment and functions of their municipal officers. Nor had their officers been slighted by the English. The typical ceremony had been the handing of the keys by the mayor to the marshal of France (Boucicault) who handed them to the lieutenant of the king of England, after which the mayor was confirmed in his office.

Nor had the administration been wholly anglicized. The seneschalship of four provinces and the custody of a few castles were in English hands, but dozens of other offices remained with their former holders. Nobles had their own interests to consider, but the conditions, as they became clear to the

---

[1] Moisant, App. III, 203.

[2] Bardonnet, 152–4. The detailed story of La Rochelle can be followed in Chaplais, 'Some Documents', 52–3, Delachenal, especially II, 204, 220, 240, 252, 331–2, 408, IV, 19; Rymer, III, i, 497 (invitation to send representatives), 504 (invitation repeated), 512–13 (letters assuring the burgesses and merchants of their privileges), 540, 548–50, Rymer, App. C, nos. 33, 36, and Bardonnet *passim*. But the abundance of evidence must not be allowed to obscure the fact that La Rochelle's circumstances were exceptional.

burgesses in 1361–2, were probably better than they had expected.

Chandos had been prudent, restrained and reasonable. He or his deputy had the names of thousands of men who had sworn on the gospel or even on the consecrated element, their oaths of obedience, and of scores who had sworn oaths of fealty, to the English king. Later generations, rendered wise by hindsight and by many conquests and many annexations, were to ascribe this and that cause for the end of the principality of Aquitaine. At its beginning, the circumstances were as favourable to its continuance as any ruler of the period could have made them.[1]

But the English had a bad name—everywhere except in the still loyal region near Bordeaux—and in many places it was deserved.[2] Not only had they invaded the land, fought the battles and carried off the prisoners. After the battle of Poitiers, groups of them had lived here and there in French fortresses and, as the forces of law grew weaker, the Companies had been formed. And these—English, Navarrais, Anglo-Navarrais, Breton, mixed—might all be regarded as sequels of the English invasions. Peace threatened to end their activities. Their brigandage, their gross misdeeds, their terrifying power lay heavily on the country. To be governed permanently by the English—when English was the brief, undiscriminating name for brigand—was a disquieting prospect. Before a decade had elapsed, a group of unforeseen circumstances was to plunge the people living south of the Loire once more into war.

[1] Delachenal says that 'the inhabitants of the principality for some years enjoyed quietness and peace which their neighbours in the kingdom of France did not know', *Histoire de Charles V*, t. 4, 20.

[2] In *Scalacronica*, 130–1, 134, 138, Gray points to misdeeds of Englishmen who, notwithstanding the truce of 1357 and the king's clear prohibition, continued to plunder and to levy tribute. During the disorder of the years following the peace, the words 'Companies' and 'English' were used without precision. A marauding band containing a few or even no Englishmen might be loosely termed English.

P.R.O. E 36/189 deals with homages in Aquitaine after the creation of the principality (19 July 1363) and may be regarded as a sequel to the documents in Bardonnet.

CHAPTER VII

Mind and Outlook

OUR aim in this chapter is to consider the minds of English men and women who went neither to Scotland, to Flanders, nor to France, but followed their callings at home. What did they know of the war? How were they affected by it? What can be known of their opinions?

Attempts to enter the minds of men and women of earlier centuries commonly start from an attitude, political, philosophical or religious, found in contemporary literature or art. Such studies are often illuminating but they do not necessarily mirror the minds of the people at large, for literature and art may be designed for a cultivated élite. Chaucer, Langland and Gower, for example, reveal phases of the outlook of the English people but their references to the war are of the slightest. Romances of Arthur and the Round Table and romances of Alexander were widely enjoyed by richer people, and accorded with the conception of war as gallant adventure. Miracle Plays were giving pleasure to the townsfolk, but we look in vain to such sources for the thoughts of Englishmen about the war in France.

To the dearth of literary sources must be added a lack of pictorial evidence. Church art was beginning to reflect the knightly class, displaying their coats of arms and sometimes their armed figures in stained glass, their portraits in brass, their effigies in alabaster. Illuminators bent over the pages of chronicles—more especially a generation or two later—to depict in pleasing colours kings holding councils of war, receiving challenges to war, setting out to war, laying siege to towns. And there are many pictures of the knightly clash of arms both in tournament and in battle. These pictures are related to our subject, but the life they depict is that of a very small section of society, and the scenes they portray form but a tiny part of the war as it was experienced by English people.

The Scots devastating Cumberland, the French attacks on Winchelsea and Southampton, the English storming of Caen, the Black Prince's 'wonderful and terrible' raid through

Languedoc—such scenes are not depicted. Nor did the illuminators portray the accumulation of arms, food and forage for an
expeditionary force, the appraisal of horses, the adaptation of
ships for the transport of horses, the treatment of the wounded
or scores of other scenes which might have cast light on the
life and thought of people below the knightly class.

If our subject is to be investigated, it must be partly by
inference from the known events. In an age of slow communications, widespread illiteracy and no regular source of
news, when peasant and townsmen were necessarily concerned
chiefly with their daily work, with seasonal changes, family
affairs and disastrous visitations of the plague, what information
can typical people have had about campaigns distant two,
three or four hundred miles from their dwelling places? Even
about activities related to the war in English counties remote
from their homes? It is with this basic question—an aspect of
consciousness—that an enquiry must start.

Inevitably—judged by more modern standards—there was
very great ignorance of the course of the war as it unfolded in
France, Flanders and Burgundy. Some of the king's messages
on his campaign in 1346 are extant as are also the formal
dispatches of Henry of Lancaster (1345–6) and of the Black
Prince (1355), and there is an informal letter on the prince's
campaign written by Wengfeld, his right-hand man. They
convey more meaning today than they can have done at the
time they were received in England for, in the absence of maps[1]
and other geographical information, many place-names had
little or no significance; and distances, difficulties and achievements could not be appreciated.

The prince's dispatch on his autumn campaign, for example,
states the route his army had travelled, but it is very doubtful
whether anyone in London would be able to follow the report
with understanding. Occasionally such messages were carried
by officers who could provide some clarification. The king sent
the earl of Huntingdon back 'to show these things more fully to
the Council', and the prince sent Sir Richard Stafford who
'will know how to tell you more at large than we could write to

[1] There were of course maps of England in the fourteenth century and
it is probable that in France there were maps of France, but I think it quite
improbable that maps of France were to be found in England during the
period of this study.

you . . .' Wengfeld resorted to two devices: he described the position of Narbonne (the turning point of the long march) by reference to Montpellier, Aigues Mortes and Avignon (places some few Englishmen might have visited) but the first is nearly seventy miles, and the others about twice that distance, from Narbonne; he compared Carcassonne with York[1] than which it was 'greater, stronger and fairer'. No better devices could have been employed, but when the best informed men in the king's Council knew so little, the mass of English people must have been extremely ill informed about the progress of English armies serving overseas.

Our enquiry therefore is limited almost wholly to conditions and events in England. For our present purpose, knowledge of the war was of two kinds: on the one hand, the unorganized mass of information derived from experience, observation and hearsay; on the other, the more organized news sent expressly for purposes of war to an official or a locality or to the nation as a whole.

Of the first kind of knowledge, dwellers in the northern counties had abundance, for border warfare was endemic. The Scots besieged Carlisle and wrought awful havoc in Cumberland. They besieged Berwick, crossed the border between the castles, thrust down into Durham, ravaged as far as the North Riding and drove away hundreds of cattle. It was largely from the northern counties that English garrisons in Edinburgh, Stirling and Perth were provisioned.[2] While the memory of Halidon Hill was still fresh, the battle of Neville's Cross was fought, and before that was forgotten, king Edward hastened northward in the late autumn of 1355 to spend weeks in the wintry borderland because of still another Scottish incursion.

Inhabitants of the ports along the Channel and the southern part of the North Sea also had direct experience of war. The French attacks on Harwich, Dover, Winchelsea, Hastings, Portsmouth, Southampton, the Isle of Wight, Swanage, Teignmouth and Plymouth must have caused widespread alarm. The attack on Southampton was very serious. On 5 October

---

[1] Avesbury, 437, 439, 444; Hewitt, *B.P.E.*, 78–9. Similarly Barfleur was said in 1346 to be 'as good and large as Sandwich' (Northburgh, printed in Froissart, XVIII, 283).

[2] References are numerous, e.g. *C. Close R.*, 1339–41, 73, 101, 103, 384; ibid., 1341–3, 22, 106, 208, 591; *C. Pat. R.*, 1338–40, 198.

1338, the unwalled town was sacked and burned. The inhabitants fled, and for months afterwards there were great efforts to build walls, to supply arms, and particularly to get the former inhabitants back to the town. From the Isle of Wight (once invaded and several times threatened) there was a similar exodus and similar pressure on occupiers of land to return. Portsmouth and Portsea were also burned. Again and again (for example in 1342, 1347 and 1360) special steps were taken for the safety of the island and neighbouring ports.[1]

The attack on Winchelsea (16 March 1360) with the threat of invasion led to the mobilization of men of London, the south-eastern and several Midland counties.[2]

It was at Orwell and at the southern ports that the armies were assembled for the campaigns in Flanders, Normandy, Brittany and Gascony. Here were seen the accumulating stores and the large numbers of horses as the men waited—usually for several weeks—till enough ships had come into harbour to convey the forces overseas. To these ports the armies and their royal leaders returned.

As the great damage wrought by the French in Southampton, Portsmouth and the Isle of Wight taught the possibility of invasion, men from the remoter parts of the southern counties were moved again and again down to defend the coastal strip.

In all these regions, therefore, people were brought directly or indirectly into the war.

Further inland, commissions of array chose, tested and arrayed the men who were to go overseas. Archers, men-at-arms and knights moved through the shires to the ports of embarkation—Welshmen crossing to Ipswich, Cheshire men marching to Plymouth, men of the Midlands finding their way to Sandwich. When the campaign ended, they returned, bringing back some of the violence they had practised abroad and provoking loud complaints from law-abiding people.

In many parts of the country, war stimulated production. Bowyers, fletchers, armourers, saddlers and smiths plied their crafts to furnish the armies. Carpenters were drawn to the ports

---

[1] Southampton: Baker, 63; Froissart (Macaulay) 48; *C. Close R.*, 1339–41, 40, 55, 64, 67 *et passim*; *R.P.*, II, 108; Rymer, II, ii, 1077; ibid., III, i, 104, 106. Isle of Wight: *C. Pat. R.*, 1338–40, 212; *C. Close R.*, 1339–41, 91, 117, 118, 121, 123–4, 352, 368; Rymer, III, i, 104, 106.

[2] See chapter I.

to build or adapt ships, and to construct engines of war. Makers of ropes and of sail-cloth helped to equip the king's ships. Purveyors and victualling officers gathered up supplies of corn, fish, wine and forage for troops serving abroad. Masons repaired castles.

The needs of transport at home led to requests (which were virtually demands) for wagons from the monasteries and, for some of the campaigns (especially that of 1359), new wagons were constructed.

Finally, eminent prisoners and hostages were moved—sometimes under heavy guard—again and again from one part of England to another. King John of France came from Plymouth to London and was lodged at the Savoy in the Strand, at Somerton in Lincolnshire, at Hertford and at Berkhampstead. The earl of Moray spent periods at York, Nottingham, Bamburgh, Windsor, Winchester. Less eminent hostages from Berwick were taken to Tavistock, Bristol and Abbotsbury.[1]

With this general background of evidence in his mind, the least informed of Englishmen could not fail to know that the war affected the lives of many of his compatriots.

To the unorganized mass of general information were added specific items of news. The full use of the nation's resources made necessary a good deal of communication between the king (and his staff) at the centre and the various sheriffs, mayors, bailiffs and other officers throughout the land, and indeed between the king and the people as a whole.

Messages from the king are of three grades of importance as news. First are those addressed to officials, directing or authorizing them to take certain action in a locality, for example, at a port where ships are to be arrested, or travellers searched, or goods intended for export detained. Reasons for the policy to be followed are not necessarily given but they are inferred and become the subject of conversation.

In the second grade are letters which not only prescribe but explain action: policy is made intelligible to those who must execute it. Officials are informed, for example, that in view of the danger of invasion, or the scarcity of victuals, or the tendency of vendors to seek excessive profits, certain action

---

[1] *Cal. Doc. Scotland*, III, 1171–3, 1205, 1213, 1280, 1317, 1337, 1342–3, 1350, 1359, 1361, 1364, 1386 and see 1308, 1322 and *C. Close R.*, 1339–41, 258.

must be taken. The officials explain and justify that action in the light of their instructions, and the neighbourhood understands something of the measures taken in the national interest for the purpose of war. Another class of message explains departures from standard practice: A, B and C are not failing in their duties: A is busy in the maritime lands 'prepared against incursions of hostile aliens'; B is waiting 'to set out against the king's enemies if they presume to invade the land'; C is ready to set out with D 'as often as there is danger of hostile attacks'.

The third kind of letter is sent expressly for publication on as wide a scale as is possible. 'Cause proclamation to be made', it usually runs, 'in seaports, market towns and other places in your bailiwick where you shall deem best, that . . .' The message is sent in Latin but it is proclaimed in English and the oldest means of communication are used. Just as for the Lords and Commons, information is 'cried in Westminster Hall', and for an army it is 'cried throughout the host', so for the people of England it is—to use a slight variant of the standard formula —'cried in the markets, fairs and other public places'. Thus the king sends information to the whole people.

It is by this means that he informs them of his assumption of the title 'king of France', of his landing in Normandy in 1346, of the victory of Crécy, of the capture of Calais, of the agreements on the truces, of the conclusion of peace.[1]

But the news items so widely diffused are not confined to past events. Some of them are warnings concerning the future and especially the nation's peril from invasion. Here again we may make a threefold distinction. There is the broad forecast couched in such words as 'The king of France is gathering a great army and a great fleet for the invasion of this country' (1345); 'cattle should be brought south from the marchland . . . as the Scots are preparing an invasion' (1345); 'the Scots have gone back to collect an army to invade England' (1346); 'the king of France does not cease to collect forces to invade the realm of England' (1351); enemy warships are assembled 'to destroy the English fleet and invade our kingdom' (1356).[2]

Next, there is the more or less explicit statement of the

---

[1] Title: Rymer, II, ii, 1109, 1111; Landing: ibid., III, i, 88; Crécy: ibid., III, i, 89; Calais: ibid., III, I, 130; Truces: *C. Close R.*, 1339–41, 636–7, Rymer, III, I, 485, Baker, 94–5; Peace: Rymer, III, i, 495.

[2] Rymer, III, i, 38–9, 62, 67, 537; *C. Close R.*, 1349–54, 356.

enemy's plan: he intends to land in (such or such a) county.
(The prompt dispatch of indications of an impending attack by
the enemy is, of course, no more than normal military procedure.) In 1338, the men of Holderness are not to be sent to
Scotland but to remain for the defence of their homeland as
'aliens . . . prepare diverse ships of war to attack those parts'.
In the same year, though Kent and Sussex are not definitely
stated to be places chosen for attack, the maritime lands in these
counties are garrisoned to resist an invasion. In 1339, the
enemy are said to be preparing to attack Orwell, to invade the
'island' of Portland and to attack Dorset and Southampton. In
1360, Southampton, Portsmouth and Sandwich have been
chosen for attack.[1]

But a third kind of message is designed to do more than alert
the defence: it is aimed at moulding opinion by foretelling
invasion together with the evils the enemy intends to perpetrate once he has stepped on English soil. This may be
vaguely 'to do much evil', as the mayor and sheriffs of London
are warned in 1338 and the people of Southampton in 1339. It
may be to 'kill, spoil, burn and perpetrate other crimes' (1360)
or 'to rescue king John from our hands' (1360) or to work even
worse havoc than he had done at Winchelsea where he had
already killed, burned, destroyed and perpetrated evils (1360).[2]

Thus to the fruits of observation and hearsay are added in-
ferences from official policy, information from official sources,
and news of major events from the king himself, while for those
who live in the coastal counties, there are predictions of invasion. The Englishman's knowledge and understanding of the
war are increased. Public opinion is moulded, and the fact that
public opinion expects a French invasion is cited in 1352 and
1355 to the keepers of the maritime lands as a warning to be
prepared.[3]

There remained another agency which had access to the
public mind. In his great undertaking the king sought to
associate the Church with the State. Its ministers were resident
in every parish, its services were frequented every Sunday, its

[1] C. Close R., 1337–9, 236, 370, 413–14; ibid., 1339–41, 12; ibid., 1360–64,
97–8; Rymer, II, ii, 1083.
[2] Rymer, II, ii, 1062, 1072, 1077; ibid., III, i, 471–2, 477.
[3] Ibid., III, i, 245, 298.

help could be valuable, for part of its mission was to influence men's hearts and minds.

The bishops were kept informed of important events and they were asked to ensure that prayers were said for the success of English arms, and thanks offered for the victories gained. (These practices were not new. Thanks had been offered, for example, for the victory of Halidon Hill in 1333.)[1] The procedure was necessarily slow: the king notified the bishops of an impending expedition and requested them to order 'preachings, prayers and processions' in their dioceses. The bishops communicated the king's wishes to the archdeacons and the archdeacons informed the clergy. There is room for research on the form in which such messages reached the parishes and on the way in which instructions were carried out. In view of all the circumstances, however, it is likely that in very many parishes the king's desires were fulfilled.

It would be an error to regard this practice (which was repeated for almost every expedition) as no more than an adjunct to a news or propaganda service. Pious leaders would regard the appeal to God for protection and a prosperous issue of a military expedition as wholly proper, and the Church as the appointed agent by and through which the appeal should be addressed. It is, however, so clearly relevant to a study of the influences affecting men's minds that it must be included at this point.

Some instances may be quoted. In July 1338, the bishops are requested to pray for a safe journey for the king in his expedition beyond the sea and to cause the clergy and people to pray for the same.[2] In August 1339, when the king is about to sail for France, there is a similar request.[3] In July 1340, the bishops are informed of the victory of Sluys, asked to pray for the king and to celebrate masses and other offices of piety and to induce the clergy and people to do the same, so that God may grant a happy issue to the expedition and give the king a heart to do justly and rule according to His precepts.[4] In 1342, 1345, 1346—Henry of Lancaster's campaigns in Gascony are remembered—1348 and 1350, requests are made for the church's aid by prayer.[5]

---

[1] *C. Close R.*, 1333–7, 128.   [2] Ibid., 520.
[3] *C. Close R.*, 1339–41, 258.   [4] Rymer, II, ii, 1129.
[5] *Exeter Episcopal Registers, John de Grandison* I, 66; *C. Close R.*, 1341–2, 650; Rymer, II, ii, 1209; Avesbury, 168; *Anonimalle Chron.*, 168–9. Rymer, III, i, 88, 81, 176; *C. Close R.*, 1349–54, 222.

In 1355, the king informed the bishops that the war would be resumed and again asked for their intercessions.[1] (Three expeditions were at that time expected to be sent overseas: one to Brittany, another to Gascony, a third to north-eastern France, but the king did not refer specifically to any of them.) In this instance (and in others), the evidence can be carried a stage or two further in the diocese of Exeter. On 11 September, the bishop wrote to the dean and chapter of the cathedral at Exeter and the archdeacons throughout his diocese informing them of the departure of the prince of Wales from Plymouth on his way to Gascony. He referred to the king's unsuccessful efforts to negotiate a peace and to the Christian duty of living in peace as far as possible; and he bade them pray that God would preserve the prince, direct his progress and enable him to return in health.[2]

In the following year when king Edward informed the bishops of the capture of king John at Poitiers, the bishop of Exeter ordered the archdeacons, abbots, priors and clergy in his diocese to hold a special service with solemn processions and High Mass.[3]

In 1359, before the king left England for his expedition in France, the bishop of Exeter instructed the archdeacons once more concerning prayers and indulgences and added that the clergy were to make processions in the usual way twice a week round their churches and churchyards.[4]

While processions are commonly requested, prayers almost invariably and preaching (sermons) often, the need for further explanation of national policy and of the church's role in relation to the war also become apparent, as may be seen in the records of the diocese of Bath and Wells. In 1337, the bishop summons the archdeacons, abbots, priors and clergy of his diocese to Wells in order that the king's 'intent and will' should be 'expounded'—it was the king's own word and request—to them.[5] In 1339, arrangements are made for an assembly at which the 'things agreed in the Parliament at Westminster' may be 'expounded',[6] and in 1340, the bishop has instructions from the archbishop of Canterbury that some notes on the financial aspect of the church's relation with the state are to be 'pub-

[1] Rymer, III, i, 303.   [2] *John de Grandison*, II, 1173.
[3] Ibid., 1191.   [4] Ibid., 1200–1.
[5] *Register of Ralph of Shrewsbury*, I, 334.   [6] Ibid., I, 379.

lished in the cathedral clearly and openly in the mother tongue'.[1]

Whether the mother tongue was used for the prayers during public worship (that is to say whether plain Englishmen understood and made the prayers for the welfare of the expeditionary forces their own) cannot be known from the instructions issued. But a still further effort to ensure public attention and understanding may be seen in orders (not requests) to the most popular of teachers, the friars. In 1346, the Friars-Preachers are directed to explain to the people the king's title to the French crown and his reasons for going to war.[2] A few months later, the Augustinian Friars, Friars Minor and the Carmelites are directed to offer thanksgivings and prayers for the successes of Henry of Lancaster in Gascony.[3] And, as if the public mind needed to be guided to right ends, the archbishop of Canterbury in denouncing Sunday markets twice in 1359, points out that people should go to church and pray for the king and his army then preparing for war and, a little later, actually at war.[4]

Thus the church was called in to focus public attention on the war, to explain its justification, to induce the people to ask for divine aid and to offer thanks for victories gained. As we have said, the terms in which the royal wishes reached the parish clergy and the zeal with which they carried out their instructions, have not been investigated. Nor can we do more than surmise the effect on the worshipping congregations. Yet it is likely that in the remoter villages, among people who frequented neither the county court nor the market town nor the seaport, references by the clergy to the war the king was waging served the purpose the king intended, and that these sayings were noised abroad in many Midland counties. In the more populous centres, they would reinforce opinions derived from proclamations and obvious war measures, and help to direct men's minds to the achievement of the royal, and indeed the national, aim.

So far we have dealt with general policy: the use of a rudimentary news service and the association in men's minds of the efforts of the expeditionary forces with God's providence. At times, the news service has the appearance of a simple propaganda organization. Such items of information as the victories

[1] Ibid., I, 425-6.   [2] Rymer, III, i, 72.
[3] Ibid., 81.   [4] *John de Grandison*, II, 1201-2.

of Halidon Hill and of Sluys are communicated not only to the archbishop of Canterbury, but to every bishop in England and Wales, while news from France in 1346 and news of the victory of Poitiers is broadcast very widely. And there are efforts to inform and influence particular groups. The provincial prior of the Order of Friars-Preachers in England is informed of the causes of the war. The prior and convent of St Augustine, London, receive similar information and a reasoned statement on the king's policy.[1] The justices of assize are shown how the king is 'compelled to fight'.[2] Churchmen, earls and barons in Nottingham, Derby and Lancashire[3] are shown 'things treated of in the last parliament at Westminster'.[4] The clergy especially need to be informed and influenced. In the northern province after 'hearing the king's affairs', they are to be induced to grant a subsidy 'as the king can have neither peace nor truce with his adversary . . . who does not cease to destroy the king's lands'.

The likelihood of invasion was, as we have seen, constantly kept before the public mind. Some of the official forecasts were mistaken, but the French attacks on English shipping, the presence of French ships in English waters (especially near the Isle of Wight) and the gravity of French attacks on English ports showed that the warnings could not be disregarded. The secret reports on which predictions of attack were based were, of course, not disclosed—they may have been entirely oral—but one valuable piece of evidence could be, and was, published. This was a document drawn up in March 1339, discovered during the attack on Caen in 1346, and promptly brought to England by the earl of Huntingdon.[5] Dated from Vincennes, it sets out in some detail a convention of the French king with the Normans for the invasion of England: the duke's part, the Normans' part, the king's part, and arrangements for finance, for the maintenance of the sea passage and the transport of food, even for the sharing of booty.

Though the arrangements had been settled so many years earlier that they must have been regarded as having lost their force, the document afforded convincing evidence of French designs. With the full publicity of a solemn procession, it was read to the Londoners at St Paul's churchyard by the

<hr />

[1] C. Close R., 1346-9, 57.   [2] Ibid., 1337-9, 523.
[3] Ibid., 1339-41, 347.   [4] Ibid., 1349-54, 356.
[5] R.P., II, 158, vide also Avesbury, 259-61.

archbishop of Canterbury 'that he might thereby rouse the people'.[1]

The prospect of a French invasion, and the certainty that Englishmen were risking their lives in France, generated a state of mind which has been manifest whenever in succeeding centuries similar circumstances have occurred—a distrust of foreigners and a strong suspicion that they served the enemy. Efforts to gain knowledge of an opponent's resources and intentions have accompanied war all down the ages. Less nefarious activities—those of the passer-by who gains knowledge for the disclosure of which he may be well paid—have also been common. Suspicion has been rife; alarm has magnified innocent episodes; scares have been generated.

That king Edward received, by one means or another, information about French intentions is certain.[2] That the kings of Scotland and of France looked for sidelights on English projects or fortifications cannot be doubted. What kind of information they sought is not clear. The king of England did not, and indeed never could wholly, conceal his intentions when an expeditionary force was being prepared. Frequently he announced the fact to the church for transmission to the nation. Moreover, between the issue of orders for mobilization—which could not be kept secret—and the departure of an army from a southern port, at least a month elapsed and almost invariably two or three months. The assembly of ships in harbour and the assembly of horses, stores and men could not be hidden. Further, some kind of inference concerning the probable point of attack could be drawn from the port of assembly. Foreign merchants or bankers living in, or visiting London, Southampton or Bristol were not unaware of impending events. When so much was evident and the arms available were common knowledge of both sides, it may be that the size of an English force in preparation and the place chosen for disembarkation were the points concerning which information was desired. At other times, up-to-date news of the fortifications of Newcastle upon Tyne, Durham, Carlisle, York or of the main ports of the south coast would be welcome.

That information—vaguely termed 'secrets'—could be, and

[1] Avesbury, 205.
[2] Baker says (of the year 1338) that Edward had reliable information from his own people. *Chronicon*, 61.

after 1340 actually was being, conveyed to the enemy, was a widespread conviction.

Distrust fell on churchmen of any kind who were not of English birth. As far back as 1295, the principle that the coastal lands of England must be free of French monks in time of war had been established, and in 1326, all secular beneficed clergy 'subjects and adherents of the king of France living near the sea or navigable rivers' were to be removed inland.[1] The principle was maintained in 1338 when directions were sent for the removal of French monks from the priories of Lewes and Saint Michael's Mount,[2] and in 1340, when the prior of Holy Trinity, York, was ordered not to admit monks from France.[3]

Few such specific measures can be traced. Usually an urgent note 'on information received' contains an order for great vigilance. It may be in the north where 'certain Scots openly or secretly enter Carlisle to spy out defects of the walls and other secrets',[4] or Robert de Preston (who had been ransomed from the Scots) is appointed to catch a spy,[5] or men in Northumberland are said to be receiving and aiding Scots.[6] More often, of course, it is in London and the South. In 1342, several men are (said to be) spying on the king's secrets and sending letters to France to forewarn the king's enemies. The authorities in all the ports are to search all suspected persons for letters and, if necessary, to detain the persons while such letters are forwarded to the chancery for inspection.[7] In London, men carrying letters prejudicial to the king are to be thrown into Newgate prison.[8] In 1346, just after the king has embarked with his army for France, the sheriffs of London are informed that several spies have entered the kingdom to discover the king's secrets.[9]

In 1347, it is reported that spies daily transmit secrets to the enemy; and there is an instance of men bringing letters into the country without showing them to the port authorities. These men 'went from place to place in London clandestinely, sometimes in clothes lined with sendal as clerks, sometimes in clothes of divers colours as squires, sometimes in gowns and other cheap

---

[1] Matthew, D. J. A., *The Norman Monasteries*, 82–4, 89. *Register of Hamonis Hethe*, Canterbury and York Society, 1948, I, 271. *C. Close R.*, 1325–7, 636.

[2] Rymer, II, ii, 1061.   [3] *C. Close R.*, 1339–41, 458.

[4] Rymer, III, i, 273.   [5] *Cal. Doc. Scotland*, III, p. 7, no. 1614.

[6] *C. Pat. R.*, 1345–8, 105.   [7] *C. Close R.*, 1341–3, 485.

[8] Ibid., 660.   [9] Ibid., 1346–9, 149.

clothes as denizens'. (It transpired that they were not spies. They were pardoned in deference to the request of high papal officials.)[1]

In 1352, it is believed that several spies cross from different English ports to France with their secrets,[2] and in 1353, the port authorities of York, Lynn, London and the Cinque Ports are ordered to permit no one to leave England without the king's special licence.[3] Suspicions continue, and at the beginning of 1360, when the king has 'learned that great numbers of letters and credences prejudicial to him and the realm are brought into England by merchants and aliens', many port authorities and many sheriffs are directed to ensure the usual rigorous search of aliens and to cause all alien merchants to take the oath ordained by the king in Council.[4]

The situation grows more complex as other currents of national feeling become apparent. Social, economic and ecclesiastical interests reveal themselves, become mingled with the political interests and call for policies scarcely distinguishable from war measures. The government appears to be defining the relation between England-at-war and the outside world. It is not only potential carriers of information, for example, who need to be watched in the ports. Some people are believed to be leaving England in order to escape the pestilence[5] and taking their money with them. There are merchants who, in the course of business or with shrewd foresight, are taking fine English specie abroad. There are soldiers of fortune who wish to continue their careers on the Continent, taking their war horses with them. There may indeed be a good market for horses abroad. And there are those who would export victuals to their own advantage when victuals are urgently needed at Calais. The national interest requires that the port authorities should

---

[1] C. Pat. R., 1345–8, 249.   [2] Rymer, III, i, 242.   [3] Ibid., 263.
[4] C. Close R., 1354–60, 662, 666. A few men, French by birth, but long resident in England, were allowed to remain unmolested under royal protection. Two of them had lived for many years in Bath and paid scot and lot; another (paying scot and lot) lived in Canterbury and others in Wells. C. Pat. R., 1345–8, 258, 348; ibid., 48–50, 553. At the request of Queen Isabella, the king gave security to a French student, William de Prato, who wished to 'obtain the estate of master in theology' in the university of Oxford. There were requests and directions for him to be treated kindly. C. Close R., 1354–60, 152–3.
[5] Rymer, III, i, 191; C. Close R., 1349–54, 149.

M

close the door firmly, permitting neither men nor horses to pass unless specially licensed to do so.

Moreover, hostility to France merges with hostility to certain aspects and practices of the Roman church. Patriotism, principle and prejudice are mingled in protests which exhibit the strength of national feeling against foreigners—especially foreign churchmen—resident in, or drawing financial advantage from, England. This hostility is seen at its height in September 1346, when the Commons in their petitions make a comprehensive attack on the practices they deplore.[1] Cardinals hold benefices in England. These benefices should be seized into the king's hands. Cardinals have received payments from Parliament while in England for the purpose of negotiating truces or peace. Such payments should cease. Cardinals receive a thousand marks each from the provinces of Canterbury and York. These sums represent a loss to England and a gain to France. They should be stopped. Alien monks should be expelled. Alien friars (of all the Orders) should leave the realm and no more should be admitted. The sums of money owed by abbots and bishops to the pope should not be taken out of the kingdom. No Englishman should take a church at farm from an alien. If any alien lands in England, the ship in which he arrived should be forfeit to the king. (At the time these complaints were made and for many months afterwards, the king was engaged in the siege of Calais. The Council gave its replies of assent, sympathy or dissent.)

To sum up, the English outlook at this period included a very marked distrust of foreigners, both lay and clerical, an insistence on vigorous scrutiny of all channels of communication between England and France, and a desire to prevent the export of English specie—in general because that conflicted with current monetary theory, and in particular because, the papacy and a French pope being at Avignon, moneys received by alien churchmen of whatever status went—it was believed—to enrich the enemy, France.

To fears of invasion and suspicions concerning spies may be added annoyance and even anger arising from purveyance, that

---

[1] *R.P.*, II, 162. The hostility is illustrated in a study of Talleyrand's benefices in England in Zacour, Norman P., *Talleyrand, the Cardinal of Perigord*, Philadelphia, 1960.

is the pre-emption of goods for royal (or national) needs. The practice gave rise to complaints in time of peace. During war, as more and more victuals, forage, munitions and other goods were required, complaints were inevitably graver. It is not with the subject as a whole that we are concerned, but only with those phases which arise from the war during the period under consideration.

War did not create new needs. It enlarged old ones, particularly:

1. The repair and extension of castles such as Dover, Leeds, Corfe, Windsor, the Tower of London, and the rebuilding of raided coastal towns and improvement of town walls especially at Southampton. There were, therefore, additional demands for stone, timber, iron, lead, lime, tiles and nails.

2. The building and equipping of ships, which necessitated supplies of timber, masts, sailcloth, anchors, cables (and the construction of a dock at Sandwich).

3. The making of munitions of war especially bows, arrows, bowstrings, steel arrowheads, engines of war; supplies of goose quills. (Armour was in demand but not, of course, obtained by purveyance.)

4. The provision of victuals including fish and wine; the provision of forage (wheat, oats, beans, peas, hay) for armies serving overseas, for certain castles in Scotland and in Gascony and, from 1347, for the town of Calais.

In order that the wide range of commodities might be obtained and the required work done, purveyors were appointed by letters patent setting out their function, the source from which payment would be made, and sometimes the area in which they were to procure their supplies. The sums payable for the goods requisitioned were recorded on tallies and, in all instances, the right to 'take carriage' for the removal of goods to the port, castle or other destination, was included in the purveyor's powers.

The complex machinery thus established called for means of prompt payment and for integrity in the purveyors. Under the circumstances of the time, delays in payment and malpractices were inevitable. Both occurred to a disturbing degree and gave rise to widespread and repeated complaints.

An episode in the business of the Black Prince affords an

illustration of delay. The army he was to command in Gascony assembled at Plymouth in the summer of 1355, some seven or eight weeks before it could sail. Supplies ran very short and purveyors had to range the neighbouring counties for victuals the total cost of which exceeded 1000*l*. On 7 September, just as he was about to leave, the prince gave orders for speedy payment to be made for these victuals.[1] The orders were not, however, carried out. By November 1356, demands for payment had risen to 'a great clamour' and by the following February, the men of Cornwall, Devon, Somerset and Dorset were making their complaints direct to the prince's council in London. Many weeks' work was spent during 1357 in dealing with the tallies cut in 1355 before all the payments were cleared up.[2]

Now delays over payments of other kinds were very common. Rewards for service, compensation for horses lost during campaigns, payments in purchase of eminent prisoners were often made many months and even years after the events to which they referred[3] had passed, and instances could be cited of payments being put off as long as possible.[4] Delays, however, were not necessarily due to slackness in administration or attempts to take advantage of creditors. Some were due to insufficiency of funds at the source from which payment was to be made. But whatever the cause, delays were grievous to those whose goods had been requisitioned. At times they were exasperating: after the death of Queen Isabella it was found that many purveyors for her household had failed to deliver the tallies without which payment could not begin.[5]

Again and again, petitions were addressed to Parliament on this grievance,[6] and some measure of redress was at times seen in instructions for prompt payment to be made as, for example,

[1] *B.P.R.*, II, 86.

[2] Ibid., 103, 107, 116.

[3] Orders for payment of compensation for horses lost or services performed during the prince's expedition of 1355-7, extend to December 1363. *B.P.R.*, IV, 253, 318, 329, 384, 450, 516.

[4] Order . . . 'to bargain for the said wools . . . buying them at the cheapest price possible and put off the day of payment for as long as he can.' *B.P.R.*, I, 82.

[5] *C. Pat. R.*, 1358-61, 157.

[6] Postan, M. M., 'Some Social Consequences of the Hundred Years War', *E.H.R.*, XII (1942), 5, 161, 171, 194, 269; *R.P.*, II, 161, 171, etc.

in the purchase of stone at Dunstable, Corfe, Eltham and
Windsor, but delays continued to be very common.[1]

As for the conduct of the purveyors, since their duty was to
acquire commodities which might have been sold in the markets, a certain heavy-handedness in taking goods and requiring
transport is not surprising, and they were subject to strong
temptation to turn the business to their own advantage. The
prior of Dover complained (1341) of victuals being taken by the
purveyors for the maintenance of mariners coming to the port
'without any satisfaction'.[2] The people of Hereford, Gloucester,
Worcester, Oxford and Berkshire stated (1346) that their
sheriffs (acting as purveyors) 'have borne themselves ill', com-
pelling the poor and simple men to supply corn and victuals,
but sparing the wealthy.[3] From Yorkshire, Lincolnshire and
Norfolk came allegations of the purveyors' extortions.[4] In
Parliament there were complaints that purveyors' malpractices
grew from day to day, and that they bought victuals very cheaply
and sold them for their own profit.[5] One man even posed as a
purveyor of the prince of Wales and managed to extort money
from the men of Devon.[6]

There were apparently instances of men posing as purveyors
to the king. This and the widespread complaints led to the
publication throughout England in 1359 of the names of all
purveyors and their deputies, with an order that purveyors'
commissions must be shown before goods were taken, and a
promise that purveyors who went beyond their commissions
would be punished.[7]

But the clearest and most comprehensive view of the malpractices the people had endured arises from a long series of
petitions presented in 1362. Requisitions (they state) should be
restricted to the households of the king, the queen and the prince
of Wales; payment should be made 'in hand' (ready cash) and
at the prices obtaining in neighbouring markets; the name
purveyor should be used no longer; the word buyer should take
its place; if buyers and vendors cannot agree, then requisitions
should be made by view and testimony of the lords or bailiffs or
constables and four good men in every town, and by indenture

[1] C. Pat. R., 1354–8, 277, 471; ibid., 1358–61, 28, 339.
[2] C. Close R., 1341–3, 342.   [3] C. Pat. R., 1345–8, 113.
[4] Ibid., 1358–61, 322.   [5] R.P., II, 140, 203.
[6] C. Pat. R., 1345–8, 169.   [7] C. Close R., 1354–60, 544.

showing the quantity of goods taken, and the price and the name of the vendor; transactions should be carried out in a seemly manner without duress, threats or crafty wickedness; they should be held in places where there is abundance and at suitable times; there should be no purchases except from willing sellers and at the agreed prices; no more than is needed for the three households should be taken and no more carriage than is necessary required; there should be fewer buyers and their functions should be clearly defined; they should have no deputies; no one need comply with the buyer's request unless he pays in hand; all requisitions of corn should be by standard measures, rased not heaped; no buyer should accept gifts or other consideration; good and loyal people should be appointed in every county where purchases are made to keep watch on the conduct of buyers, and malpractices should be punished.[1]

That group of petitions affords (by implication) the most revealing picture of purveyances in the period 1338–62, and explains the nation-wide indignation they aroused.

On the conclusion of the truces and of the peace, large numbers of English troops came back to England. Concerning their state of mind and subsequent lives the evidence is insufficient for generalization.

There are glimpses of men who had served in two theatres of war, at least one who had served in three,[2] and the campaigns of the late 1360's soon afforded further opportunities. Of the Cheshire archers who had accompanied the prince of Wales in Gascony, two were charged with dishonesty over their share in a prisoner of war, two had been overpaid while serving in France and were asked to refund some money, but many of them sought and gained little grants of rights or privileges or exemptions in their home county which would be acceptable rewards for service.[3] Many of the prince's household staff received very substantial rewards in Cheshire or elsewhere.[4]

Two types of men probably stood out among the returned

---

[1] *R.P.*, II, 269.

[2] Roland de Penfound (Cornwall) was granted a pardon in 1350 'in consideration of good service in Aquitaine and in Brittany and at the siege of Calais'. *C. Pat. R.*, 1348–50, 538.

[3] Hewitt, *B.P.E.*, 162–3.   [4] Ibid., 160–2.

soldiers. One was the garrulous, boastful raconteur described in *Piers Plowman*:

> With a look like a lion and lordly in speaking;
> The boldest of beggars; a boaster who has nothing;
> A teller of tales in towns and taverns;
> He says what he never saw and swears to his honesty;
> He devises deeds that were done by no man,
> Or is the witness of his well doing and will say sometimes:
> 'Look! if you believe me not, or think, I lie basely,
> Ask him or ask him, and he can tell you
> What I suffered and saw.[1]

Such men were to be found in France also, for something of the same characteristic may be seen in a poem by Deschamps about the less glorious aspects of war:

> Each of them eagerly answers the [king's] order,
> And rushes to the army that he may say
> 'I was there.'[2]

The other type was prone to lawlessness. In the 1340's and 1350's there were at any moment, as we have seen, several hundred men who had been indicted of murder and, after due process, outlawed. These men saw in military service a means of gaining pardon for their crimes and restoration to civic status.

The recruitment of such men for the wars had two immediate effects: it afforded a supply of men who were not *prima facie* inferior to their fellows in such qualities as courage, fortitude and skill in arms, and it diminished the number of criminals at large.

On their return to England, these men had not only their pardons and resultant freedom of movement, but also the habits acquired by a year or two years of rough but often exhilarating life in the *chevauchée*, unhampered by the restraints of 'civil' life. There had been a companionship in violence for personal advantage.

That such men could not be readily integrated again into English society is evident. On other young men, indicted as yet of no crime, the life of the *chevauchée* had the same effect. The

---

[1] Quoted in Bennett, H. S., *Life on the English Manor*, 124. The Everyman edition of *Piers Plowman*, 73–4, has another version.
[2] *Le Lay des douze estats du monde*, Rheims, 1870, 11.

general results are seen in the outbreaks of disorder which marked our period.

In 1347, an increase in robberies was met by heavier punishments.[1] But it is the group activities, the work of armed bands, such as the serious wounding of the king's bailiffs in the fairs at Holderness (1347) and at Wells (1347),[2] the rescue of a criminal from the king's bailiff at Kingston-upon-Hull (1351),[3] the angry attack on the justice holding the session at Eynsham (1350),[4] the bold attacks on ships in the port of Bristol (1348) and at Newcastle-upon-Tyne (1354),[5] the existence of armed gangs infesting the fairs and markets of Gloucestershire (1348),[6] or overawing the people of Bridgnorth (1353)[7]—it is such group activities (and we have cited merely a few examples) that are the significant marks of disorder in our period. A 'confederacy' of such men in Salop (1358) is described as 'arrayed as for war'.[8]

Contemporary opinion linked the disorder with the practice of granting pardons, and expressed itself in petition after petition. In 1347 the Commons drew attention to the prevalence of murders, violence, robbery and rape, all of which they held to be increased by charters of pardon.[9] In the following year, they stated that throughout England, thieves and other evildoers on foot and on horse infested the roads committing robberies.[10] In 1350 (as in 1347), they petitioned that no charters of pardon should be granted to murderers or notorious felons.[11] In 1353, attention was drawn to a common and deceitful practice: criminals gained pardons on the understanding that they would remain overseas for service in the wars. In fact, however, they returned quickly and continued their misdeeds in England.[12]

As with the purveyors, so with the pardoned soldiers (and indeed with disbanded soldiers in general), nation-wide con-

---

[1] Baker, *Chronicon*, 92.
[2] *C. Pat. R.*, 1345–8, 317, 106.
[3] Ibid., 1350–54, 102, 154.
[4] Ibid., 1348–50, 594.
[5] Ibid., 72; ibid., 1350–54, 542.
[6] Ibid., 1348–50, 72.
[7] Ibid., 1350–54, 519.
[8] Ibid., 1358–61, 160. There were marks of disorder in Cheshire in 1360 and 1361. *B.P.R.*, III, 401, 421. It is impossible to show to what extent—if at all—disorder increased at this period. Our aim is to illustrate the *kind* of disorder which engaged contemporary opinion and the causes assigned at that time for that disorder.
[9] *R.P.*, II, 172.
[10] Ibid., 207.
[11] Ibid., 229.
[12] Ibid., 253.

cern reached a climax at the close of our period. After the peace of Bretigny, most of the English troops came home; disorder increased, and it became evident not only that felons who gained pardon by military service might prove to be bad citizens, but also that military service itself had made some men into bad citizens.[1] The conviction is revealed not in a petition, but in a statute of the realm directing the justices to 'inform themselves . . . touching all those who have been plunderers and robbers beyond the seas and are now returned and go wandering and will not work as they were used to do'.[2]

The outlook and the practices adopted in the campaigns had been transferred to England. In order that 'the people be not by such rioters troubled or damaged, nor the peace broken, nor merchants or others passing on the high roads of the realm disturbed or put in fear of the peril which may arise from such evil-doers', the justices are to divide indicted or suspected men into two classes: those of 'good fame', who can give security for their behaviour, may be liberated; all others are to be punished.[3]

Punishment, however, was not easily inflicted, for the returned soldiers—'those who lately lived by plunder and robbery in foreign parts'—had, as we have seen, formed bands and resorted to beating, robbing, mutilating, holding to ransom and killing. In Wiltshire, Berkshire and Hampshire, they were 'arrayed as for war', and the posse of the counties might be needed to overcome them.[4] England was, in fact, enduring in a mild form some of the evils which were afflicting France, where disbanded soldiers were forming Companies and dominating the countryside.

Though there were waves of annoyance and even anger over spies, purveyors and returned soldiers, the broad attitude of English people throughout our period was—as is well known—favourable to the war. We have emphasized that the mass of the nation had of necessity only a meagre knowledge of the course of events in France and, for long periods, few reports reached even the Council, though one purpose of the fleet[5] gathered in

[1] Cf. *Shorter Cambridge Medieval History*, II, 893-4.
[2] Crump, C. G., and Johnson, C., 'The Powers of Justices of the Peace', *E.H.R.*, XXVII, 1912, 226-38.
[3] Ibid., 227.   [4] Ibid., 236.
[5] *C. Close R.*, 1354-60, 600.

1359 was to 'bring back to the Council in England news of the king and his army'. Such information however as was available was presented to the prelates, magnates and Commons at their occasional assemblies at Westminster. The procedure tended to follow a pattern: Bartholomew de Burghersh or Sir Walter Manny gave an account of the situation (the campaign or the negotiations or the truce); the parliament or more often the Commons were asked to consider the matter and to offer counsel and aid; the Commons made their reply.

At no point was aid refused (though it was associated with demands for redress of grievances). As for their counsel, they assented to the maintenance of the truce in 1343 because it was 'profitable to the king and all his people'; they asked the king to 'make himself so strong that he could cross the sea with assurance of God's help and his righteous quarrel to end the war by way of peace or force' (1344); they said they were 'too ill informed to offer any advice' (1347); they granted aid 'having regard to the need for the defence of the realm' (1353); they stated that 'whatever decision the king and magnates made would be acceptable to them' (1354) and in 1355, when the war had been resumed, they unanimously granted a subsidy for six years.[1]

In considering this ready assent to the war, and its bearing on the outlook of the people, two aspects of the conflict must be borne in mind. First, the scanty news available during much of the period pointed to French aggression, actual and prospective. The repeated warnings of French invasions, the actual attacks on the south-coast towns, the very serious Scottish incursions of 1345 and 1346, the readily quoted French violations of the truces and French bad faith in the negotiations, confirmed the conviction formed in parliament in 1344, that the French king was 'trying his utmost to gain possession of English territories in France and that he was determined to occupy England itself unless his course could be stayed by force'.[2] It followed that French aggression needed not only to be resisted, but to be ended.

Secondly, the legitimacy of Edward's claim to the French throne was not widely debated in England. Parliament approved the claim, received much information about the king's needs in

[1] *R.P.*, II, 136, 150, 165, 238, 262, 264.
[2] Ibid., II, 147.

pursuit of that claim, supported his efforts financially, thanked God for the victory of Crécy (since it was clear that the money had been well spent) and, at the end of the period, decided again to thank God 'who had given them such a lord and governor'.[1] Historians may dispute over Edward's statesmanship or his military strategy. They are agreed that his conduct of the war satisfied his contemporaries.

In view of the pope's unceasing efforts to secure peace between the contending kings, the church was more tepid in its support of the war, but—so far as is known—the many requests for prayers (described above) were duly forwarded to the clergy on whom lay the duty and the onus of putting them into effect.

For the majority of the people, it was a period of confidence and occasionally of elation. War had of course led to additional taxation and withdrawn thousands of men from their normal, necessary work, but it had not been a continuous strain, for there had been periods—including one quite long period—of truce. The quarrel between the Plantagenet and the Valois became the conflict between the English and French peoples. Its victories became part of that stock of common memories which produced national feeling. The French had not invaded England. On the contrary, the English had invaded France—repeatedly; and the only French men who had remained for forty-eight hours on English soil were prisoners. They were not the crew of a galley caught in the Channel or bowmen captured near Calais. They were the very greatest of the French: the king himself, his son, and his most distinguished nobles. Further, the king of Scotland also was a prisoner. All these men had to pay large ransoms in order to gain liberation. Thus money came into England.

Spoils also were brought to England. After the fall of Calais, says Walsingham, it seemed to the English that a new sun had arisen because of the abundance of peace, the plenty of goods and the glory of the victories; and he goes on to describe the widespread use by English women of wearing apparel brought over from France.[2]

Eminent men returned from the wars pleased with their experience and enriched by the prisoners they had ransomed

[1] Ibid., II, 159, 219. See also McKisack, M., 'Edward III and the Historians', *History*, February 1960, 9–10.

[2] Walsingham, 292.

or sold to the prince or the king. Some—especially those who had served the prince—were rewarded with lands or incomes;[1] many gained pardons. Even bearers of the first news of victories received big rewards.[2] If there were any who had neither reward nor pardon nor prisoner nor a share in the loot, they had at least had a period of well-paid service with the companion-ship and exhilaration of army life.

Great satisfaction there must have been, and in the closing years of the reign when adversity and defeat were falling on English arms, men looked back with pride to the period which ended at Bretigny and the treaty of Calais. 'The king of England was for many years spirited and gracious in victories,' declared Thomas Brinton, bishop of Rochester. 'In his days, England might have been called a kingdom among kingdoms: so many victories were gained, so many kings captured, so many terri-tories occupied . . . God was wont to be English . . . How often a few years ago, our princes crossed the seas to defend our rights and won manly triumphs over their enemies.'[3]

English pride had reached a climax in 1357 in the greatest celebrations London had ever known. The prince of Wales had conducted his royal captives from Plymouth to the south bank of the Thames and on Wednesday, 24 May, made the formal entry into the capital.

Great preparations had been made for an impressive occasion and wine was available in abundance and free for all who wished to drink. The mayor, aldermen and members of the guilds, mounted and newly apparelled, went out to meet the cavalcade at the head of which rode the prince, king John, his son Philip and thirteen of the most important prisoners. Then they turned about and led the long procession over London Bridge, through streets decorated with arms, armour and tapestries, past St Paul's churchyard where the bishop of London and the clergy were stationed and, by way of Ludgate and Fleet Street to Westminster, where the king of France entered the royal palace and met the king of England.[4]

In conclusion, two points must be emphasized. First, this short sketch of the thoughts of English people as they were

[1] Hewitt, *B.P.E.*, 160–3.

[2] Neville's Cross: *C. Pat. R.*, 1345–8, 198; Poitiers: Hewitt, *B.P.E.*, 138.

[3] *The Sermons of Thomas Brinton*, Camden Society, 3rd series, LXXXV, LXXXVI, 62, 335, 335, 112.

[4] Hewitt, *B.P.E.*, 149–50.

affected by war during our period is, of necessity, limited to aspects of national life for which evidence was created and has survived. There were, of course, aspects for which very little or no evidence exists. Collective fears—of invasion, for example— led to administrative action and therefore to the creation of documents. Collective joy at the news of a victory might cause festivities to be held in scores of places without leaving any documentary evidence whatever. The news of the capture of king John led to the command for thanksgiving to be offered in the churches throughout England, and Froissart reports 'great joy when they heard tidings of the battle of Poitiers . . . and the taking of the king; great solemnities were made in all churches marvellous to think of' (to which a translator added 'and great fires and wakes throughout all England').[1] Yet, for the success of Crécy, the capture of Calais and the conclusion of peace, though the nation's joy may be inferred, it is not recorded.

Secondly, the sentiments which we have isolated for treatment must of course be restored to the field of the mind—a man could in a single hour experience fear of invasion, hatred of spies, anger against purveyors, exasperation at the conduct of disbanded soldiers—and woven into the broad consciousness of men and women occupied with the hundred and one circumstances of daily life. The war was important, but so was the export of wool and the great pestilence and the enforcement of the Statute of Labourers and the rise in prices. So also were local affairs such as the silting of a harbour, the repair of a bridge, the changing patterns of trade. So also was personal and family life: the marriage of a daughter for example or the sharing out of a divided inheritance. For the great majority of English people the war was a frequently recurring theme, but not a constant and inescapable preoccupation.

[1] Froissart (Macaulay), 133.
Other aspects of opinion—some local, some temporary—may be traced or inferred:
1. Resistance to the burden of the *garde de la mer*, Rymer, II, ii, 1025, III, I, 115, *R.P.*, II, 104–5, 161, 194.
2. The conflict over the payment of wages from county boundaries to the coast. See Powicke, *Military Obligation*.
3. The assessments to provide archers.
4. The demands for taxes from areas which had suffered devastation (e.g. Cumberland, Southampton) or borne great burdens.

Transport of horses

EQUIPMENT A: FITTINGS

By a writ dated 6 March 1340, the king had ordered the arrest of all vessels of 30 tons and upwards in the ports of the counties of Essex, Suffolk, Norfolk, Lincolnshire and Yorkshire for the passage of himself, his magnates and others to parts beyond the seas. The said ships were to be in the port of Orwell by Palm Sunday.

For the transport of horses in these vessels, William de Wauton, sheriff of Essex, was directed to provide gangways, hurdles, empty tuns, boards, racks, ropes, staples, rings, iron nails and other goods and have them brought to Orwell.

The sheriff in due course sent in his account of the expenses incurred in executing his orders:

4 oaks and 60 beams bought in Ferring wood in Essex for making 4 gangways for shipping horses at Orwell; felling, stripping, sawing and making them 30 feet long, 5 feet wide; carriage from the wood to the port of Manningtree (14 miles)	14s.	6d.	
Rods and stakes for making 418 hurdles bought at Maldon and other places; making the hurdles, laying them together, carriage to the port	4l.	18s.	2d.
Timber for making 116 racks bought at Maldon and elsewhere; making them and carriage to the port	3l.	6s.	6d.
864 boards bought at various prices in Bromfield and elsewhere; carriage to the port	5l.	14s.	1d.
717 yards of canvas bought in London for making mangers at 1l. 12s. 6d. a hundred; carriage to the port	11l.	15s.	10¼d.
400 fathoms of rope bought at Woodbridge and Marlford in Suffolk for the mangers; portage to the port		11s.	5¼d.
413 stables, 413 rings, 14,550 large nails bought at Easterworth, 2 barrels to hold the staples, rings and nails; carriage to the port	4l.	2s.	10d.
Rent of an empty building at the port for receiving and storing the above goods from 2nd April to 22nd May (59 days); 2 large boats hired at Ipswich for six journeys to convey the goods from the port to Orwell, portage from the storehouse to the boats, carriage by boat, unloading at Orwell, portage from Orwell to a storing place hired in Harwich to hold the goods till the king's passage	2l.	2s.	0d.

Wages of a clerk stationed at Manningtree to receive
and guard the goods for 59 days at 2*d*. a day, and of a
man riding from Colchester to London (44 miles) and
back, to buy the canvas (2 days) and also from Colchester to Woodbridge and Marlford in Suffolk and
back, to buy the ropes (20 miles) (one day) at 8*d*. a
day   10*s*. 2*d*. (sic)

                                              33*l*. 15*s*. 6½*d*.

(The above goods were handed over to John de Coggeshal who
succeeded William de Wauton as sheriff of Essex, and John de
Coggeshal acknowledged receipt of these goods.)

E 372/185, m. 5, and see *C. Close R.*, 1339–41, 391

EQUIPMENT B: TUNS

Peter de Veel, sheriff of Devon, produced details similar to those
shown above for work done in the arraying of 47 ships in 1338–9.
His account included:

134 tuns bought to hold water for the horses in the ships,
together with washing out, binding and wedging of the tuns
and carriage from Exeter where they were bought, to the
port of Exmouth   17*l*. 16*s*. 8*d*.

From E 372/184, m. 4

In 1340 the sheriff of Essex is directed to send to the port of
Orwell quantities of hay, oats, litter and 20 tuns for carrying water.
C. Close R., 1339–41, 391.

APPENDIX II

Ships used for the transport of Henry of Lancaster's troops to Bordeaux in 1345[1]

Port and Ship	Master	Constable	Mariners	Boys
DARTMOUTH				
Alle Halewelle Cog		J. Gray	26	4
Seinte Marie Cog	William de Asshedon	J.Wady	36	2
Cog Johan	William Weryn	Roger Knollyng	28	2
Lithfot	Simon Randulf	—	13	1
Leonard	John Squyer	—	9	2
Maryon	Henry Rogter	—	11	2
Seynt Esprit	John Gegge	—	11	1
Godier	John Scheter	Henry Royer	18	2
Clement	John Hurtyn	—	16	2
Seynt Marie Cog the Second	John Pegyn	Hugh de Whytel	20	3
Seynt Marie Cog the Third	Walter Passur	—	13	3
FALMOUTH				
Seynte Marie Cog	Richard de Burton	Richard Greywe	21	4
POLRUAN				
Michel	Thomas Stodleigh	—	7	2
Michel the Second	Thomas Kerner	—	20	3
Cog Johan	John Attegate	—	14	2
Katerine	John Adam		8	2
James	John Pelpek		11	1
James	Stephen Wagoun		8	2
FOWEY				
Godbertte	Roger Riche		7	2
Seinte Favores Cog	Michael Mayntourn	John Carver	24	4
Seint Marie Cog	John de Clifton	Richard Bryan	18	2
Gracedieu	Robert Warman	—	15	2
Cog Johan	Peter Elys		18	2
Seint Magie Cog the Second	Martin Saundre		12	3
Seint Marie Cog the Third	John Blakeman		12	2
PORT NOT STATED				
Sauvoye	John Tynnere		15	2
Sauvoye the Second	Henry Karner		12	1
Alisot	John Porthalle		14	2
Petre	John Samson		10	1

[1] From E 101/25/9.

182

Port and Ship	Master	Constable	Mariners	Boys
MELCOMBE				
Cog Johan	Thomas White	Thomas Colynber	28	5
Welfare	John Smith	—	8	2
WEYMOUTH				
Godier	Richard Caunsenele	John Seydon	18	2
Alle Halewelle Cog	Gilbert Pinche	J. Basset	18	3
COMBE				
Margarete	John Benet		13	1
Seinte Marie Cog	Walter Holde		17	3
EXMOUTH				
Bouremaide	Richard Roulfe		16	1
Michel	Roger Gyde		13	2
Cog Thomas	William Elys		10	2
George	John Neel		13	—
Trinite	William Otery	Richard Garland	26	2
PLYMOUTH				
Seinte Marie	Edward Bondy	Will Herward	24	4
Seinte Marie II	Reginald Attepole	Stephen Bach	16	4
Cog John	John Holman		15	4
James	Richard Teynere		11	2
Rodecog	John de Westen		14	2
Seinte Saveur	John Bowere		14	2
Seinte Marie III	Will Blerak		18	—
Seinte Marie IV	John Phelip	J. Slye	25	4
Godbegote	Richard Bole		20	3
Gracedieu	John de Taunton	Will Cornys	22	2
Thomas	Roger Dogel	J. Hamelyn	23	4
Godbegote II	Henry Chopyn		8	1
Seinte Marie V	Richard Stede	J. Fischacre	18	4
Gracedieu II	Will As	Robert atte Mor'	21	4
Trinite	Simon Garston		14	1
Sente Savour	Martin Richard		15	3
(10 of the above were cogs)				
SOUTHAMPTON				
Seinte Anton	John atte Pole		12	3
Mariote	William Bryan		16	3
Seinte Marie Cog	William Colyn		15	2
Mariote the Second	Reginald atte Dane		11	1
Trinite	Nicholas Goute		11	1
TYNEMOUTH				
Nicholas	Robert Hunte		23	2
Seint Marie Cog	Robert Stote		13	4
Michel	John Clyne		14	4
Nicholas the Second	Walter Power		—	—
POOLE				
Rode Cog	Richard More	1	31	3
SIDMOUTH				
George	John Hals and John Vinter		19	3
Seinte Marie Cog	Richard Hok		17	3
Alle Halewe Cog	Walter Gyfford		10	1

N

Port and Ship	Master	Constable	Mariners	Boys
TOTNES				
Godyer	John Samiger		19	2
LONDON				
Cog Thomas	Richard Gokyng		17	2
Katerine	William Chirchegate		11	2
Welfare	John Sterne		15	2
Margerye	Richard Wowere	Simon William	18	2
Trinite	John Reynale		11	2
Katerine the Second	Symon Springge		15	2
Nicholas	John Waite	Thomas Parkere	20	2
Barnabe	Thomas Clere		13	2
James	William Adam		9	2
Michel	Henry de Lyme		15	3
Nicholas the Second	John Henry		12	2
Cog Thomas	Hugh Burgoys		15	3
Alice	Richard Cartere		11	4
Cog Johan	Andrew Aunger		14	1
SEATON				
George	Robert Cade		15	2
SEAFORD				
Christemasse	William Bourne		13	2
James	Henry Brovlyng		12	2
HASTINGS				
Jonette	Simon Goldyng		9	1
WAREHAM				
Cog Johan	Thomas Cosh	John Curays	25	1
Seinte Marie Cog	John Hogge		12	2
LYNN				
Mariote	John Sergaunt		10	1
Nandieu	Peter Colyn		12	1
Cristofore	Hugh Antoyne	John Lange	20	2
LYMINGTON				
Jonette	Henry Redyng		13	3
Cog Johan	John Wolf		13	2
Seinte Marie Cog	John Wulles		14	2
HOO				
James	Robert Frend		9	1
MEDWAY				
Welfare	William atte Welle		6	2
SHOREHAM				
Nicholas	John Leche		11	2
BOURNEMOUTH				
Clement	Thomas Fishere		11	2
HOOKE				
Godebegete	Robert Cole		7	3

Port and Ship	Master	Constable	Mariners	Boys
BAYONNE				
Seinte Marie	Amand d'Angresse	Bydon	27	–
Seinte Marie the Second	Jean de la Vache	Jean de Herne	31	–
Seint Esprit	Jean de Bekeron	Bernard de Gares	28	–
Seint Pierre	Pierre Derbyns	William Bernard	33	–
Cog Johan	Menaud de Benesse	Pierre d'Aynoghton	43	–
BRISTOL				
Cristofore	John de London	Maurice de Lynn	22	4
Dieu la Gard	Robert Leyr	Walter d'Endesbourn	36	4
Assumption	Laurence Geest	John Palmer	35	7
GOSFORTH				
Malve	Robert Gardyner	William Twyte	26	–
Godyer	William Scot	John de Oxeneye	24	3
Margaret	William	1	18	1
BOSTON				
Blithe	John Pouton	John Poynton	24	2
Welfare	Adam Alman	John de Bradfeld	17	2
Katerine	Walter Westfare	—	18	3
Godyer	Simon Farman	—	11	1
HULL				
Godyer	Walter Reynoldesson		8	1
LYME				
George	John Merseye	Simon Bottele	19	2
Godzer	John Tyd		17	2
James	Simon Scot		16	1
Katerine	Adam Musele		14	1
Nicolas	Thomas Stokketh		11	1
James the Second	Robert Brown		11	1
YARMOUTH				
Bonette	Alan French	Eustace Masun	20	2
James	Nicholas Gymmengham	1	18	2
Mariele	Walter Scot	1	21	1
Margarete	Reginald Slyng		11	1
Annote	John Laurence		13	1
Cog Johan	Walter Man		13	1
Nicolas	Thomas Smyth		11	1
Jonette	John Robynson		10	1
BLAKENEY				
Nicholas	John de Thorp	1	22	2
Blythe	Simon Dameson		15	2
COLCHESTER				
Seinte Marie Cog	Bartholomew Gerard	1	31	2
Leonard	John Lucas	1	34	2
Seinte Marie Bote	William Bacon	–	9	1
Laurence	Peter Podde	–	5	1

Port and Ship	Master	Constable	Mariners	Boys
MAINTRE				
Margerye	Bartholomew Reve	–	7	1
Welfare	Robert Baker	–	10	1
HARWICH				
Nicholas	John Elys	1	20	2
Emond	John atte Scone	–	17	1
Seinte Marie Cog	William Priour	–	15	2
BRIDLINGTON				
Swalowe	John Schipman		17	2
Petre	John Williams		8	–
MALDON				
George	Adam Cole	–	8	1
WITLONESSE				
Nicolas	John Hubbard	–	7	1
DONCASTER				
George	William Fishlak		7	2
HORNCASTLE				
Fluve Johan	Walter Chyke		20	2

Sources and Bibliography

ORIGINAL AUTHORITIES

I. *Unpublished*

At the Public Record Office:

Exchequer Accounts Various.
Gascon Rolls, Treaty Rolls.
Pipe Rolls.

At the City Library, Exeter:

Miscellaneous Rolls, No. 6 (Materials for the repair of the towers, walls and gates of the city).

II. *Published*

Official Records:

Ancient Correspondence
Calendar of Close Rolls
    ,,   Documents relating to Scotland
    ,,   Fine Rolls
    ,,   Inquisitions Ad quod damnum
    ,,   ,,   Miscellaneous
    ,,   Patent Rolls
    ,,   Papal Letters
Exchequer Rolls of Scotland
Parliamentary Writs
Pell Records, ed. Devon, F., London, 1837.
'Procès Verbal de délivrance à Jean Chandos des places françaises', ed. Bardonnet, A., *Mémoires de la Société de Statistique des Deux Sèvres*, Niort, 1867.
Register of the Black Prince, 4 vols., London, 1930–3.
Register of John of Gaunt, Camden Society, 3rd Series, XX–XXI.
Rolls of Parliament.
Rolles Gascons, Catalogue des, ed. Carte, T., London, 1743.
Rymer's *Feodera*, Record Commissioners, London, 1816–19.
'Some Documents regarding the Fulfilment and Interpretation of the Treaty of Bretigny', 1360 ed., Chaplais, P., *Camden Miscellany XIX*, vol. XXX, 1952.
Some New Documents illustrating the Early Years of the Hundred Years War (1353–1356), ed., Bock, F., Manchester University Press, 1931.

The Knights Hospitallers in England, ed. Larking, L. B., Camden Society, vol. 65, London, 1857.
The Register of John de Grandison, Exeter Episcopal Registers, ed. Hingeston-Randolph, F. C., London, 1894-7.
The Register of Hamonis Hethe, ed., Johnson, C., Canterbury and York Society, Oxford, 1948.
The Register of Ralph of Shrewsbury, ed. Holmes, T. S., Somerset Record Society, 1895-6.
The Sermons of Thomas Brinton, Camden Society, 3rd Series, Vols. LXXXV, LXXXVI, 1954.
Literae Cantuarienses, ed. Sheppard, J. B., Rolls Series, 1888.
La Guerre de Cent Ans vue à travers les Registres du Parlement 1337-1369, ed. Timbal, P. C., Paris, 1961.
Les Journaux du Trésor de Philippe VI, ed. Viard, J., Paris, 1899.

Chronicles, etc.:

A. *Anonimalle Chronicle*, ed. Galbraith, V. H., Manchester, 1914.
Anonymi Cantuarensis, ed. Tait, J., Manchester, 1914.
Avesbury, Robert, Chronica Adae Murimuth et Roberti de Avesbury, ed. Thompson, E. M., London, 1889.
Baker, Galfridi le, ed. Thompson, E. M., Oxford, 1889.
Chandos Herald, ed. Pope, M. K. and Lodge, E. C., Oxford, 1910.
Eulogium Historiarum, ed. Haydon, F. S., London, 1863.
Guisborough, Walter of, Chronicle of, ed. Rothwell, H., Camden Society, LXXXIX, 1957.
Knighton Henrici, Chronicon, ed. Lumby, J. R., London, 1895.
Lanercost, Chronicon de, 2 vols., Edinburgh, 1839.
Melsa, Chronica Monasterii de, ed. Bond, E. A., London, 1866-8.
Memoirs of the Crusades (Everyman edition).
Reading, Johannis de, ed. Tait, J., Manchester, 1914.
Scalacronica, ed. Maxwell, H., Glasgow, 1907.
Vita Edwardi Secundi, ed. Denholm-Young, N., London, 1957.
Walsingham, Thomas, Chronica Monasterii S. Albani, ed. Riley, H. T., London, 1863-4.

B. *Bel, Jean le*, ed. Viard, J. and Duprey, E., Paris, 1905.
Chronique Normande du XIVe siècle, ed. Molinier, A. and E., Paris, 1882.
Chronique des Quatre Premiers Valois, ed. Luce, S., Paris, 1862.
Chronique des Règnes de Jean II et de Charles V., ed. Delachenal, R., Paris, 1910.
Les Grandes Chroniques de France, Paulin Paris, Paris, 1836-8.
Froissart, J., Oeuvres, ed. Lettenhove, K. de, Brussels, 1876.
Froissart, The Chronicles of, ed. Macaulay, G. C., London, 1924.

Lescot, Richard, ed. Lemoire, J., Paris, 1896.
Textes et Documents d'Histoire, ed. Calmette, J., Paris, 1937.
Venette, Jean de, The Chronicle of, ed. Newhall, R. A., New York, 1953.
Bonet, Honoré, Tree of Battles, ed. Coopland, G. W., Liverpool University Press, 1949.
Deschamps, Eustache, Oeuvres inédits de, Reims, Paris, 1849.
Deschamps, Eustache, Le lay des douze estats du monde, Reims, 1870.

OTHER WORKS

General:

ARENHOLD, L., 'Ships earlier than 1300', *The Mariners' Mirror,* vol. I, 1911.
ARMITAGE-SMITH, S., *John of Gaunt,* London, 1904.
AUDINET, E., 'Les Lois et Coutumes de la Guerre à l'Epoque de la Guerre de Cent Ans', *Mémoires de la Société des Antiquaires de l'Ouest,* t. IX, Poitiers, 1917.
BAGLEY, J. J., *Life in Medieval England,* London, 1960.
BELTZ, G. F., *Memorials of the Order of the Garter,* London, 1841.
BENNETT, H. S., *Life on the English Manor,* Cambridge, 1960.
BOUTRUCHE, R., *La Crise d'une Société,* Paris, 1947.
—— 'La Dévastation des Campagnes', *Etudes historiques,* Université de Strasbourg, Fascicule 106, 1947.
BRINDLEY, H. H., 'Medieval Ships', *The Mariners' Mirror,* vols. II and III.
BROOKS, F. W., *The English Naval Forces, 1199–1272,* London, 1962.
BROWN, A., COLVIN, H. M., TAYLOR, A. J., *The History of the King's Works,* London, 1963.
BROWN, H., *History of Scotland,* Cambridge, 1911.
BRYANT, A., *The Story of England,* vol. 2, London, 1963.
BURLEY, S. J., 'The Victualling of Calais 1347–65', *Bulletin of the Institute of Historical Research,* vol. 31, 1958.
BURNE, A. H., *The Crecy War,* London, 1955.
—— *The Agincourt War,* London, 1957.
—— 'John of Gaunt's Grande Chevauchée', *History Today,* Feb. 1959.
CAM, H., 'The Legislators of Medieval England', *Law Finders and Law Makers in Medieval England,* London, 1962.
CAPES, W. W., *A History of the English Church in the Fourteenth Century,* London, 1909.
CAROLUS-BARRÉ, M., 'Benoit XII et la mission charitable de Bertrand Carit', *Mélanges d'Archéologie et d'Histoire* (Ecole française de Rome, t. LXII), 1950.
CLAUSEWITZ, G. VON, *On War,* London, 1956.
CLOWES, W. L., *The Royal Navy,* London, 1897.

COLLIS, M., *The Hurling Time*, London, 1958.
COVILLE, A., *Les états de Normandie*, Paris, 1894.
―― 'France: The Hundred Years War', *C. Med. Hist.*, VII.
CRUMP, C. G. AND JOHNSON, C., 'The Powers of Justices of the Peace', *E.H.R.*, vol. 27, 1912.
DARBY, H. C., *Historical Geography of England before 1830*, Cambridge, 1936.
DELACHENAL, R., *Histoire de Charles V*, Paris, 1909.
DENIFLE, H. S., *La Désolation des Eglises, Monastères et Hopitaux en France*, Paris, 1897-9.
EVANS, D. L., 'Some Notes on the History of the Principality of Wales in the Time of the Black Prince', *Cymmrodorion Society Transactions*, 1927.
EVANS, JOAN, *Life in Medieval France*, London, 1957.
FALLS, C., *The Place of War in History*, Oxford, 1947.
GASK, G. E., 'The Medical Staff of Edward III' in Cope, Z. (ed.), *Sidelights on the History of Medicine*, London, 1957.
GREEN, V. H. H., *The Later Plantagenets*, London, 1955.
HAY, D., 'The Division of the Spoils of War in Fourteenth Century England', *Trans. R.H.S.*, 5th series, vol. 4, London, 1954.
HEWITT, H. J., *The Black Prince's Expedition of 1355-57*, Manchester, 1958.
HOWARD, M., 'Military History as a University Study', *History*, XLI, 1956.
―― *Soldiers and Governments*, London, 1957.
HUIZINGA, J., *The Waning of the Middle Ages*, 1955.
HUNNISETT, R. F., *The Medieval Coroner*, Cambridge, 1961.
KEEN, M., *The Outlaws of Medieval England*, London, 1961.
―― 'Brotherhood in Arms', *History*, XLVII, no. 159, 1962.
LANE POOLE, A. (ed.), *Medieval England*, Oxford, 1958.
LANE-POOLE, R. H. O., 'A Medieval Cordage Account', *Mariners' Mirror*, vol. 42 (i), Feb., 1956.
LAVISSE, E., *Histoire de France*, Paris, 1902.
LEWIS, N. B., 'The Organization of Indentured Retinues in Fourteenth Century England', *Trans. R.H.S.*, 5th series, vol. 4, London, 1954.
―― 'Indentures of Retinues with John of Gaunt', *Camden Soc.*, 4th series, vol. I, 1964.
LOT, F., *L'Art militaire et les armées*, Paris, 1946.
LUCE, S., *La Jeunesse de Bertrand*, Paris, 1876.
MACKINNON, J., *History of Edward III*, London, 1900.
MACKLIN, H. W., *The Brasses of England*, London, 1907.
MATTHEW, D. J. A., *The Norman Monasteries and their English Possessions*, Oxford, 1962.

McFARLANE, K. B., 'England and the Hundred Years War', *Past and Present*, no. 22, July, 1962.

McKISACK, M., 'Edward III and the Historians', *History*, XLV, no. 153, 1960.

—— *The Fourteenth Century, 1307–1399*, Oxford, 1959.

MOISANT, J., *Le Prince Noir en Aquitaine*, Paris, 1894.

NYS, E., *Les Origines du droit international*, Paris, 1894.

OMAN, C., *A History of the Art of War in the Middle Ages*, London, 1924.

PANTIN, W. A., *The English Church in the Fourteenth Century*, Cambridge, 1955.

PATOUREL, J. LE, *The Medieval Administration of the Channel Islands*, Oxford, 1937.

—— 'The Treaty of Bretigny', *Trans. R.H.S.*, 5th series, vol. 10, 1960.

—— 'Edward III and the Kingdom of France', *History*, October, 1958.

PERROY, E., *The Hundred Years War*, London, 1957.

POSTAN, M., 'The Trade of Medieval Europe', *Cambridge Economic History II*, Cambridge, 1952.

—— 'The Costs of the Hundred Years' War', *Past and Present*, no. 27, April, 1964.

—— 'Some Local Consequences of the Hundred Years War', *Economic History Review*, vol. XII, 1942.

POWICKE, M., *Military Obligation in Medieval England*, Oxford, 1962.

PRINCE, A. E., 'The Indenture System under Edward III', *Historical Essays in honour of James Tait*, Manchester, 1933.

—— 'The Payment of Army Wages in Edward III's Reign', *Speculum*, XIX, 1944.

—— 'The Strength of English Armies in the Reign of Edward III', *E.H.R.*, XLVI, 1931.

—— 'The Army and Navy', *The English Government at Work*, 1940.

—— 'A Letter of the Black Prince', *E.H.R.*, vol. 41, 1926.

RAMSAY, J. H., 'The Strength of English Armies in the Middle Ages', *E.H.R.*, XXIX, 1916.

REDLICH, F., *De Praeda Militari*, Wiesbaden, 1956.

RENOURD, Y., 'Les Cahorsins, hommes d'affaires', *Trans. R.H.S.*, 5th series, vol. 10, 1961.

RICHARDSON, H. G., 'The Commons in Medieval Politics', *Trans. R.H.S.*, XXVIII, 1946.

RICKERT, E., *Chaucer's World*, Oxford, 1950.

RILEY, H. T., *Memorials of London and London Life*, London, 1868.

SCHUBERT, H. R., *History of the British Iron and Steel Industry*, London, 1957.

SISAM, K., *Fourteenth Century Verse and Prose*, Oxford, 1933.

STONES, E. L. G., 'The Folvilles of Ashby-Folville', *Trans. R.H.S.*, 5th series, 7, 1957.

SUMNER, B. H., *War and History*, Edinburgh, 1945.

THOMPSON, A. H., 'The Art of War to 1400', *C. Medieval H.*, VI.

THOMPSON, J. W., *Economic and Social History of Europe in the Later Middle Ages*, New York, 1960.

TOUT, T. F., 'Medieval and Modern Warfare', *Bulletin of the John Rylands Library*, vol. V, Manchester, 1919.

—— *Chapters in Administrative History*, Manchester, 1928–37.

—— 'Firearms in England in the Fifteenth Century', *E.H.R.*, XXVI, 1911.

TREASE, G. E., 'Spicers and Apothecaries of the Royal Household in the Reigns of Henry III, Edward I and Edward II', *Nottingham Medieval Studies*, vol. III, 1959.

—— *Pharmacy in History*, London, 1964.

TREUE, W., *Art and Plunder*, London, 1960.

UNWIN, G., *Finance and Trade under Edward III*, Manchester, 1918.

VILLEFOSSE, R. H. DE, *Charles le Sage*, Paris, 1947.

WEDGWOOD, C. V., 'The Common Man in the Civil War', *Truth and Opinion*, London, 1960.

WILKINSON, B., *Constitutional History of Medieval England, 1216–1399*, London, 1952.

WILLARD, J. F. AND MORRIS, W. A., *The English Government at Work 1327–1336*, Cambridge, Massachusetts, 1940.

WROTTESLEY, G., *Crecy and Calais*, London, 1898.

Local:

GARDINER, D., *Historic Haven* (The Story of Sandwich), Derby, 1954.

HOPE, T. M., 'Essex and the French Campaigns of 1341–7', *The Essex Review*, July, 1942.

HUDSON, W., 'Norwich Militia in the Fourteenth Century', *Norfolk Archaeological Society*, XIV, 1901.

MILLER, E., *War in the North*, University of Hull, 1960.

PHILIPOT, T., *Villare Cantianum*, Lynn, 1776.

RUSSELL, P., 'Fire Beacons in Devon', *Reports of the Devonshire Association*, LXXXVII, 1955.

The Oak Book of Southampton, vol. II, Southampton, 1911.

The Sign Manuals and Letters Patent of Southampton, vol. I, ed. Tudden, H. W., Southampton, 1916.

'Le Livre des Bouillons', *Archives municipales de Bordeaux*, I, 1867.

'Documents sur la ville de Millau', *Archives historiques de Rouergue*, VII, Millau, 1930.

Archives de la ville de Perigueux, Perigueux, 1894.

Index of Persons and Places

Ships mentioned in the text are indexed below, but see also Appendix II

Subject Index

administration, 170; in Gascony, 140, 147–9, 150, 152
admirals, 53, 77, 80–1, 95
ale, 52, 61
aliens, 165, 167, 167n, 168
anchors, 76, 169
apothecaries, 73
archers, 19, 31, 70, 82, 94–5, 135, 157; array of, 36–8; clothing, 37–9; equipment, 40, 63; health, 37; indentured, 35–6; kept for home defence, 14; mounted, 34, 36; movement of, 42–5, 49; pay of, 34–7, 40–2, 88; serve on ships, 38, 77, see discipline
archery, 37, 84, 94
armour, 14, 50, 73, 89, 169, 178
arms, 6, 40, 63–73, 83–4, 169, 178; issue of, 69–70; lists of, 60, 69–72, 118; manufacture of, 68, 169; orders for, 64–6, 68–9, 71; purchase of, 65, 68–9; shipment of, 84–5, 90; storage of, 68–9; transport of, 65–6, 70, see bowstrings, engines
arrayers, 7, 9, 11, 20, 36–7, 93–4, 157
arrows, see arms
art of war, see war
artillers, 68, 70, 72
atrocities, 121–3
attacks on England, 1, 2, 12, 16, 19–20, 51, see invasion of England
attorneys, 42

baggage train, 39, 50, 102, 109
band, military, 39
battle confused with war, 135
beacons, 4, 5, 7, 9, 16–18
bishops, 161–2
booty, 105, 134n; sharing, 107, 164, see pillage, spoils of war
bows, see arms
bowstaves, 73
bowstrings, 65, 69–70, 71, 84, 169
bowyers, 65, 68, 157
bridges, 104, 112, 152, 179
burning, 31, 106–7, 112–15, 120, 125–7, 132–5, 140, 160; of ships, 2, 3, 23;

of English ports, 2, 19, 156–7; by the Black Prince, 96–7

cables, 76, 169
cannons, 72, 85n
carriage, see transport
cardinals, 168
cattle, 99, 102–3, 105, 107, 109, 112, 125, 156
cheese, 55, 84
chevauchée, 93, 99, 103, 109, 111, 115; activities, 96, 121; aim of, 100, 105; discipline, 96; effects, 124, chapter V passim, 173
children, 97, 125–6, 132–3, 138
chivalry, decline of, 134–5; flower of, 91; ideals of, 32–3, 99; orders of, 33, 99, 131–2
chroniclers, 94, 99, 132; absence of evidence in, 97, 100, 102, 122, 126, 135; atrocities, 122–3; exaggeration, 122, 131; imprecision, 124; terseness, 107, 109, 114–15, see Anonimalle, Baker, Froissart, Walsingham in Index of Names
church, 28, 160–8; attitude of, 177; Roman, hostility to, 168
churches, bells, 5; destruction of, 114, 123, 125, 132–5; prayers, preachings, processions, 161–4; protection of, 96–7; rebuilding of, 130; robbery of, 138; shocking scenes in, 123
civilians, non-combatants, viii, 28, 94, 96, 111, 115, 117, 121, 125–7, 129–30, 156–8, 162–3 and passim. See also news and poor
coastal defence, see maritime lands
companies, formation, 136, 153, 175; growth, 143; losses caused by, 124, 148–9, 152
confessors, 22, 110
convoys, 23, 62, 77
corn, see victuals, export forbidden, 61–2
council, king's, 155–6, 167–8, 175–6; and the maritime lands, 8, 10, 11, 18
craftsmen, 38, 60, 68, 142, 157–8